An RAF Time Capsule

COPYRIGHT NOTICE

© Sandra Hemsworth, 2025

All rights reserved by the author. This book is copyright. Apart from any fair dealing for the purpose of private study, research, criticism, or review, as permitted under the Copyright Act, no part may be reproduced by any process without written permission from the publisher.

No part of this book may be used or reproduced by any means, graphic, electronic, or mechanical, including photocopying, recording, taping or by any information storage retrieval system without the written permission of the copyright owner except in the case of brief quotations embodied in critical articles and reviews.

The views expressed in this work are solely those of the author and do not necessarily reflect the views of the publisher and the publisher hereby disclaims any responsibility for them.

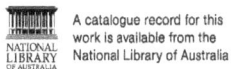
A catalogue record for this work is available from the National Library of Australia

ISBN (sc): 978-0-6454869-6-4

Published by Footprints Publishing Pty Ltd

DEDICATION

I dedicate this book to my parents, my father Roy Albert Blackburne and my mother Hilda Kathleen Blackburne (Peggy), née Short, who, both at a young age, stepped into the unknown for King and Country. Both were from ordinary backgrounds who unfalteringly did their duty at a time of great global uncertainty.

ROY'S WAR

An illustrated story as told through the contents of his kitbag

CONTENTS

DEDICATION
INTRODUCTION
ROY'S WAR
PART 1
   PRE-WAR
      The Boy behind the Man 1
      The RAF Kit Bag 7
      Volunteering 23
      Recruitment and Training 38
      No. 7 School of Technical Training, ... 39
      The Point of No Return, 1st June 1940 49
PART 2
   WARTIME
      The Battle of Britain 51
      Biggin Hill 57
      Unsung Heroes, the 'Erks' 62
      RAF Acklington. 73
      John Ellis. Flight Lieutenant. 79
      RAF Woolsington 83
      Westhampnett. 85
   Overseas Deployment
      Leaving from Liverpool 101
      A Brief Respite in Durban 105
      Order of Roy's RAF postings in India 111
      Alexandria Docks, Bombay 112
      Deolali Camp 15th March 1942 114
      Ambala 115
      Quetta Arsenal 129

RAF Hill Stations 137
    Naini Tal 137
    Solan 139
Winter in the Murree Hills 152
    Junior Non-Commissioned Officer Course 153
    RAF Ranchi 154
    Burma 159
The Circumstances of the War in Burma 165
Correspondence 182

PART 3
  POST-WAR
    Demobilisation 197
    Roy's Medals 202
    Homecoming 205
    Over but Not Forgotten 252
ABOUT THE AUTHOR 273
ACKNOWLEDGEMENTS 274
REFERENCES 275

Likely Timeline inferred from R.A.F. Service Record and Dates from Personal Effects Found in the Kitbag

23.2.1939 -	Enlisted with 610 (County of Chester) Squadron Auxiliary Air Force
24.8.1939 -	610 Squadron, RAF Hooton Park, Cheshire
2.2.1940 -	RAF St. Athan Technical Training College, Glamorganshire
2.6.1940 -	610 Squadron, RAF Biggin Hill, Kent
9.1940 -	610 Squadron, RAF Acklington, Northumberland
2-3.1941 -	610 Squadron RAF Westhampnett, Sussex
25.4.1941 -	9/1941 - Hut 23, 2 Wing, RAF Station, Innesworth Lane, Gloucester. (see postcard).
9.9.1941 -	SHA Echelon Flight, Hut 63, RAF Station, Honiley, Kenilworth, Warwickshire.
7.2.1942 -	Departure – Liverpool
3.1942 -	Bombay, India
15.3.1942 -	Deolali Transit camp, 100 miles North East of Bombay
21.3.1942 -	Ambala
4.1942 -	Ambala
5 -15.4.1942 -	New Dehli
6.1942 -	Punjab
9.1942-	Naini Tal
9.1943-	Kashmir
10.1943 -	Ambala
16.11.1943 -	South East Asia 322 Maintenance Unit, RAF Cawnpore
14.3.1944 -	Adm. BMH, (Admitted British Military Hospital).
24.3.1944 -	Calcutta M/E

- 11.1944 - 1.O.C.T.U. (1. Officer Cadet Training Unit), Murree Hills, Upper Topa)
- 26.12.1944 - South East Asia 322 Maintenance Unit, RAF Cawnpore
- 12.1944 - RAF Ranchi S.L.A.I.S. (Specialised Low Attack Instructors School)
- 1.11.1945 - BHQ Karachi, (Base Headquarters, British)
- 5.11.1945 - UK 104 P.DE. (Demobilisation Unit)
- 10.12.1945 - 104 P.DE. Hednesford - Release

INTRODUCTION

For those recently bereaved going through the contents of the family home can be a very emotional time which is often full of surprises about the deceased person's life particularly for those whose relatives had fought for King and Country, my family was no exception.

As a family, we knew very little of our father's World War II years, except that he had served with the RAF and had been deployed to India and Burma. Not only his family but sadly none of his dear friends or neighbours, who had known him for many years, had any idea that he had worked as ground crew with the 610 (County of Chester) Squadron during the Battle of Britain, had worked tirelessly in India and was involved in the Burma Campaign. He had preferred never to burden others with his experiences. It wasn't until the day of his funeral when solemnly entering the church they saw an RAF flag draped across his coffin. In the congregation, paying their respects were members of 610 (County of Chester) Squadron Association some of whom had served with him, one standing proudly at the front of the church holding the RAF standard.

As WW II came to an end, my father Roy was told by a senior officer to, *'Forget everything you have seen or you will go mad.'* Like many heroic men of his generation, he took that advice.

A familiar sight in many homes: long forgotten photo albums with yellowing paperwork, all shoved into the back of a drawer or cupboard or a kit bag! A treasure trove of family history waiting to be rediscovered.

Unbeknown to his family however, he had not only mentally but also physically, packed those memories away, away into his kit bag in a dark corner of the loft in the family home. There it remained, undiscovered for over 55 years until the time came to empty the home prior to sale. My family and I were intrigued, we had no idea where he had served during the six years of war, nor what he had endured and achieved during those long years away from home. He never spoke of the personal deprivation, the tragic loss of friends and colleagues and how very hard he and his fellow airmen had worked in the worst possible conditions and locations. At times, reading this book and viewing his many photographs, it may seem his war was one long holiday. Nothing could be further from the truth, my father had recorded not only the happy times during the war, but also the hardships, of course there would have been restrictions as to where and when he could have taken his camera, but he tried his best!

Intrigued by our unexpected find and as the family historian, I felt the need to delve deeper and write about our father's war years, my intention was to write a short pamphlet for the 610 (County of Chester) Squadron, under whom my father proudly served, but the deeper I delved through all the memorabilia left behind, more questions were raised.

What was going to be a pamphlet became a book.

PART 1

PRE-WAR

The Boy behind the Man

Roy Albert Blackburne was born on 20th November 1918 in a country in turmoil, arriving just nine days after the end of the first World War and with the Spanish Flu Pandemic of 1918-1919 sweeping the country. In 1929, barely 10 years later as Britain was still coming to terms with the 'war to end all wars', the US stock market crashed, causing a global economic downturn followed by a decade of depression around the world. During these inter-war years, the County of Cheshire, a dairy county of beautiful, verdant countryside and picturesque villages, suffered from gross unemployment. Its industrial areas were particularly affected, resulting in abject poverty for many. Despite this, Roy's hometown of Ellesmere Port, situated on the Manchester Ship Canal, continued to develop as an industrial town. In 1924, at nearby Stanlow, Shell UK Ltd built a large refinery, followed ten years later by Burmah Oil Trading Ltd, creating a significant number of jobs for the rapidly growing population and enticing an influx of workers from Liverpool. John (Jack) Blackburne, Roy's father was one of them. John, a World War I veteran himself, worked as an industrial insurance agent for the Prudential earning a comfortable living, which meant the family lived well even in such tumultuous times. When Roy was born he became the second son and fifth child of John and Alice Blackburne, a younger brother to Alice 7 yrs, John 5 yrs, Beryl (deceased), and Millicent 1 yr.

At the time of Roy's birth, his mother was an invalid and confined to a wheelchair following a bad fall whilst hanging out washing. Life must have been a daily struggle for her and her four very young children, but despite Roy's mother's infirmity, life was happy at no.72 Princes Road. They were a good-humoured family that always supported each other. Perhaps because of his upbringing, Roy became quite self-reliant and resourceful from an early age. This would stand him in good stead for the challenges that lay ahead, particularly during his war years.

He and his siblings attended the local Catholic school. Coming from an industrial town, on leaving school it was expected that a trade was generally the best career path. Roy had other plans, however, so on completing his education he went on to do a 'Senior Technical Course' from 1935-36, followed by a course in the 'Civil Service' in 1937. He also qualified in English and Business Training at the Cestrian Commercial College in nearby Chester, all completed before the age of twenty.

Skerry's Colleges were a series of colleges that ran courses for people who intended to enter the civil service, post offices or other government posts by preparing them for competitive Civil Service examinations. Founded in 1878 by George Skerry, Skerry's was the first college in England to run correspondence courses for those unable to attend personally. The nearest College to Ellesmere Port was at Rodney Street in Liverpool. No doubt such a prestigious course held him in good stead in future endeavours. (schoolandcollegelistings.co/Skerry's College on Rodney Street).

Roy, like many other youngsters growing up between the wars, had the freedom to roam, took very little for granted and appreciated what little he had. When money was tight he did without, when plentiful, (which was rare), he saved for a rainy day. That alone gave him the incentive to try and do better and have ambition in life. From a very young age, he had the drive and determination to alter the path set out for him. His decision to enrol in the Auxiliary Air Force at Hooton Park and the impending war became a turning point in his young life, his immediate future mapped out for him, at the very least for the duration of the war.

Roy and my mother Hilda Kathleen (Peggy), née Short met at the Majestic Dance hall in Ellesmere Port, Cheshire prior to the war, where he politely asked, 'May I have the pleasure of this dance?' They decided against marrying until the war was over because Peggy 'did not want to be left a widow.' Surprisingly, there were no letters of their ongoing romance found amongst the numerous contents of the kitbag, but I am sure there must have been many, possibly too personal for prying eyes.

Peggy, on leaving school at the age of 14, as was then the norm, became an apprentice hairdresser, on completion of which she bought her own salon 'Peggy's' in Little Sutton Village.

Peggy's salon in Little Sutton

At the outbreak of the war, encouraged by her father, Peggy decided to lease her shop and become a nurse. She commenced training as an auxiliary nurse for her badge in the 'Civil Nursing Reserve' at Winwick Hospital near Warrington, working there until 1945. The hospital, initially known as Winwick Hall, opened in 1897. During World War I (hereafter WWI) it's named changed to Lord Derby War Hospital (1915-1920), and later became Lancashire County Mental Hospital Winwick, or Winwick Asylum.

Throughout World War II (hereafter WWII), Winwick still operated as a mental asylum, but had one separate wing for use as an emergency war hospital for the treatment and care of orthopaedic casualties. The large, forbidding red brick building with its tall laundry chimney must have seemed very imposing to such a young woman who had rarely ventured far from the small Cheshire village. Barely out of her teens, she saw and treated the worst injuries imaginable, nursing 'our boys' with the greatest of respect and compassion. Here Peggy witnessed the true reality of war, patients with injuries such as exposed spines, numerous amputations and complicated fractures - many having little hope of survival. The hospital treated not only British Servicemen, but also prisoners of war in a locked ward, of whom Peggy recalled, 'looked no different to our lads'. The job was both physically and mentally exhausting, and the horrific images she saw throughout her time there still haunted her many years later. The hospital closed in 1997.

Peggy (centre front) with other hospital staff of Winwick emergency Medical Hospital

Between July and October 1942 Peggy was given compassionate leave to help care for her bereft mother who was having trouble coping following the death of her beloved son William (Billy). On 8th June 1940, along with 151 other men, Billy died when their ship HMS Ardent, was torpedoed and sunk whilst escorting the aircraft carrier HMS Glorious by the German battleships Scharnhorst and Gneisenau off the coast of Norway.

NATIONAL SERVICE ACTS, 1939 to 1941

MINISTRY OF LABOUR AND NATIONAL SERVICE,
Local Office,

60 BRIDGE STREET,
BIRKENHEAD

CERTIFICATE OF POSTPONEMENT OF LIABILITY TO BE CALLED UP FOR SERVICE IN THE ARMED FORCES OF THE CROWN OR FOR CIVIL DEFENCE.

(This certificate should be signed by the applicant as soon as it is received.)

This is to certify that the liability of (Name in full) _Hilda Kathleen Short_ Regn. No. _W._

(Address in full) _4 Dapleston Road, Little Sutton_

to be called up for service in the Armed Forces of the Crown or for Civil Defence has been postponed to and including _31 Dec 1942_ (date). After that date this certificate will cease to be in force. The ground on which postponement is granted is _Domestic Hardship_

Signature of Local Officer _[signature]_

Date _25 JUL 1942_

Signature of Applicant _____

NOTES.

1.—Any application for the renewal of this certificate must be made to a Local Office of the Ministry of Labour and National Service not later than 14 days before the date when the certificate will cease to be in force, i.e. not later than _7 Dec_ otherwise the Minister will be bound to dismiss it, unless there are special circumstances which in the Minister's opinion justify the delay.

2.—The Postponement Certificates Regulations provide that the period for which a postponement certificate may be granted or renewed should as far as possible be adjusted to the time which the applicant might reasonably be expected to require in order to make alternative arrangements with respect to his domestic position or the carrying on or disposal of any business or to deal with any other relevant matter as the case may be, so however that—

(1) the period for which a certificate may be granted shall in no case exceed a period of six months, calculated from the date on which the applicant applied to the Minister for the certificate, or in any case in which there has been an appeal to the Umpire, a period of six months calculated as aforesaid or a period commencing on the date on which the applicant applied to the Minister for the certificate and ending on a date not later than one month after the date of the decision of the Umpire in that case whichever period is the greater;

(2) the period for which a certificate may be renewed shall in no case exceed a period of six months, calculated from the end of the period for which it was granted or last renewed or, in any case in which there has been an appeal to the Umpire, a period of six months calculated as aforesaid or a period commencing on the date on which the applicant applied to the Minister for the renewal of the certificate and ending on a date not later than one month after the date of the decision of the Umpire in that case whichever period is the greater;

(3) no certificate granted on the ground of business responsibilities and interests should be allowed to remain in force for longer than twelve months in all, unless it is renewed on some other ground and accordingly (save as aforesaid) the maximum period for which such a certificate may be renewed must be ascertained by deducting from the said period of twelve months the period for which the certificate was originally granted and any other period or periods for which the certificate has since been renewed, and

(3) no certificate renewed on the ground of business responsibilities and interests but granted on some other ground shall be allowed to remain in force for longer than twelve months calculated from the beginning of the period for which it was first renewed on the ground of business responsibilities and interests.

N.S.78.

Following the Normandy landings in 1944, Peggy's mother received another telegram saying her other son Thomas (Tom) was missing in action, presumed dead. Unbeknown to his distraught family, Thomas, although badly wounded, had been dramatically rescued by the Free French and smuggled through occupied France back to the safety of England.

1939. Peggy aged 19 yrs. A nurse at Winwick Hospital

1939. Roy, 21yrs. Enlisted with 610 Auxiliary Squadron

The RAF Kit Bag

This book is an illustration of 'Roy's War' as told through the many items found in his kit bag and through the lens of his trusty folding Ensign camera. Roy was a keen amateur photographer and had methodically taken and recorded hundreds of photographs in his time away, the majority found still in their negative form. Roy's photographs in this book are original, and unpublished and are an account of his war years. Perhaps they were taken and hidden away with a vision that one day they would come to light and be published as a record so all could see as his version of events? The majority of negatives were found in his kitbag, others in long forgotten photograph albums in the back of cupboards, despite their condition the photographs do give a reference point as to my father's actions and whereabouts during the war. Roy, being typical of his generation, threw nothing out, resulting in the huge number of photographs and documents found. Throughout 'An RAF Time Capsule', Roy's descriptions alongside the photographs in the albums are included wherever possible. Unless stated otherwise, (where every attempt has been made to contact third parties so as not to contravene copyright rules), the photographs, documents and item in this book, are original and from my father's own memorabilia.

Roy's pride and joy, an 'Ensign' folding camera, a popular camera of its day. Almost indestructible when folded completely flat making it ideal to pack in a kitbag

Numerous large format high definition negatives from which Roy's wartime photographs were developed

Roy's identity disc. On the disc was AAF (Auxiliary Air Force), Roy's number, his surname and his initials, his religion RC (Roman Catholic) Rank wasn't included as it could change during the time of service. In case of death, the lozenge shaped tag stayed on the body, the other was for identification and administration by the Grave Registration Unit

April 1943
Me with the old bush hat on

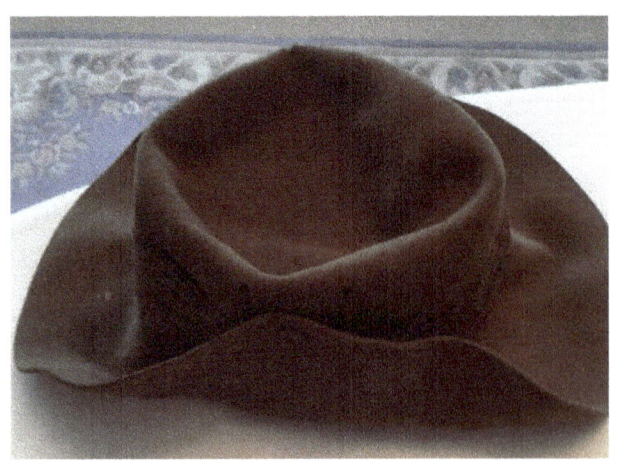

Field Dressing Kit

On the waxed exterior were instructions on using the field dressing. Inside was a large pad of absorbent cloth/gauze attached by the middle to two long pieces of fabric enabling the pad to be fixed and compressed against a wound. The instructions also state that in the case of a head wound where respirators have to be worn, care should be taken to adjust the pad so that it does not interfere with the fit of the facepiece. The company producing these kits was Arthur Berton Ltd., London. The dressing was kept on the person and in the same pocket used by each and every RAF personnel so in times of injury or panic it could be found quickly

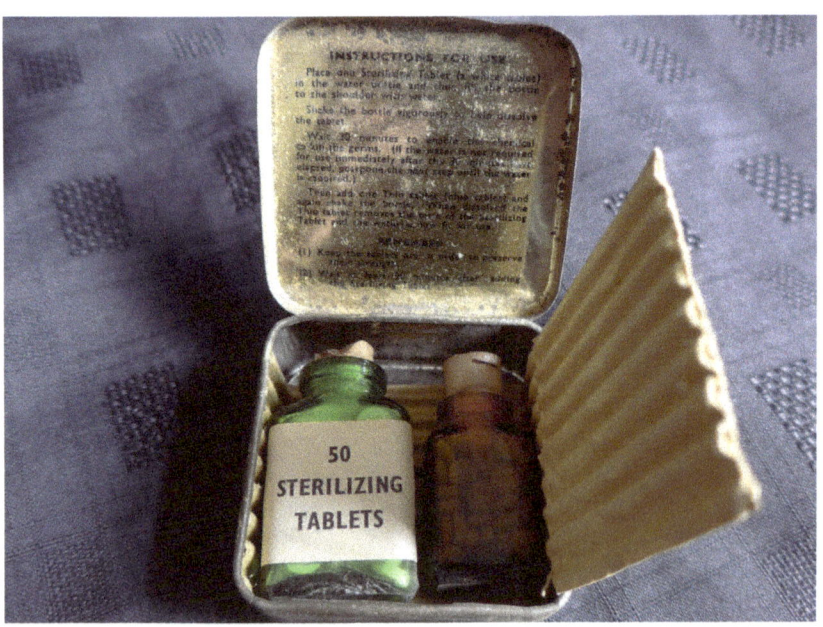

Above is a tobacco tin plus small silver tube containing pills, likely morphine tartrate standard issue, part of the field first aid kit. The tube would have been kept on the person for speedy access, rather than in a kitbag.

Below contents of tobacco tin.

Red RAF eagle badges were worn on khaki uniforms. On the left sleeve 2 stripes denoting Roy was a corporal

Roy's sergeant stripes

Other clothing found in the kitbag; a tropical uniform and the 'demob' suit shown below

Kit bag lock and brass button shield, used when cleaning brass buttons to prevent the cleaning solution staining the uniform

Malayan carved dagger

A propaganda photograph above and it's reverse below

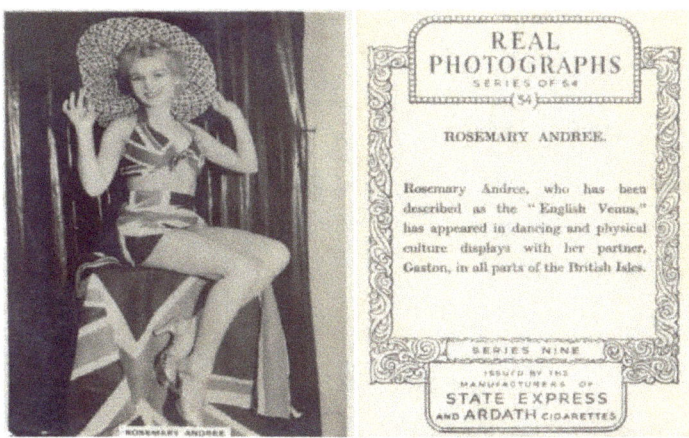

Cigarette card of Rosemary Andree, a forces sweetheart

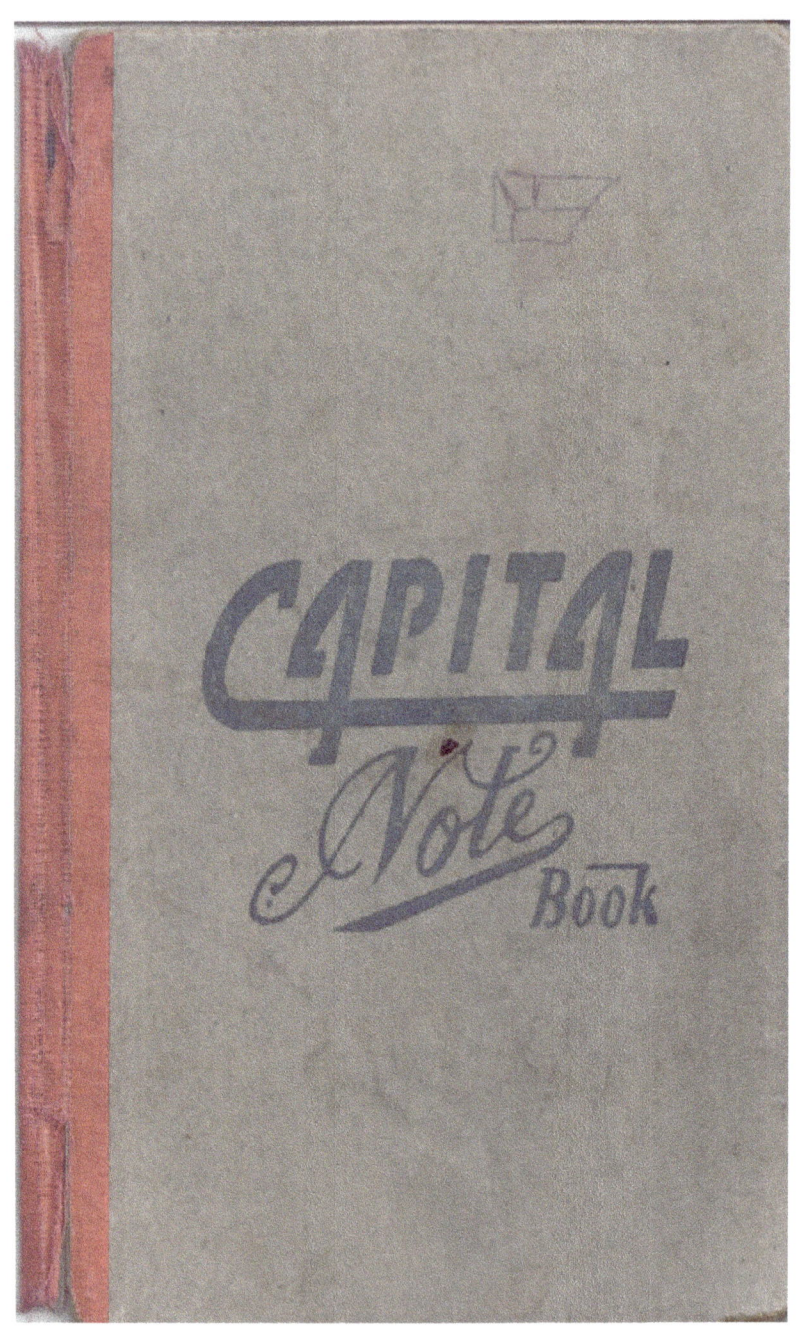

Roy's notebook written while on a Junior Non-Commissioned Officers course in Upper Topa, India (now Pakistan)

Religious Items

As a child, Roy was brought up as a Roman Catholic, attending the local catholic schools. There were numerous religious items in the kitbag, obviously finding some solace in his faith whilst away at war. The irony being despite his dedication to his faith, in later years due to his marriage to Peggy an Anglican, Roy was excommunicated from the Catholic Church. Several years later he was denied entrance to a local catholic church on the occasion of the christening of his nephew.

PRAYER FOR PEACE

(Pope Benedict XV)

Dismayed by the horrors of a war which is bringing ruin to peoples and nations, we turn, O Jesus, to Thy most loving Heart as to our last hope.

O God of Mercy, with tears we invoke Thee to end this fearful scourge; O King of Peace, we humbly implore the peace for which we long.

From Thy Sacred Heart Thou didst shed forth over the world divine Charity, so that discord might end and love alone might reign among men.

During Thy life on earth The Heart beat with tender compassion for the sorrows of men; in this hour made terrible with burning hate, with bloodshed and with slaughter, once more may Thy divine Heart be moved to pity.

Pity the countless mothers in anguish for the fate of their sons; pity the numberless families now bereaved of their fathers; pity Europe over which broods such havoc and disaster.

Do Thou inspire rulers and peoples with counsels of meekness, do Thou heal the discords that tear the nations asunder; Thou who didst shed Thy Precious Blood that they might live as brothers, bring men together once more in loving harmony.

And, as once before to the cry of the Apostle Peter: *Save us, Lord, we perish*, Thou didst answer with words of mercy and didst still the raging waves, so now deign to hear our trustful prayer, and give back to the world peace and tranquillity.

And do thou, O most holy Virgin, as in other times of sore distress, be now our help, our protection and our safeguard. Amen.

Imprimatur: — SALESIUS LEMMENS O. F. M.
Sup. Miss. Karachiensis.

Rotti Press.   Pilgrim Road.   Karachi.

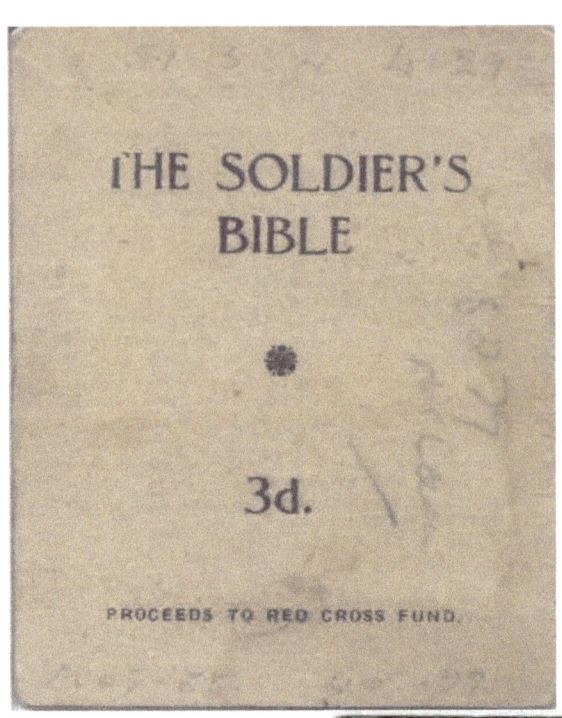

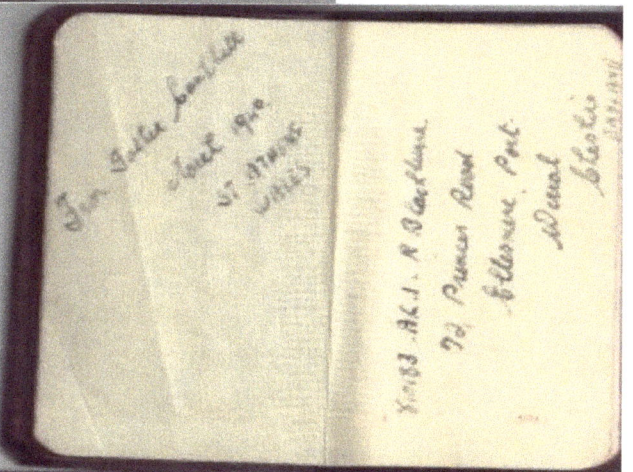

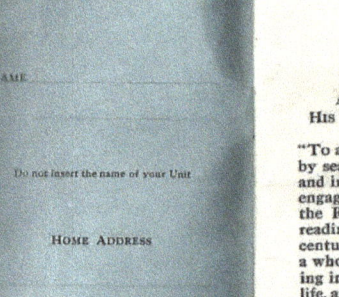

NAME

Do not insert the name of your Unit

HOME ADDRESS

A MESSAGE FROM
HIS MAJESTY THE KING

"To all serving in my Forces by sea or land, or in the air, and indeed, to all my people engaged in the defence of the Realm, I commend the reading of this book. For centuries the Bible has been a wholesome and strengthening influence in our national life, and it behoves us in these momentous days to turn with renewed faith to this Divine source of comfort and inspiration."

September 15, 1939.

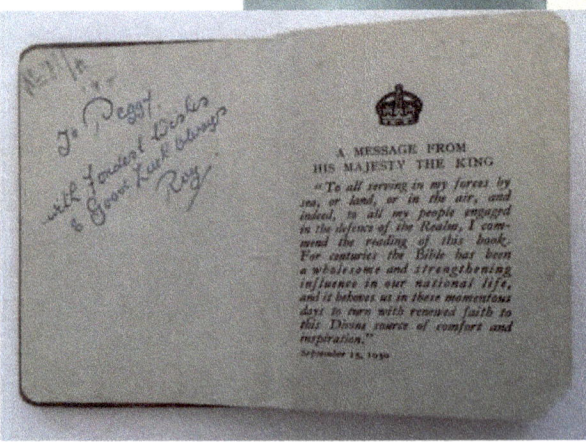

To Peggy,
with fondest wishes
& loving thoughts
always
Roy

Roy, like many other servicemen, took out a policy in case of injury or death. Roy took his out through his father, Jack. Jack, having fought in WW1, must have felt a great sense of foreboding as he watched his young, naïve son leave home for an unknown destination and indeterminate length of time during such global turmoil.

Volunteering

23rd February 1939 - February 1940

Below is an extract taken from The *Cheshire Observer,* August 1938, detailing a camp that 610 (County of Chester) volunteers enjoyed at RAF Airfield Abbotsinch, Scotland.

'The 610 (County of Chester) Bomber Squadron Auxiliary Air Force have returned to their home station at Hooton, after spending a fortnight under training at Abbotsinch Aerodrome, Paisley, Scotland. Today this is Glasgow International Airport, then it was the headquarters of 269 (General Reconnaissance) Squadron RAF.

The 610 Squadron was raised from volunteers in the following areas: - Chester, Ellesmere Port, Wallasey, Birkenhead, Northwich

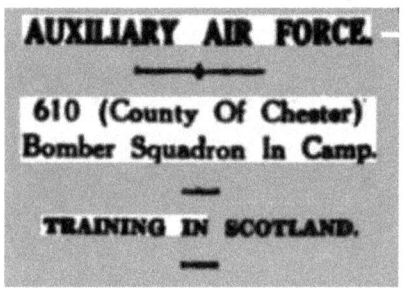

and other intervening districts. All these men had occupations in civil life varying from plumbers to bank clerks and even company directors. They voluntarily gave up one evening a week and weekends for training. They were reimbursed for travelling expenses and receiving an annual bounty and special pay based on hours of attendance throughout the year. Many joined with directly transferable skills particularly the engineers and pilots – many of whom had learned to fly with university air squadrons. Training is given in the following R.A.F. trades: - Fitter, rigger, armourer, photographer, wireless operator, clerk; general duties, clerk; accounting, equipment assistant, and drivers; petrol. Selected airmen may be trained as air observers or air gunners and when qualified are eligible to receive extra pay for such duty.

For their journey to Abbotsinch the main party travelled to Scotland by train from Hooton, with P.O. Albrecht in command, while a favoured few – the pilots - were given the opportunity to fly North. The Squadron transport section travelled by road and made good time on a tedious journey'

'On arrival in camp the Squadron quickly settled down, the older members in barracks and the recruits under canvas. Reveille was sounded at 6 each morning and the routine of the day began with breakfast followed by the Colour Hoisting Parade. A touch of local colour was added to this daily parade by the R.A.F. station pipe band, and everybody on camp was soon whistling the Scottish airs they played. After the parade work was the order of the day and as soon as the daily inspections had been carried out by the ground staff the machines took to the air. Some went bombing at Dalgety Bay near the Forth Bridge others on photographic flights and the remainder on various routine flying duties of the Squadron. The recruits under training were now able to put their theoretical knowledge into practice in the workshops and for the first week several of the more advanced members were to be seen in the classrooms studying for the examinations which were held on the Monday and Tuesday of the second week, the examining officer being Squadron Leader Reason.'

Photograph of the Annual Camp Abbotsinch.

A Hawker Hart with ground crew of 610 Abbotsinch summer camp. Aircraft was squadron coded JE which was later changed to DW

(Photograph courtesy of 610 Squadron Association)

Work finished at 4:00 p.m. each day and various means of passing the leisure time were available. Cricket, tennis, billiards, darts and other games were provided at the camp, while Paisley offered picture houses and theatres. Glasgow was also a popular rendezvous but the biggest attraction, was of course, the Empire Exhibition. A squadron trip was arranged on the first Saturday at camp and three bus loads left for a tour down the Clyde Coast and on to the Three Lochs - Loch Long, Loch Doil and Loch Lomond. The weather which had been indifferent until then, suddenly took a turn for the better and helped make the tour the success it was.

During the second week passenger flights were arranged for all personnel on the ground staff and the trips in the Avro Ansons of the 269 Squadron were very popular, the favourite route being over the Exhibition and then on to Clydeside where a magnificent view of the new Cunard liner Queen Elizabeth was obtained. Blackburn 'Shark' and Fairey 'Swordfish' types of aircraft were usually surrounded by a crowd of interested airmen, discussing the various features of these craft.

The big day of the fortnight was on the second Wednesday when the A.O.C. inspected the Squadron and took the salute at the march and the fly past. Just as all the kits had been carefully laid out in front of the tents a squall came on and everything was thoroughly wet through just one of the vicissitudes of Air Force life.

Soon the time came for leaving and a busy day was spent packing all the tools and implements so necessary to modern aircraft and on the Sunday the main party again entrained arriving at Hooton, the best station of all, about 4 p.m. The flying party followed the next day and the transport section returned by road.

The general opinion of the Squadron was that the fortnight's training was really enjoyable and most of the members are keenly looking forward to next year.

Training is now being continued on Thursday evenings and at week-ends and vacancies shortly will be available for recruits. Full particulars as to the conditions of service may be obtained from the Commanding Officer, 610 (County of Chester) Bombing Squadron, Hooton Park, Wirral. Facilities for sport and recreation are available at headquarters.

August 1939, 610 (County of Chester) Squadron Annual Camp at Abbotsinch, Scotland. Roy 7th from right 2nd row down. Just days following the end of the annual camp, war was declared on 3rd September 1939 when Germany invaded Poland. (Copyright Diane Reid nee Woodfine, via 610 Squadron Association).

As the Cheshire Observer was a local paper, it very likely that this article appealed to a large number of potential volunteers, Roy being amongst them. He enrolled with 610 (County of Chester)

Squadron 23rd February 1939, shortly after the article was printed. Even at this early stage of 1939, the rumblings of war must have been heard, but not yet certain. Roy, like many young men of his generation, would have been looking for excitement and adventure.

An early photograph of a non-flying group. Possibly taken at Abbotsinch. Roy, 4th row, 4th from left

One way a boy from a working-class background could find it was by becoming a volunteer in the armed forces. Roy would have attended Hooton Park once or twice a week for training in airmanship which would have included various disciplines. He would have gone away on regular camps, under canvas, held at regular RAF stations, and of course the annual camp that he attended in August 1939 at Abbotsinch. Discipline, challenges and comradeship would mold him into the airman he eventually became. He may well have held an ambition to become a pilot himself; many ground crew eventually did.

610 (County of Chester) Squadron of the Royal Auxiliary Air Force

'The history of 610 is brief covering just twenty years. Despite this short existence the Chester Squadron distinguished itself both during the war years and in peacetime. It comprised around 200 members at any one moment but the total number of personnel serving with 610 during the life of the Squadron amounted to well over 1000 individuals of fourteen different nationalities. The Squadron was formed at Hooton Park in February 1936 and commanded by an Auxiliary officer, supported by 56 regular airmen. Most of the personnel were local men from Merseyside and from Cheshire. At that time 610 was a light bomber Squadron and operated Hawker Hart and Hind biplanes. The Training Flight included Avro Tutor and de Havilland Tiger Moth aircraft. By 1938 the personnel had increased to twenty officers with one hundred and forty-five men. During this year six men were selected from the air gunners to train as pilots with the rank of sergeant on qualifying. In January of 1939, 610 Squadron was transferred from Bomber to Fighter Command and embodied into the regular RAF. In September of that year its first Spitfires began to arrive at Hooton Park. On the 10th October 1939, the Squadron moved to its first war station - RAF Wittering in Northamptonshire and became operational. On 10th May 1940 Germany invaded Holland and Belgium and orders were received for 610 to move immediately to RAF Biggin Hill, which became the most famous fighter station in the RAF.'

'The Squadron badge of 610 (County of Chester) Squadron was designed by T.J. Heaton-Armstrong who was Chester Herald and Inspector of RAF badges at the College of Arms. It depicts the Chester City badge – 'A garb, party per pale, gules and azure'. (A wheatsheaf divided vertically red and blue). This was approved and signed by HM King Edward V111 in July 1936...' The motto of 'Alifero Tolitur Axe Ceres' translated means, 'Ceres (The Goddess of Corn' Rises in a Winged Car (chariot) and is a quotation from Ovid. The image of a sheaf of wheat represents Cheshire's agricultural farmland.

610 Squadron Spitfires and to the far right a redundant Hurricane at Hooton Park, prior to departure to RAF Wittering at the start of the war. Photo Don Stephens (via 610 Squadron Association)

A Hawker Hind, a standard light bomber of the RAF during the 1930s. Many Battle of Britain pilots gained their wings on the trainer variant between 1935 and 1939. Photo 610 Squadron Association

Royal Auxiliary Air Force

The Royal Auxiliary Air Force originally the Auxiliary Air Force as part of the RAF provided a reinforcement capability for the regular service if needed. It offered additional frontline capability for the regular service if needed During the WW II, the AAF provided 14 of the 62 Squadrons in the RAF Fighter Command's Order of Battle and accounted for approximately 30 per cent of the accredited enemy kills. In recognition of their achievements during the WW II, the prefix 'Royal' was added to the title of the Auxiliary Air Force in 1947.

No. 610 (County of Chester) Squadron was founded on 10th February 1936 at Hooton Park, Cheshire as one of the twenty-one Auxiliary Air Force Squadrons. A few former Royal Auxiliary Air Force Squadrons have recently been reinstated to provide support functions alongside existing RAF units.

(Michael Lewis 610 (County of Chester) Squadron Association) Personal Communication March 9th 2020/610squadron.com.

Aerial view of Hooton Park Belfast Truss type hangars
(Phil Butler via 610 Squadron Association)

Hooton Park was once one of a small number of airfields in the North-West of England prior to Liverpool's Speke airport across the River Mersey and later Manchester Ringway (now Manchester International Airport) being opened. (*Hooton Park, Abandoned and Little-known Airfields in Europe*). The site was acquired by Vauxhall Motors in 1961, and used to establish a motor vehicle manufacturing plant. The use of the actual hangars from the old airfield by Vauxhall for industrial purposes ended in the late 1980s, by which time, the historical significance of the old airfield site was becoming recognized. Initially listed as Grade II in 1988, a later review recognized the hangars rarity and were immediately included on the Heritage at Risk Register. Built from basic materials they were becoming unsound. Before they could be repaired and renovated however, the asbestos roof panels had to be replaced. The site has been managed since 2000 by Hooton Park Trust.

(*Historicengland.org.uk.*)

Rare image of a bleak winter at Hooton Park. Note one of the three pairs of Belfast Truss Hangars, which had a unique latticed timber roof construction which was first used in the Belfast Shipyards. The roofs were able to span large unobstructed working areas. The hangars being completed in 1917 and the airfield was first used during World War 1. Some of the pilots killed in accidents during that time are buried at the ancient church of St. Mary's, Eastham

Becoming a Technician in the RAF
Flight Mechanic

There is a big demand and consequently wide scope for intelligent men in a variety of Royal Air Force trades, in which they not only enjoy comfortable living conditions, good pay and full and interesting life, but acquire much knowledge and skill which will be most valuable to them when they return to civil life.

Men between the ages of 18 and 42 yrs. of age, with a mechanical turn of mind, may find an opening in the RAF. Even a man merely interested in machines or handling of tools as a hobby may have sufficient knowledge to be trained as a Flight Mechanic (E) Engine or (A) Air Frame. Recruits in this trade begin as aircraft hands under training and are paid at the rate of 17s.6d. per week. At the end of their training course they become Flight Mechanics (Group 11), which means their pay is increased to a minimum of 28s. a week.

The Flight Mechanic could then undertake a conversion course to Fitter 11 (E) or (A) (Group 1), which carries a minimum pay rate of 29s. 9d. a week for an Aircraftman 2nd Class. As he acquires further skill or even on completion of his course he may become an Aircraftman 1st Class and be paid 35s. a week, or Leading Aircraftman at 42s. a week. Skilled fitters from civil life may become Fitters 11 € or (A), without first serving as Flight Mechanics and are put in Group 1 while under training.

These rates of pay compare very favourably with civil life when it is remembered that clothes, food, living quarters, recreation, medical services, and many other amenities are provided in the RAF free of charge. For married men also there are married and family or dependents allowances which considerably increase the rates of pay quoted above. (ABC of the RAF, How to Become a Technician in the RAF, page 33).

RAF trades and pay groups are placed in six groups for pay purposes covering all trades, administration, nursing and medical. Roy as a fitter, grade II (engine) was in group 1 where his rates of pay were as follows;

AC2 - Aircraftman 2nd Class – rate of pay – 3s.9d. - 16s.6d per day. Equivalent rate today - £7.38 – £32.46

AC1 - Aircraftman 1st Class – rate of pay – 4s.6d - 16s.6d. per day. Equivalent rate today - £8.85

L.A.C – Leading Aircraftman – rate of pay - 5s.6d per day. Equivalent rate today - £10.82

On 24th August 1942 Roy received a Good Conduct Badge resulting in a further 3d. per day. Equivalent rate today - £0.49

In 1944, on becoming a non-commissioned officer, obtaining the rank of Corporal, his basic daily rate of pay increased to 7s. 6d. Equivalent rate today £14.75, *(Equivalent rates of pay, currency converter 1270-2017, Equivalent rates of pay, currency converter 1270-2017 The National Archives, www.nationalarchives.gov.uk)*

Prior to the end of the war Roy was promoted to acting sergeant where his basic daily rate would have been 9s.6d. Equivalent rate today - £18.69

Good Conduct Badges and Pay - *badges are awarded for very good conduct after 3, 8 and 13 years qualifying service rendered after attaining the age of 18 yrs. Good conduct pay of 3d. a day is awarded for each badge.*

Additional pay. *– Non-substantive pay at daily rates varying from 3d. to 1s. is issuable as follows:*

1. *Qualifications pay granted for definite qualifications*
2. *Duty pay for performance of specific duties.*

War pay *at the rate of 6d. a day is issuable in addition to the rates of pay set out above.*

Trades and Pay Groups of the RAF, *(ABC of the RAF page 12, London the Amalgamated Press Ltd.)*

Within each trade group aircraftmen second class (AC2) is the lowest of the pay range and Warrant Officer the highest.

These were the basic pay rates, calculated on a daily basis, but additional payments were made in individual cases for various reasons. For instance, certain specialist qualification directly relevant to some trades could bring the holder extra payment of 'non-substantive' daily 'bonus' pay varying from 3d to 1s. All air men and women having a service record of very good conduct were also awarded 3d per day additional to basic rate at each stage of completing 3, 8 and 13 years 'service in the RAF. Once enlisted, an airman's 'terms of service' during the war were relatively undefined. Beyond the certain knowledge that he/she was unlikely to be released from the service until the close of war unless for medical reasons, or other individual possibilities. He could be posted at short notice to far-flung places with no re-dress. If such a posting was to an overseas theatre of operations, his stay outside home was undefined, which could mean his stay could be months - two, three or four years away from family with no known date for repatriation to his homeland.' Hammerton, John, ABC of the RAF, The Amalgamated Press, Ltd., 1943, p. 12.

Once enlisted, an airman's terms of service' during the war were relatively vague, beyond the certain knowledge that he was unlikely to be released from the Service until the close of the war unless for medical reasons, or other individual possibilities He automatically became subject to all and every rule and regulation to be found in KRs and AC1s, was bound in disciplinary matters by the imposing volume MAFL, apart from a host of temporary wartime impositions placed upon all servicemen and civilians. He could be (and often was) posted at the shortest of notices to far-flung corners of the globe, with no redress. If such a posting was to an overseas theatre of operations, his stay outside his homeland was undefined in the context of specific length of sojourn, i.e. there were no laid down, set parameter to an overseas 'tour of duty. This might be mere months, or more often, two, three or even four years away from kith and kin, with no known date for repatriation to his homeland until only weeks before actually leaving his unit abroad. Even 'working hours' depended on myriad considerations on the particular unit, station, or Command he might be on or in. Traditionally, then, no Serviceman could belong to a trade union, hence his working life became a simple matter of 'Service exigencies' – a term sufficiently vague enough to 'cover' all of any imposed work structure.

(The Royal Air Force, 1939-1945, page 10. Chaz Bowyer, Pen and Sword Paperbacks, Barnsley)

MUSTERING.		Date	Rank	Character	Trade.	Proficiency.			Recs. for Prom.
Authy. C. Form.	Description and Date of Effect					A.	B.	C.	
On Entry	ACH/F.A.E. 23/2/39	31/12/39	AC2	VG	ACH U/T F/mech	JL			
		31.12.40	AC2	VG	F/M(E)	SGT.			
		31-12-42	LAC.	VG.	F2E	Sup			
		31/12/43	LAC	VG.	Fit. 2. G.	Sup.			
		31 Dec	LAC	VG	F.2.E.	Sup			

Abbreviations; Ex – Examiner, F11 E – Fitter 2 engines

Ground Crew, ranks and roles during WW II

AC2 Aircraftman 2nd Class - Lowest rank

AC1 Aircraftman 1st Class

LAC Leading Aircraftsman

CPL Corporal

SGT Sergeant

F/SGT Flight Sergeant

W/O Warrant Officer - Highest rank

A slang term during the war for a non-commissioned airman below the rank of corporal, was an 'Erk', taken from the cockney pronunciation of aircraftsman – 'erkraftsman'. To qualify for an RAF ground crew trade, the recruits would first have to participate in several months of introductory training of life in the RAF, consisting of drills, physical training, introduction to firearms and a host of other disciplines. They progressed to an individual specialist training programme in a chosen trade such as fitter, armourer, rigger, flight mechanic, which involved practical and technical studies. On completion they would take a written and oral test both of an extremely high standard. *(Airfix, Aerodrome Magazine, Keep 'em Flying/Ground Crew Support Operations During WW II).*

It took a team of people to get a pilot and his aircraft airborne. Without this back up, loyalty and hard work from the ground crew there would have been a very different outcome. A huge effort was required from a host of non-flying crew who dealt with all manner of emergencies during operations. The ground crew, besides ensuring a clear runway, re-armed, serviced and repaired aircraft many of which had been damaged during operations. They were the unsung heroes of any operational station. The work they did was not glamorous but as vital to the war effort as any other. Working hours for ground crew varied depending on whether they were on an operational station or non-combative. Generally, they worked six and a half days a week with forty-eight hours off once a month.

Roy was trained to work on Rolls-Royce Kestrel and Rolls-Royce Merlin engines. He was also qualified to work on the Bristol Pegasus engine. The Rolls-Royce Merlin powered the RAF fighters, Hawker Hurricane and the Supermarine Spitfire along with the fighter/bomber de Havilland Mosquito fighter/bomber and heavy bombers including the Avro Lancaster and Handley Page Halifax. Roy worked on both the Hurricane and Spitfire at Biggin Hill during the battle of Britain.

Rolls-Royce Merlin and Bristol Hercules aero engines noted in his special qualifications were used in Hurricane and Beaufighter aircraft respectively – two types of aircraft SLAIS were equipped with during the time it was based at RAF Ranchi which was during the time Roy was stationed there.

(Alan Thomas, Air Historical Branch (RAF) Personal Communication December 15th 2020/, Ruislip, London)

Roy achieved a respectable 69% B pass during his Junior Non-Commissioned Officers Course (Murree Hills). His exams results were very good particularly the L.T.T.B. (Local Trade Test Board)

SPECIAL QUALIFICATIONS.
Exams., Courses, Engines, etc.

Authy., C.F. and Date.	Description and Degree of Proficiency or Assessment.
136/40	Ex. Rem. 7/4. 26/6/40. 57%
8/41	Ex Remust F.T.E 25-6-41 53.4%
164/42	Ex L.T.T.B. 30.6.42. 75.05%
24/12/43	Ex LTTB. 12.10.43. 81.7%
1942	Kestrel.
1943	Kestrel, Pegasus.
?/44	Ex. No.7. JNCO's. Course 13/11 - 9/12/44 63.9%
?/45	Ex Rulers JNCO's course 11.12. - 23 [?] 69% B.
1944	Hercules, Merlin

DATED 2nd MARCH 1959.

4908

Recruitment and Training

'*Pilots constituted only a fraction of total air force personnel. Those recruited for non-flying purposes came from a wide variety of backgrounds, including members of university air squadrons (UASs), private and commercial pilots as well as those trained in the military. In most air forces which were based on conscription there was a certain degree of choice for those conscripts who volunteered for one service in preference to another. Almost all air forces depended to some extent in recruiting personnel from unofficial and semi-official air organisations that existed before the war broke out, for these tapped sources of enthusiasm and interest in air affairs from the civilian population.*

'*In Britain the volunteer air reservists, such as the Royal Auxiliary Air Force proved an important source as did the Cadet scheme which did not fully materialize until 1938 as the Air Defense Cadet Corps. The existence of an informal procurement is for air service both simplified the selection process and provided a large reserve of men with an interest in, and experience of, air activity. This fact was more important from the point of view of acquiring suitable ground personnel than pilots since pilots required long periods of intensive training…*'

'*During the war the supply of large numbers of skilled ground crew and engineers was an essential factor in keeping an air force in being. No air force was unaware of this necessity, but there were limits imposed on the amount of maintenance and engineering personnel available. Part of the problem lay in the fact that much of the skilled labour was required more urgently in the aircraft factories, and the air force and economic ministries fought over how it should be divided.*'

'*Without doubt one of the most significant attributes at the outset of WWII was the effectiveness of its ground crew training regime. Under the stewardship of Hugh Trenchard, Marshall of the RAF, Britain had an apprenticeship programme that was arguably the most advanced of its kind in the world. It produced large number of ground trade professionals, who were extremely capable and highly qualified in all aspects of aviation preparation and maintenance. The Halton Apprenticeship Programme founded by Hugh Trenchard ran from*

1920-1966. Obviously, impending conflict resulted in many more people being required to train for this important role and although the training programme would have been modified somewhat to accommodate the increase in numbers, the effectiveness of this established system would continue to produce well trained ground crews. '

No. 7 School of Technical Training

11th May 1940

R.A.F. St. Athan, Glamorgan

Near Cardiff, Glamorgan, Wales

No. 7 School of Technical Training ran from February 1941 – June 1944, Hut No. 2 - No. 4 Wing, R.A.F. St. Athan, Near

Cardiff, Wales. At St. Athan, ground crew were trained on Hawker Harts and Avro Tutors - both biplanes.

St. Athans, Cardiff. Feb - June. 1940.

St. Athan, in the Vale of Glamorgan, has played a vital role in aircraft maintenance and training since the airfield's official opening on 1 September 1938. The first unit to form at St. Athan was No 4 School of Technical Training (SoTT) and it has been continuously present at the airfield ever since… The unit was initially formed to train airframe and engine fitters and mechanics but also trained Flight Engineers from 1942 due to the increased wartime demand for aircrew. A huge number of both military and civilian staff has been based at the airfield. In 1944 there was accommodation for 14,000 personnel, a very large number for a wartime station… The airfield's location meant that a number of training units were moved to St. Athan in an attempt to protect them from air attack, though Luftwaffe raids did cause some serious damage and fatalities during 1941.

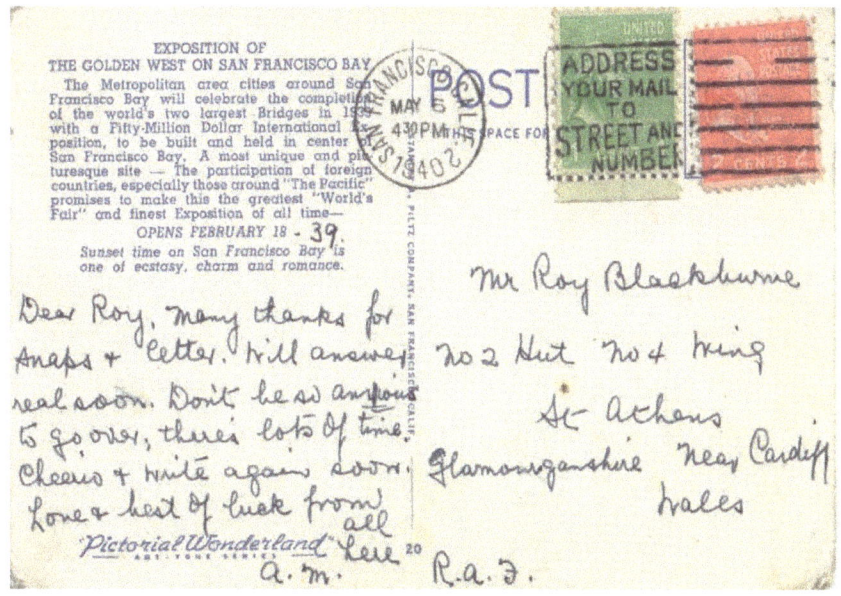

During the war a dummy airfield was built using wood and cardboard, a few miles west from the original airfield and successful efforts were made to hide the proper airfield. Aircraft and buildings were made of cardboard and wood and some real, but old tractors were driven around the site. The Germans attacked the dummy airfield a number of times and it was rebuilt each time. forums.x-planes.org. On the nights of the 28th and 29th July 1940 and 28th April 1941 St. Athan was bombed but no casualties reported.

Ingenious ways were used to camouflage valuable aircraft from attack, this 610 Squadron Spitfire pictured at Gravesend was disguised as a shed.

Roy, 1st left. LAC Banton, Joseph 810134 of Wolverham Road, Ellesmere Port joined 610 Sqn 28th February 1938 – 4th January 1946, he died in 2012. Jones, William G. (Bill) 810027 of Thamesdale, Ellesmere Port. Clowes, Russ also of Thamesdale, Ellesmere Port. All local men, their paths would have crossed many times pre and post war, as some worked for Shell

Left-Right, Banton, Chen, Beesley, Roy, Clowes. Cycling 22 miles from Cardiff to Portcawl

On the rocks, Roy, Chen, Beesley, Banton, Clowes

Roy 21 years old, In the barracks - 2nd April 1940 - training to be a flight mechanic

Training Aircraft

Having an 'M' suffixed serial number indicates it was primarily a training aircraft for ground crew. Formerly K8283 with 10FTS at Ternhill, Shropshire. When it became obsolete it was given a new identity as 1720 M (an instructional airframe) with a large batch of surplus Furies on the 10th January 1940. The 'M' indicated maintenance use only serial numbers.

Between April and September 1941, Roy underwent further ground crew training at RAF Innesworth where these photographs of tethered Armstrong Whitworth Whitley Bombers were taken. The photographs are of instructional aircraft for training crews. The Whitley Bomber was always intended for night operations. *It was the largest bomber at the outbreak of the war. In 1939 it soon became obsolete due to its slowness and vulnerability.* (paradata.org.uk/Whitley Bomber/26th September 2020). Aircrew nicknamed the cramped Whitley Bomber 'the flying coffin'.

(*Backroom Boys, Personal Stories of Britain's Air War 1939-1945/ Edward Smithies/Cassell Military Paperback*)

Hawker Fury Mark 11

Whitley Bomber

Whitley Bomber

Vickers Wellington GR Mk. VIII Bomber: This particular aircraft, serial N 2754, was used as a ground based instructional airframe for training aircrew and was never operational. On the fuselage, a rotable aerial a high frequency wireless direct finder. (Personal Communication Michael Lewis 18th August 2016/610squadron.com)

A Wellington displaying anti-submarine radar masts and a Lorenz Beam approach aerial. The Vickers Wellington was the most massed produced bomber of the Second World War. 11,461 were, made in Weybridge (Brooklands), Chester (Broughton) and Blackpool (Fylde). (www.baesystems.com/ Vickers Wellington)

Westland Lysander

Designed by W.E.W. Petter, the Westland Lysander was an aircraft with the ability to fly safely at low speeds. It had a short take-off and landing capability along with good visibility for the pilot. These capabilities enabled it to operate from small clearings with makeshift runways making it ideal for clandestine operations. RAF 138 Squadron, Special Operations Executive, made at least 400 Lysander sorties between 1941 to the end of 1944. RAF Tangmere was used as a refuelling stop for these aircraft en route to France. This was possibly where the next photograph was taken by Roy. 610 Squadron as part of 11 Group was stationed at nearby RAF Westhampnett, now known as Goodwood, in early 1941.

ARMY. CO-OPERATION. LYSANDER.
WITH. BOMBS. AND. RUBBER DINGY
18.4.40

Young recruits taking a break

The Point of No Return, 1st June 1940

With initial ground crew training at Hooton completed, and five months of their training at St. Athan behind them, Roy and his fellow airmen stand ready with kitbags packed, travel details around their necks, their destination Biggin Hill. Roy 2nd from right

Wartime greeting postcard

Order of Roy's Postings to RAF Stations in Britain

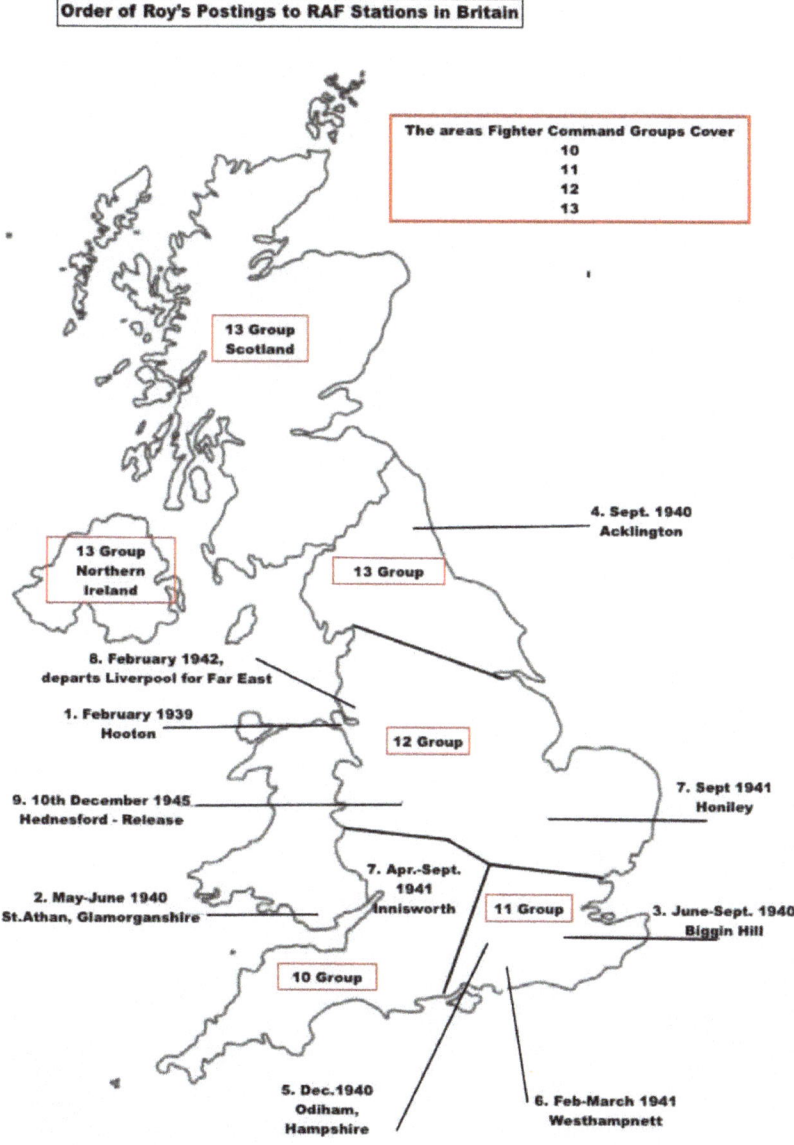

PART 2

WARTIME

The Battle of Britain

10th July - 31st October 1940

The Strongest Link' *(historylearningsite.co.uk/RAF Biggin Hill)*

Biggin Hill

The Battle of Britain was 'the first major battle to be fought entirely in the air and Nazi Germany's first major military defeat... At the height of the Battle of Britain, The RAF had only 749 fighter aircraft available against 2,550 Luftwaffe aircraft.'

Hitler's plan was to invade middle European countries followed by France in preparation for the invasion of Britain. Once France had been taken, Hitler ordered his generals to organise the invasion of Britain, code name, 'Sea Lion.' The Germans were to destroy the RAF in the air and on the ground, giving them air superiority to allow the invasion armada to head up to the Southern English Coastline, the Luftwaffe having four times as many pilots as the RAF were a far superior force. The Battle of Britain began with German air attacks on coastal shipping, followed by airfields and aircraft factories. 'Adler Tag' or 'Eagle Day' on the 13th August was the day Goering selected for the major air attacks. Thankfully much of the impact was lost due to bad weather and poor communication. 610 Squadron operating from Biggin Hill, Hawkinge, put up a magnificent show with 40 enemy aircraft confirmed destroyed during August. The Squadron lost eleven pilots and five ground crew during the Battle. In the final analysis 610 could be ranked around fifteenth most effective of all the 62 squadrons taking part. 'Over thirty ground crew in total were killed at Biggin Hill. During this tremendous period of history, the ground crews worked miracles of skill in keeping the Squadron's aircraft up to the fullest operational efficiency. Rarely was a damaged aircraft allowed to remain unserviceable for more than a few hours, even if it meant the crews working every minute of the day and night to affect the necessary repairs. 610 (County of Chester Assoc., a brief history of)

'Although ground crew seldom left the ground, all too often they found themselves the target of air attacks. They suffered terrible casualties, first in France supporting the Hurricanes sent over by Churchill and later on, the British airfields that took the brunt of the German bombing. Their job was one of almost total hardship. Their accommodation rarely rose above the rudimentary, sometimes not even that - they would make do with tents, outhouses, anything with a roof.'

'Their daily regime involved servicing the aircraft that were undamaged, before facing the Herculean task of repairing the many, many aircraft that limped home riddled with bullets and scarred by fire. Squadrons were flying four or five sorties a day; each time requiring the fitters to refuel and rearm the aircraft before moving on to a host of engine checks. Oil, Glycol coolant and oxygen supplies had to be replenished - and all of this accomplished in around half an hour. Their work never ended; much of it had to be done in the open, exposed to all the weather could throw at them, and invariably into the night. Sleep was something snatched in bursts or neglected altogether. During August and September, the ground crew were bombed and strafed by the Luftwaffe formations that had made the airfields their principal target. What scant accommodation they had was often the first thing to be destroyed by bombs and machine-gun fire. It would be their job to emerge from the smoking ruins, and get the airfield working again as soon as possible, filling holes in the runways before perhaps transferring to the satellite airfields which acted as alternative landing grounds for those aircraft still operating'.

WASHING DAY
RIDGEWAY. JACKSON.
TURNER.
8·9·40.

J. KING. MY TENT FOR THREE MONTHS
9·9·40

'In total some 312 RAF personnel were killed on the ground during the Battle of Britain, and 467 injured. When considered against the toll of 535 RAF aircrew killed during the Battle, it will be seen the loss of life and injury on the ground was indeed significant. To the aircrew went the glory, of the unsung ground crew, however, it should always be remembered that they also served.'

Al fresco lunch with 'A' Flight out on the airfield at Biggin Hill. Photograph courtesy of 610 Squadron Association

German and British Aircraft Of WWII

German	British
Messerschmidt Bf109 350 mph Fighter	Supermarine Spitfire 369 mph Fighter
Junker – Ju 87 240 mph Dive Bomber/Fighter	Hurricane 335 mph Fighter

Messerschmidt Bf110
348 mph
Fighter/Bomber

Boulton Paul Defiant
300 mph
Night Fighter

Junker – Ju 88
317 mph
Bomber

Mosquito
200 mph
Fighter/Bomber

Heinkel He 111
275 mph
Bomber

Avro Lancaster
280 mph
Fighter/Bomber

Dornier 215
312 mph
Bomber

Handley Page Halifax
280 mph
Fighter/Bomber

Dornier 17
310 mph
Bomber

Short Sterling
282 mph
Fighter/Bomber

Goring once boasted, 'Our aircraft are definitely superior to those of the British'.

The above information reflects the enormity of the task ahead for the RAF: the German Luftwaffe was considered a far superior force. During the Battle of Britain ground crew would have been extremely proficient at servicing the Spitfire, Hurricane and the Defiant at speed and whilst under enormous pressure to keep the aircraft airborne. Each aircraft had its own ground crew, prior to a flight the crew would do a pre-flight examination on the engine.

Pre-flight examination

Checking everything thoroughly, oil tank full, eighty-five gallons of petrol in the petrol tank, all ok in the cockpit, when it was ready it would be brought up to 'readiness'.

Flight Mechanic engine - check any damage to the engine, check fuel and oil tanks were full, check cockpit.

Rigger - check wheels, tyres, airframes and hood, polish hood.

Armourers - check the ammunition and re-arm the eight wing-mounted machine guns with ammunition.

The aircraft was often brought to a point of 'readiness' in just thirty minutes.

After-flight examination

Again, all trades would check to see if there was any damage and to what extent.

'Flight mechanic (engines) would have checked the engine for any problems reported by the pilot and also check that the fuel and oil tanks were full - a Spitfire holding 85 gallons of fuel. It would take half an hour to ready the aircraft for the next flight. This routine was similar to the pre-flight but with the additional problem of repairs to any damage such as bullet holes.

The armourers had to fill the magazines of the eight machine guns with ammunition, the instrument man had to replace oxygen bottles, the radio man had to check such a lot, the rigger had to check the wheels, tyres and airframes and the Perspex hood this required scrupulous cleaning – a speck on it, it might be mistaken for a German aircraft. Often the situation was not so straight forward. It would be immediately apparent that the aircraft had been in action by the red patches being torn from the machine gun ports. Frequently, the aircraft would need a simple after flight refuelling. At other times there might be damage to the airframe, propeller, radio or cockpit instrumentation. The engine was able to take quite a battering before it would pack in. The team would work together and help each other out wherever possible.'

Fitters were the skilled technicians who were responsible for the engines and other mechanical parts.

Biggin Hill, situated due south of London, was responsible for the protection of the south-east of England and the approaches to the nation's capital. During wartime, fighter squadrons were divided into two, 'A' flight and 'B' Flight. Between 2nd June 1940 and 13th September 1940, Roy, barely 21yrs old and with just six months basic training behind him, became part of 'B 'Flight of 610 Squadron. They were stationed for 105 days at Biggin Hill, the majority spent during the height of the Battle of Britain. The Battle lasted 82 days from 10th July 1940 to 31st October 1940. Along with other ground crew, he worked on aircraft in extreme conditions, and often whilst under heavy aerial bombardment by the enemy.

Sergeant, later Squadron Leader, Iain Hutchinson of 222 Squadron at Hornchurch, aptly describes the danger imposed on the ground crews and their dedication in 'Life on a Battle of Britain Airfield': '

The airfield was under attack and chunks of shrapnel were raining down. When I taxied towards the dispersal no-one was to be seen; they were all in the airfield shelters taking cover. Before I rolled to a halt and cut the engine, B Flight ground crew, under their flight sergeant, were swarming around my Spitfire, the bowser racing out to refuel the aircraft, while the armament men, laden with ammunition, were re-loading the guns. The noise from the explosions going on around us was terrifying but not one of those magnificent men faltered in the tasks. I was frankly relieved to be taking off.'

11 Group RAF Crest

"When 610 Squadron arrived for the first time at Biggin Hill they were visited by a plump fellow dressed in a dark siren suit who said, 'So this is the Cheshire Squadron.' In those days Winston Churchill lived not far from Biggin Hill and visited the station regularly. He was well aware that these were the men who were to serve Britain in 'Her Finest Hour'"

As European nations fell, Hitler and the third Reich set their sights upon an invasion of the English coastline. Hitler was heard to have said, 'I shall succeed where Napoleon failed, I shall land on the shores of Britain' in preparation for the planned invasion.

On August 18th, the Luftwaffe launched a major attack on Biggin Hill itself. In just ten minutes 500 bombs were dropped and the base was severely damaged. Immediately after the attack, all personnel at the base used whatever they could find to fill in the craters that pockmarked the runway. By late afternoon, the runway was in use again and 32 and 610 squadrons continued with their work. Over three days, from 30th August to 1st September, Biggin Hill was attacked six times, yet as Roy states below, *'No matter how many times the runway was put out of action it was always ready at dawn every morning.'* The ground crew worked around the clock to maintain the runway and keep the aircraft flying.

Hawkinge was the Forward Operating Base that 610 often used while based at Biggin Hill. It enabled the fighters to patrol the Channel and give air cover to the shipping entering Dover Harbour.

A C. R. Blachford wrote of 'being at readiness' from about three-thirty in the morning until eleven-thirty at night, day after day. Meals were taken 'as and when' and the rare days when we made to the airmen's mess for a meal were usually interrupted by an air raid'. (The Battle of Britain, the Greatest Air Battle of WW II/Richard Hough and Dennis Richards/pg.168/W.W. Norton &Company)

The Luftwaffe force launched another major attack on the 30th August 1940, which the Allies met with 16 squadrons. The Biggin Hill fighter station was spared during the first wave, but the village was not so lucky. The second wave destroyed a number of coastal radar stations, which left Biggin Hill more vulnerable. These radar stations provided an early warning system for the airfields. That evening, Biggin Hill narrowly avoided destruction. The attack destroyed its communication system, severing the link with Fighter Command Headquarters at Bentley Priory. Repair shops were all destroyed, and a shelter was hit, resulting in the deaths of 40 base personnel.

DAWN PATROL OFF TO HAWKINGE, DOVER

READY FOR TAKE OFF.

Weather conditions would determine if there was a likelihood of an attack by the enemy, if the weather was fine squadrons were put on a 'high state' of preparedness, if the weather deteriorated the 'high state' was relaxed somewhat. Squadrons were put into one of three degrees of readiness, 1. Readiness 2. Advanced Available 3. Normal Available. Should a squadron in 'readiness' be ordered to take off, Advanced Available changed to a state of Readiness and Normal Available to Advanced Available, making squadrons available to defend vital targets such as aerodromes and aircraft factories or act as reserves should there be other waves of attack. (*[15]Ref: The Battle of Britain, An Air Ministry Account of the Great Days from August –31st October 1940, Published by His Majesty's Stationery Office, London. (www.forces-war-records/page 8)*

Roy 1st right

*Some of the boys
A FLT. 610.
Searle. King. Birschell. Fairbain
Parry. Dowle.*

According to the Operations Records Book for 1st September 1940, 'All airmen of 610 Squadron are authorized to draw 'War Pay' at the rate of 6d per diem.

Unsung Heroes, the 'Erks'

Without the aircraftsmen, the Spitfires and Hurricanes could not have taken off, and certainly not survived the battle. These two aircraft won the Battle of Britain, and Roy was a proficient flight mechanic of both. Every aircraft that landed from each operation was serviced. Ground crew did just that, playing a major role in the Battle of Britain, servicing, assessing and repairing battle damaged aircraft, occasionally whilst under fire when ME 109s strafed the airfield.

The following extract is another from Pilot Iain Hutchinson, taken from 'Spitfire Ace, Flying the Battle of Britain', '*I thought they were terrific. One of the times when I landed to rearm and refuel, the airfield was being attacked. I got out the cockpit and they got the machine-gun rounds out. And I could hear this banging going on all over the place. I got under the wing, ostensibly to look and see if the guns had been reloaded, but basically, I was trying to keep clear of any shrapnel that might come our way. Then I was glad to get back into the aircraft and take off again, I may say. But they were out there in the middle of it, ignoring it all, and they were fantastic. You could depend on them to the last man. And the great thing was it was that they were engineers of skill; they did an absolutely precise job - there was no skimping any job, everything was done to perfection.' They looked after their pilots better than anyone could have done.*'

Following operations, the crew would prepare the aircraft for its next sortie. Armourers were to rearm the Spitfire's eight Browning Machine Guns, which all had to work perfectly in order for the pilot to survive. There was also a team that refuelled the aircraft. Often the ground crew would work all night to prepare a flight if it was to leave in the early hours. Ground crew worked incredibly hard during the long weeks of the Battle of Britain, having very little sleep, rarely changing their clothes and grabbing their meals on the job.

Each aircraft had two flight mechanics or aircraftsmen assigned to it to repair, rearm and refuel. If needed, however, they would call upon specialists with greater expertise in a particular field, for example, specialist electrical or radio fitters. Once the aircraft was ready for action it had to be signed off by an NCO, and the pilot also signed it off before departing for yet another dogfight in the sky. As the battle intensified and the demands on the pilots become greater, the strain on some squadrons and ground crew became intolerable. To get the aircraft airborne, not only skill but speed was required. The fighting record of each squadron depended as much on the efficiency and skill of the ground crew as it did of the pilot. During combat, when the pilot ran out of ammunition, he would return to his home station to be rearmed and refuelled.

ME! August 40.

The pilot's seat control was adjustable for differing heights by means of a lever on the right-hand side of the seat. To facilitate entry to the cockpit, a portion of the coaming on the port side was a hinged door.

Whilst Roy was doing his part to defend the South of England at Biggin Hill, Roy's family were also under heavy enemy fire back home in Ellesmere Port in the north-west of England. 'Between July and December 1940, 278,300 bombs were dropped on Liverpool and Merseyside alone.' When the Battle of Britain was at its height, 'On the night of the 29/30th of August the bombers were back over Merseyside to unload more explosives on the docks area, still smouldering from the night before.' No doubt Roy was totally unaware of the immediate danger his family faced and they were equally unaware of what was unfolding at Biggin Hill; that he too was in the midst of one of the major events of the war. Of interest is the number of RAF stations Roy was posted to following the Battle of Britain. No longer a newly qualified recruit, Roy was sent straight from training at St. Athan to the firing line at Biggin Hill. Now battle weary, he was sent for further mechanical training to various aircraft stations around the country, such as Innesworth, where he trained on the Whitley Bomber. These postings gave him the abilities to work proficiently in all aspects of mechanical work and on all types of aircraft prior to his posting to India.

Obviously a very stressful and traumatic time for Roy and fellow ground crew. The note was written from memory after the bombing took place, his date mistaken for the 6th rather than the 4th September. Prior to the bombing of the hangar there had been continual raids by the Luftwaffe on Biggin Hill for weeks, often two a day.

> *Salvage operations were still underway on 1st September, the first signs of activity over the French coast were seen on the radar screens at 10.30 hrs. and once again a high-level attack made for Biggin Hill at noon. The Spitfires of 610 Squadron which had been flying out of Biggin since May, had just departed for a rest period at Acklington but the ground crews had yet to leave and were waiting on the north side of the airfield for their transport to arrive when another raid began. They quickly took cover in the woods nearby as the bombs rained down on the landing area.*
>
> *Once again the airfield was a mass of bomb craters but these were filled in and the airfield was able to reopen later in the day. There was a further low-level bombing and ground strafing attack at 1800 hrs. which caused further damage, however the fires were quickly brought under control.'*

After the attack, very little of the infrastructure remained standing, hence the decision by Group Captain Grice to blow up the little that was left. Should the bombers return they would fly straight over, thinking the station had been totally destroyed, giving Biggin Hill the chance to regroup.

'At 1800 hrs. on 4th September the order was given to blow up the hangar. This was the time the Luftwaffe usually showed up but on this particular day they decided to give Biggin a miss which was unfortunate for Grice as he could not blame it on the enemy. He was severely reprimanded at the Court of Enquiry that was set up afterwards but everyone at the station felt he should have been commended.'[27]

Roy's date differs to the official record

A note Roy had written (typed as read):

'This photograph was taken on the 6 September 1940 at Biggin Hill during one of the heavy bombing and strafe raids. We blew up the hanger ourselves and let the Germans think that they did it. It was blown up because it was so heavily damaged in previous air raids by Germans bombers. I was strafed and bombed and shot at. But ironical as it may seem after this day 6.9.40 it all changed the enemy came less frequent and without that domination and only spasmodic raids. We knew then that he may have lost the battle'.

Operated by British Fleet Arm, the Blackburn B24 Skua was a two-seater, single engine aircraft, a dive bomber and a fighter.

An Armstrong Whitworth Ensign aircraft with a collapsed undercarriage, possibly at RAF Chipping Warden which was nearby to RAF Wittering in Northamptonshire, where 610 were briefly stationed.

It was Douglas Bader, echoing the words of William Shakespeare, who said, 'The Royal Air Force seemed to breed unusual characters. Generally, the brotherhood that made up the RAF fighter squadrons in the Summer of 1940 were the happy few, a band of brothers unique in British military history who came from all walks of life and from all over Europe and all the far flung reaches of the Empire. Canadians, Australians and New Zealanders.'

'The members of 610 (County of Chester) Squadron who died in action during WW 2, 63 from Great Britain, 2 Australia, 5 New Zealand, 1 Bahamas, 3 Canada, 1 Poland, 3 Belgium and 1 Sweden'. (Oliver Aviation Collection, 610 (County of Chester Squadron), compiled by Mark Oliver.

Below - Spitfires returning after a 'sweep'

German bomber, 1 of 57 brought down by 610. A lull in B flight during an air raid, September'

Winston Churchill spoke those stirring words, "The gratitude of every home in our Island, in our Empire and indeed throughout the world, except in the abodes of the guilty, goes out to the British Airmen, who, undaunted by odds, unwearied in their constant challenge and mortal danger, are turning the tide of the world war by their prowess and by their devotion. Never in the field of human conflict was so much owed by so many to so few."

He was speaking at a time when the battle was still at its height, for it was not until the end of October that the Luftwaffe abandoned its daylight attacks and began to rely on night raids: an admission of defeat.

32 Squadron returning to Biggin Hill after a sweep

Silhouetted against the night sky three Hurricane aircraft coming into land after a sweep, thankfully all three returning safely. Ground crew would wait in anticipation for their pilots to return, if only two returned they would know something terrible had happened to one of their pilots. 'No. 32 Squadron was one of the most successful Hurricane squadrons of the Battle of Britain, and was credited with 102 victories in the first half of the battle.'

32.SQDN.

At Supermarine Aviation there was a team of designers who worked on the Spitfire design. The chief designer of the aircraft was Reginald Joseph Mitchell, an aeronautical engineer who died in 1937. Sadly, he did not live to see his design used in combat. Mitchell was keen to have the aircraft named the 'Shrew' or the 'Scarab' but was outvoted by the board of Vickers. The head of Vickers Aviation, Robert Mclean, named the aircraft 'Spitfire' after his little daughter Annie who he said was like 'a little spitfire', meaning 'spirited'. 'In all, 20,351 Spitfires were produced for the RAF'

Spitfire of 610 Squadron. Note the sleek fuselage compared with that of the Hurricane below. DW was the squadron code and the third letter 'N' was the individual aircraft identifier letter. To the rear of the aircraft a smaller individual black serial number could be found, which was different on each aircraft, and stayed with it during its lifetime. Hurricanes followed a similar squadron coding. (web.archive.org 610 Squadron Radio Code was 'Dogrose')

Hurricane of 32 Squadron, (GZ) serial number V7060. The Hurricane was slightly larger than the Spitfire with a 'drop' to the tail. The photograph of the Hurricane was likely taken at Biggin Hill as 32 Squadron were there at the same time as 610 Squadron in 1940.

Wing Commander Michael Nicholson Crossley, Commanding Officer of 32 Squadron for part of the battle said: 'The ground crews were past all praise. If we had long hours they had longer ones by far. There was always laughing and ragging around the place, betting cigarettes or drinks as to whether A flight would do better than B. A lot of publicity and glamour comes the way of the pilots but not all the praise in the world would do justice to these back-room boys.'

Both the Spitfire and Hurricane had Merlin engines, which meant Roy was qualified to work on both aircraft. The Hurricane had a wooden fuselage and wings covered in fabric whilst the Spitfire was made completely out of metal, consequently it was easier to repair any damage on the Hurricane, as the fabric could be patched up. (*uk/thespitfireandthehurricane/21st August 2020*)

Whilst the Hurricane was the most numerous and most successful of British fighter planes, it was the faster and lighter Spitfire that caught the imagination of the public. In the words of one of its test pilots Jeffrey Quill, "a symbol of defiance and of victory in what seemed a desperate and hopeless situation."

RAF Acklington

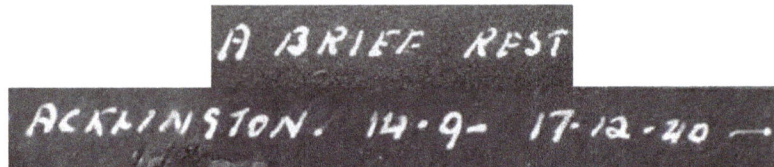

The Latin motto translates as 'yesterday it had to be taught, today it has to be carried out'. (RAF Acklington, Guardian of the Northern Skies/Malcolm Fife/National Archives

Following the Battle of Britain, in September 1940, 610 Squadron moved to RAF Acklington to regroup and for some to enjoy a few days leave. During the 'brief rest,' maintenance work continued for Roy and fellow ground crew. RAF Acklington, 13 Group, Fighter Commands most northerly operational airfield during the Battle of Britain and one of the most important in the north-east of England. During the period of Roy's posting there, 610 Squadron received an intake of new, inexperienced pilots to replace those who were lost in the Battle of Britain or those who had been sent to give the benefit of their hard won experience to other units. Some of these new pilots were involved in several incidents/crashes at both Acklington and also at nearby Eglingham keeping the ground crew busy with repairs:

2nd November - a 610 Squadron Spitfire made a belly landing, pilot safe, aircraft damaged;

5th November - Spitfire X4011 crashed on take-off, pilot killed, aircraft destroyed;

19th November - 610 Squadron Spitfire R6686 crashed landed, pilot safe, aircraft damaged;

9th December - 610 Squadron Spitfire P9311 belly landed, pilot safe, aircraft damaged in Eglingham;

4th November, 610 Squadron Spitfire L1094 crashed into the ground during aerobatics practice, pilot killed, aircraft destroyed;

19th November 610 Squadron Spitfire R6891 crashed, pilot killed, aircraft damaged.

> *Now, the Squadron's role was to train new recruits from the OTUs in order to get them ready to join an operational frontline Spitfire squadron in 11 group, while also allowing the veterans some respite from being at constant readiness and the strain of aerial combat.*

RAF Acklington was a station located just over three miles from Amble, Northumberland. The airfield reopened in 1938 and was renamed RAF Acklington where no. 7 armament training station was formed. There were two decoy airfields sites situated nearby, 'K' site – a daytime dummy airfield complete with decoy Hurricanes situated at nearby Long Houghton, and 'Q' site - a night time dummy airfield erected south of Acklington at Widdrington. (*RAF Acklington, Guardian of the Northern Skies, Malcolm Fife, page 132*). RAF Acklington was used by the RAF until 1975 when it was handed over to Her Majesty's Prison Service for the building of two new prisons.

RAF Acklington as identified by the 'slag heap' of Broomfield Colliery: a landmark near the boundary of the airfield. Acklington is situated on the edge of the Northern coalfield. This photograph, printed from Roy's negatives, shows Spitfire 'DW-W' positioned in a revetment (blast pen) designed so any blast would go upward and not outward, thereby not damaging neighbouring aircraft, preventing a chain reaction. The pennant painted below the cockpit identifies the Spitfire as Squadron Leader John Ellis's who was Commanding Officer of 610 Squadron.

H. David Denchfield a sergeant pilot of 610 Squadron wrote of ground crew in his recollections of a Spitfire pilot at Acklington; 'I think the original pilots were all gone, one way or the other but the ground staff as usual with Auxiliary squadrons remained. They could not be posted to another unit against their wishes, hence spent most of the war with their original units. A great spirit resulted.' *(RAF Acklington, Guardian of the Northern Skies, Malcolm Fife, Recollections of a Spitfire Pilot at Acklington, pg. 11).*

Although Roy originated with 610 (County of Chester) Auxiliary Squadron he did not remain with them for the duration of the war because as stated on his service record under 'miscellaneous' he was willing to go to any other RAF or AAF Unit.

This Spitfire X4649 was delivered to 610 Sqn at Acklington on 7th November 1940.

On 4th November 1940 754347 F/Sgt. Hugh Biggans McGregor, was posted to 610 Sqn from No. 7 O.T.U. (Operational Training Unit), Hawarden in North Wales. Barely a month later on 11th December 1940 when flying Spitfire P9451 he was killed when he was involved in a mid-air collision with another 610 Squadron Spitfire - X4649 (above). The other aircraft was flown by P/O Ross who managed to bail out and parachute to safety. McGregor was aged 24 yrs. and son of Robert Clark McGregor and Elizabeth Harkness was buried at Larkhall Cemetery, Dalserf (*personal communication Michael Lewis, 22nd July 2020/ 610(County of Chester) Sqn. Assoc.,*)

An original photograph printed from one of Roy's negatives, shows a Spitfire 'DW-K' serial number X4241 of 610 Squadron in a 'Category 3' (unspecified) accident with a Bristol Blenheim bomber following a ground collision on 2nd September 1940 at Acklington. The badly damaged propellers of the bomber indicate its engine was running at the time of impact and *it* had crashed into a stationary Spitfire.

The Handley Page H.P.54 Harrow, aka 'Sparrow', a transport aircraft, was used between 1937-1945. The Sparrow could accommodate 12 injured/sick soldiers as stretcher cases. (*www. neversuchinnocence.com/Handley Page H.P.54 Harrow*). The transfer of ground crew from airfield to airfield would generally have been by rail, but because of the distance and logistics involved, Roy and fellow ground crew flew on a Handley Page Harrow from Newcastle to RAF Odium, Portsmouth 17th December 1940.

Ground crew would invariably feel the loss if their pilot did not return from a sortie, it was often the younger more inexperienced pilots who never returned. The average age of a Battle of Britain pilot was 20yrs and the average life expectancy was just four weeks. In a newspaper article by Group Captain Douglas Bader CBE, DSO, DFC written in later years he stated, 'Like other battles in our history, the Battle of Britain became important only in retrospect to those who fought it. In that desperate year of 1940 only the Prime Minister, the War Cabinet, and the Commander in Chief of Fighter Command knew without doubt what was at stake. The pilots certainly did not know .'

John Ellis Flight Lieutenant

Photograph courtesy of 610 (County of Chester) Squadron on the occasion of receiving his DFC from the King for 'Gallantry in operations against the enemy.'

Roy was one of the ground crew (engine) for John Ellis

Ellis became a:

Temporary Squadron Leader,
Squadron Leader,
Temporary Wing Commander,
Group Captain.

Later awarded two Distinguished Flying Crosses for his heroic actions during the war.

Post war decorations:

January 1947 - MiD (mentioned in dispatches)

May 1956 - OBE (Order of the British Empire)

June 1957 – MiD (mentioned in dispatches)

June 1960 - CBE (Commander of the Order of the British Empire)

John Ellis, service number 37850, joined the RAF as a regular in March 1936. Following the outbreak of WW II, he was posted to 610 Squadron at Hooton Park for flying duties on 15th September 1939, on the 16th September he was promoted to Acting Flight Lieutenant.

Distinguished Flying Cross (DFC)

Period: WW II (1939=1945)
Rank: Acting Flight Lieutenant
Awarded on: August 13th, 1940

'This officer was employed on offensive patrols over Dunkirk during the evacuation of the British Expeditionary Force and led his flight with great courage. On two occasions whilst deputising for his Commanding Officer, he led a patrol of four squadrons, displaying great initiative and leadership. During these patrols Flight Lieutenant Ellis destroyed two enemy aircraft. Later, whilst engaged on home defence duties, he shot down one enemy bomber. In July 1940, whilst leading the squadron, he destroyed two enemy aircraft and on the following day he shot down a further three of eight enemy aircraft destroyed by his squadron. Flight Lieutenant Ellis has displayed courage and leadership of a high order.'

Distinguished Flying Cross (DFC)

Period: WW II (1939-1945)
Rank: Acting Squadron Leader
Unit No. 610 (County of Chester) Squadron, Royal Air Force
Awarded on: May 2nd 1941
(The London Gazette Issue 3515 published on the 2nd May 1941/ tracesofwar.com)

Ellis shot down five enemy aircraft before the Battle of Britain, three of them were fighters. He destroyed a Bf 109 over Dunkirk on 29th May 1940 and a Do 215 E in Dover on 29th May 1940.

John Ellis sitting on top of the Spitfire.
(Photograph courtesy of 610 Squadron Association)

On the occasion when the then 'Acting Flight Lieutenant' John Ellis received his DFC, Distinguished Flying Cross, 13 th August 1940, his ground crew must have felt an enormous sense of pride, not only with his achievement but with their own contribution towards his success.

On the 7th June 1940, he destroyed a Bf 109. On 12th June 1940 a He 111 of Wekusta 51 flown by Oblt Derd Nessen, the

Staffelkapitan was shot down off Margate. The He 111 was attacked at 0700 by two Spitfires flown by the 610 Squadron, F/Lt John Ellis (P9451/DW-M) and Sgt. Stanley Arnfield (P9495 DW-K), the crippled reconnaissance machine then ditched several miles offshore. Three of the crew managed to get out before it sank but two others, Uffz Franz Bolinski and Uffz Willi Stiegelmeir were lost.

However, one of the survivors, Reg. Rat. Hermann Freudemberg, a weather specialist, drowned before the fishing boat *'Golden Spray'* arrived. The boat's crew of three, including 16yr old Ken Ross, dragged the two injured airmen aboard including the pilot who had head injuries and a bullet in the arm. Young Ken ripped his underwear into shreds to make bandages. The other survivor Obfw Hans Peckhaus was also seriously injured, on reaching shore both were rushed to hospital for emergency treatment. On the occasion of the then Acting Flight Lieutenant, John Ellis receiving hs Distinguished Flying Cross (DFC) on 13th August 1940, the ground crew must have felt and enormous sense of pride, not only for Ellis achievement but with their own contribution to his success.

In the latter part of 1942, Ellis was sent to Khartoum in Sudan. 'In the Spring of 1943 he was restationed at Malta to lead the Krendi Wing but on June 13th he was shot down by a Me 109s when escorting American B-24s who were going to attack Gerbini Airfield. He bailed out over sea and was picked up by a German search and rescue party. He was sent to Stalag Luft III and became active in the escape committee as no. 2 under Roger Bushell.'

Following the war, John Ellis held various positions within the RAF until he retired on the 28th February, 1967. He ended the war with 14 enemy aircraft destroyed. He took part in the first Battle of Britain Commemorative Fly Past September 1945. Post war he lived at Petersfield in Hampshire.

The following letter was sent to Roy from Group Captain John Ellis

From: Gp. Capt. J. Ellis CBE DFC.

FAIR OAKS
DURFORD WOOD
PETERSFIELD
HANTS GU31 5AW
Liss 3360

15 June 81

Dear Mr Blackburn,

I should like to thank you for subscribing to the beautifully bound copy of "The Battle of Britain" which Arthur Hufford and Wallace Howard kindly presented to me recently on behalf of all known surviving ground crews of 610 Squadron.

It is a marvellous present which will always be a reminder to me of those memorable days at Biggin Hill in 1940 and the vital part you and your colleagues played in keeping our Spitfires flying.

Very many thanks and maybe we can all meet in Chester on the 50th anniversary

All the best

Yours sincerely
John Ellis

RAF Woolsington

A satellite station (not self-administrating) of both Acklington and Ouston, Woolsington opened as a civil airport in 1935 but was requisitioned by the RAF at the advent of WW II. It served at various times as a satellite for both RAF Acklington and RAF Ouston but saw little operational flying. Woolsington's main operational role was as the base of 83 Maintenance Unit which salvaged crashed aircraft over much of the region. 'Its main task was to salvage the remains of aircraft that had crashed in the northern England and bring them back to Woolsington.' After the war, civil flying resumed at this airfield and it is now known as Newcastle International Airport.

'Wheatsheaf' Woolsington after pay parade.

RAF Westhampnett

According to the squadron's Operations Records Books (ORB), orders were received 14th December 1940 from 11 group for the Squadron to move from RAF Acklington to RAF Westhampnett in West Sussex. On 19th December, F/Lt. (Acting Squadron Leader) John Ellis D.F.C. (37850) along with seven other pilots proceeded by air from RAF Acklington to RAF Westhampnett. The transfer of ground crew from airfield to airfield would generally have been by rail. Westhampnett opened in 1940 as an RAF emergency landing airfield for fighter aircraft during the Battle of Britain when it was home to two Spitfire Squadrons. The airfield was a satellite of Tangmere Airfield, located two miles away. During this period, air and ground crew were housed under canvas, several months later moving into Nissen huts and barracks. The officers' mess was in a nearby manor house.

WEST HAMPNETT. SUSSEX. 18·12·40 — 25·5·41

Roy on guard

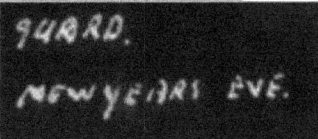

Ensigns were a type of aircraft that were mainly used for transport duties during WW II. Only 14 were made. One of the first duties was following the German invasion of the Low Countries (Holland and Belgium), for ferrying supplies to France. This was followed by evacuation before France capitulated in June 1940.

Pilots of 610 Squadron at RAF Westhampnett with Squadron Leader Holden, C/O of the Squadron at that time (wearing forage cap, centre).

Photo Courtesy of 610 Squadron Association

Fifteen pilots of 610 Squadron were killed whilst operating from RAF Westhampnett.

Unfortunately, the ORBs did not record the movements of the ground crew, they only recorded the movements of aircraft and pilots, but in doing so they do indicate the enormity of the daily operations at a given airfield. Westhampnett was no exception. It was an operational airfield facilitating numerous daily sweeps, patrols and several circuses. To keep these aircraft in good mechanical order and airborne throughout would have been an enormous task for ground crew who, with discipline and team work, would have likely worked around the clock.

To keep the aircraft in the air would have taken a highly specialized team of ground crew requiring great attention to detail to ensure the aircraft were ready for their next mission. For ground crew assigned to a bomber squadron on night operations, the working day would start early in the morning with the daily inspection. The crew that had flown the aircraft on the last operation discussed with the ground crew any issues they experienced with either the aircraft equipment or engines during the mission. Anything highlighted as a problem was noted on a Form 700, which was colloquially referred to as a 'snag sheet', but was a significant document on an RAF airfield. As long as Form 700 was in the hands of the ground crew, that particular aircraft 'belonged' to them and it was unavailable for operations; no one on the airfield could order an 'erk' to sign off the aircraft until everything on the snag sheet had been rectified and checked. Once all the work had been completed and the pilot of the aircraft was happy, he would be asked to sign the form and responsibility for the aircraft would pass back to him.

Roy 2nd left

Roy 1st left

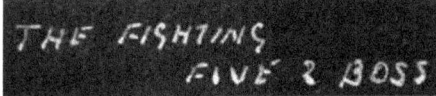

Below; An excerpt from Ellesmere Port Pioneer at the 40th Anniversary Reunion; 'Accommodation left a lot to be desired at Westhampnett, the squadron was obliged to sleep some of its members in a shippon. They removed the cows and everything else except the smell joked Mr. Banton. the rat hunting' incident brought more laughs. Rats were hunted by putting oily rags down their holes, setting light to them and smoking the rats out. 'The only trouble is, they went straight from there to the NAAFI,' said Mr. Blackburne. If they thought of the danger of their situation, they never let it worry them. 'It was all rather a laugh and a giggle, ' said Mr. Swinnerton, while *Mr. Blackburne said, 'Biggin Hill was just another station.'* We did not know what we were going in for when we went there. It was never us who got it, it was always the other guy. It was whilst based at Westhampnett that the 610 Squadron escorted the plane that flew a new pair of legs out to Douglas Bader when he was a prisoner of war in Germany.

The number of footprints in the snow indicates the enormous amount of activity that had taken place.

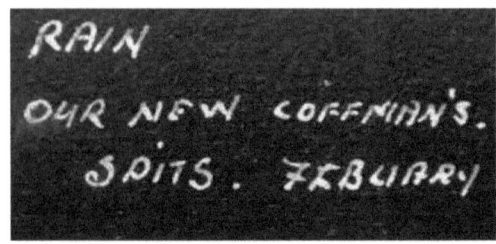

Coffman starters were an engine starting system (also known as the 'shotgun starter') used on many aircraft piston engines including the Rolls-Royce Merlins used in Spitfires.

The highly specialized work of ground crew continued in all weathers. Above, Roy was wearing the standard ground crew issue: wet weather gear, a black sou'wester hat that had a 'gutter' at the front which sloped downwards toward the back to keep the neck dry and a long oilskin coat.

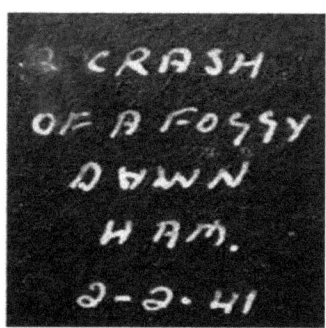

Damage to the propeller of the aircraft on the left indicates that this is the aircraft that was in motion at the time of the collision.

RAF Innsworth School of Technical Training, Gloucester

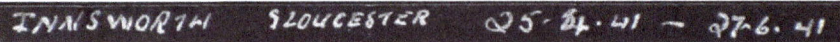

Roy attended Innsworth No. 7 School of Technical Training at RAF Innsworth from 25th April 1941 to the 27th June 1941. Innsworth was a non-flying RAF station which opened in 1940 for the training of engine and airframe fitters and mechanics. Roy's unit was the first based there. 'Over 2,000 officers and men were based at Innsworth by the time training began in earnest in 1941, this being delayed due to the arrival of 1,500 RAF evacuees from Dunkirk.' Innsworth closed in March 2008. In 2010 it was renamed 'Imjin Barracks' and became home to the Allied Rapid Reaction Corps, ARRC. *(Forces-war-records.co.uk)* wikivisually.com)

A post card from Roy's Uncle Albert.

'Hello Roy, how are things going now, sorry have not replied to your letter will do so later, I am on holiday at the moment, you know where at and who with, Yours Albert'

RAF Honiley

A.C. Blackburne 810183, S.H. A. Echelon Flights, Hut 63, RAF Station Honiley, Kenilworth.

RAF Honiley is located 1 kilometre north-west of Honiley, in the vicinity of Coventry. At the time of its construction in 1940/41 the airfield was referred to as RAF Ramsey, changing its name to RAF Honiley at its opening in August 1941. The station's primary focus was the defence of the Midlands by night fighter squadrons. The airfield held 15 hangars, a technical workshop, as well as a cinema.

'Dear Roy, hope this finds you quite o.k. Pleased to say we are having a good time, quiet and happy for a few days. Hope to see you soon, Albert'

Speke Airfield (Liverpool)

The following photographs were taken by Roy when he was stationed at Speke Airfield in September 1941 whilst awaiting deployment to the Far East. Speke opened as a 'civil' airport in 1934 but was operated by the military during the war. It is now known as John Lennon Airport. As Roy's service record states, he was HH whilst at Speke: this is the Command reserve or Headquarters Holding, which means the man does not make up the establishment of the unit but is supernumerary and is owned by headquarters as an area reserve. The officer commanding a unit cannot post this man but must ensure he is fully trained and supported and equipped ready to be shipped off elsewhere if needed. (*RAF Commands.com Ross McNeill, 13th November 2011*).

With Roy's hometown of Ellesmere Port tantalizingly close and visible across the River Mersey from Speke, it is to be hoped he had home leave prior to setting sail on the hazardous journey to India.

During WWII, de Havilland DH86 aircraft operating for Railway Air Services were seconded for military service, communications and radio navigational training purposes.

A Martin Marauder, a twin-engine bomber built by Glen L Martin Company, pictured at Liverpool, Speke Airport. Due to the high incidence of crashes on take-off and landing it became known as 'The 'Widow Maker'.

A Boulton Paul Defiant nicknamed 'Daffy' by the pilots. In the background are American built aircraft and the distinctive hangars of the old Speke Airport.

The Defiant was designed to an Air Ministry Specification under the direction of J.D. Nord. It was an interceptor aircraft that served with the RAF during WW II. It was designed as a 'turret fighter' with no forward guns, which became a weakness when in action, particularly during daylight hours.

'The concept of a two-seater single-engine fighter with all of its armament concentrated in a massive power operated turret was based on the belief that a gunner with no responsibility for flying the aircraft and able to traverse his battery of guns through '360 degrees' had more chance of hitting the enemy than a pilot that had to point the aircraft in the direction in which he wanted to fire. Not properly appreciated by those who fostered this concept was the way it divided responsibility between pilot and gunner and required the pilot not only to fly the aircraft, but also to think in abstract terms as to his gunners' line of sight.'

Bristol Blenheim Mk V1 (Long nose), built by Rootes Securities at Speke. This was taken at Speke while the bomber awaited collection by the squadron to which it had been allocated. The squadron code was X-LW Serial number V5794. The LW indicated the aircraft was attached to 75 Calibration Flight/Signals Flight. The engines are 'Vokes' filters indicating the aircraft was to be used in dusty areas such as desert. (Blenheim Society). 44 Personal communication/Tony/blenheimsociety@yahoo.co.uk//20thApril 2018

The Bristol Blenheim was an aircraft ahead of its time. Originally built as a civil aircraft, because of its excellent flying characteristics, Lord Rothermere, the owner of Associated Newspapers Ltd, donated the aircraft to the nation. As well as bombers both Mk 1 and Mk 1V were adapted as fighters by the addition of a gun pack located in the bomb bay which contained four Browning .303 machine guns. The Mk 1V was used as a long-range fighter which was used as a maritime patrol aircraft. Both aircraft were used as bomber/gunnery trainer. (*Blenheim society. com*)

Bristol Blenheim close-up

Lockheed Hudson bomber. The American designed Hudson, nicknamed the 'Old Boomerang' due to its ability to withstand enemy fire and safely return home, would go on to earn innumerable accolades during the war. It primarily served with the RAF Coastal Command hunting German and Japanese submarines, but Hudson crews also provided convoy escort, participated in the RAF's first thousand-aircraft raid into Germany, performed reconnaissance missions and dropped spies behind enemy lines.

(www.lockheedmartin.com/TheHudson/ theoldboomerang23rdAugust2020).

Lockheed Hudson aircraft on the apron at the old Liverpool Speke Airport

Overseas Deployment

Leaving from Liverpool

During the war, the movement of servicemen from England overseas was mainly by sea. On a chilly February morning heading into the unknown, Roy, 23 years old, would not return home for another four years. As the ship sailed out of the Mersey, no doubt he would have looked back at The Liver Buildings and wondered if he would ever return home, and if so, whether it would be a country under German occupation.

The Liver Buildings

LEAVING LIVERPOOL FOR THE SEA
STUCK ON SAND BANK.
7.2.42

En route to Singapore, India via Freetown, Sierra Leone, Cape Town and Durban

CONVOY

After 18 days, the convoy arrived at Freetown on 25th February 1942. 'Freetown, the capital of the British West-African colony of Sierra Leone, was central to the Allies' strategy during World War II. It served as a convoy station, with up to 200 cargo and military vessels moving in and out of its well-protected harbour at the height of wartime activities. In 1939, Great Britain introduced a general militarization of the city and the US built installations and stationed officers and troops there.'

(Ascieiden.nl/Freetown, Sierra Leone and World War II:Assessing the Impact of the War and the Contributions Made/ seminar date: 17th March 2011/Location: Pieter de la Courtgebouw/ Faculty of Social Sciences, Wassenaarseweg 52,2333 AK Leiden/ Leiden University/accessed 10th Sept. 2020).

An unidentified convoy troop ship

Ex German Ice Breaker now under Dutch Ensign used as Armed Cruiser.

South Atlantic

A Brief Respite in Durban

Durban was a transit point for the movement of convoys, troops and materials during the war. Personnel in transit were billeted at Clairwood Camp, previously known as the Imperial Forces Trans-Shipment Camp (IFTC). The large camp was located eight miles from Durban, and overlooked the Clairwood Racecourse.

HM Troopship Somersetshire, 7,456 gross tonnes.

The photograph was possibly taken whilst Roy was in Durban, as the Somersetshire operated from the Red Sea to South Africa, Australia and New Zealand, repatriating wounded soldiers from early 1941. The Somersetshire was one of the Bibby's line of troop ships with accommodation for 1,300 troops. 'In September 1939, the Somersetshire was requisitioned and converted into HM Hospital Ship No. 25 with 507 beds, 118 medical staff and 171 crew members.'

Trans-Shipment Camp (IFTC) located eight miles from Durban, and overlooked the Clairwood Racecourse 22nd February 1942

The Gang

Due to the numbers of disembarking servicemen in Durban, many used rickshaws, pulled by Zulus, for transportation

Vast numbers of servicemen passed through the port of Durban en route to war zones in Asia and the Far East. During their stay public transport was freely available, many servicemen opted for the novelty of riding in rickshaws pulled by Zulu's. Special concessions were available at cinemas and free concerts were performed at the City Hall, all run by the Municipal Entertainment Department. At Durban, Roy was transferred onto the Dutch ship MS Christiaan Huygens, which had arrived at Durban on February 13th 1942 for refuelling. The Christiaan Huygens had accommodation for 638 passengers. After hostilities commenced the ship was operated by the Orient Line and used by the Allied Forces as a troop carrier. 'Nine ships sailed from Durban on February 22nd 1942 as convoy DM3 for Singapore, this included the Christiaan Huygens. However, events overtook the convoy, Singapore had fallen to the Japanese, the new destination of Batavia was later amended to Columbo, then Bombay as the Japanese advance through East Asia quickened. Bombay was reached on March 6th 1942.' According to a letter Roy's father Jack had written, Roy had 'been to Singapore' but thankfully, contrary to what it states above, this was not correct.

PART OF CONVOY LEAVING US TO GO TO CAIRO AND BOMBAY.

22.2.42

INDIAN OCEAN LAT 15. LONG 60

It was at this position the convoy split.

DESTROYER H.80 AND "WOODLARK"

CENTRAL ATLANTIC

24.2.42

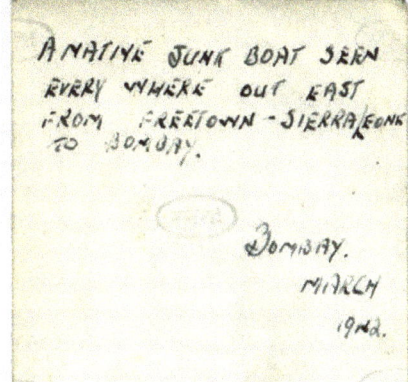

A NATIVE JUNK BOAT SERN EVERY WHERE OUT EAST FROM FREETOWN - SIERRA LEONE TO BOMBAY.

BOMBAY.
MARCH
1942.

Order of Roy's RAF postings in India

India was one of the principal bases for conducting operations against Japan in Asia.

Alexandria Docks, Bombay

MS Christiaan Huygens docked at Bombay on March 6th 1942. RAF personnel were transferred to a nearby RAF station, others posted to RAF Ranchi, a two-week train ride away across the plains of India or further north to Cawnpore 322 M.U. (Maintenance Unit). On arrival in Bombay, Roy was transferred to Deolali Camp, 100 miles North East of Bombay, whilst he awaited a posting to an active service unit.

The ship *Mauretania* was built at Cammell Lairds, Birkenhead, and launched on 28th July 1938. At the start of the war, The Ministry of War requisitioned *Mauretania* and the ship was refitted as a troop ship in Sydney, Australia, to carry up to 6,500 servicemen and women.

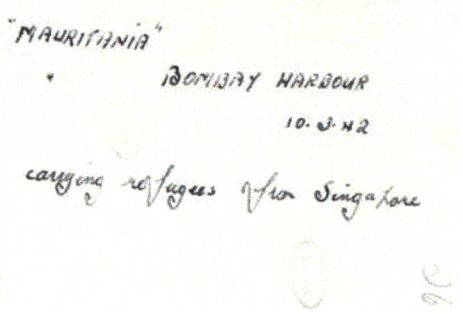

"MAURITANIA"
Bombay Harbour
10.3.42
carrying refugees from Singapore

Deolali Camp 15th March 1942

Situated 100 miles north-east of Bombay, Deolali camp was an army transit camp for British Troops in India. Troops were transported there by rail from Bombay and stayed for several weeks in order to become acclimatised to the Indian heat. The camp was where the British slang noun 'doolali-tap' originated, which loosely means 'camp fever,' referring to the apparent madness of men waiting for ships back to Britain after finishing their tour of duty.

By the 1940s the term had been shortened to just 'doolally,' an adjective meaning 'mad (insane) or eccentric'. The town was the setting for the British sitcom 'It Ain't Half Hot Mum' set in 1945. The servicemen were allowed into the nearby town of Nasik where, with its bars and brothels, venereal disease was common. Malaria was also a problem in the area and was a major source of concern for the forces on the Indian continent.

Roy at Deolali camp 15th March 1942, while awaiting his posting to Ambala. He most likely travelled the 1,568 kms overland to Ambala by train, in stifling heat and cramped carriages. Roy, 2nd from left front row, Beesley (unknown first name in St. Athan with Roy), 2nd from right

Ambala

Ambala is a city in the Ambala district in the state of Haryana, north-west of India, approximately 100 miles north of Delhi. RAF Ambala began operating in 1919 and in 1941 became an RAF sub depot. Today it is still an active station; the Indian Air Force station in Western Air Command. Roy arrived at the base along with 40 other B.O.R's (British Other Ranks), where he was stationed between 31st March 1942 until October 1943. At the time Roy was stationed there the base consisted of:

No 303 Maintenance Unit;
No.1 School of Technical Training;
No.1 Service Flying Training School;
Central Map Section;
Base Accounts Office;
Personnel Reception Centre;
Central Trade Test Board;
No. 144 Repair and Salvage Unit arrived later, in February of 1944.

One stripe on the sleeve denoted a Lance Corporal and the badge of a propeller denoted a leading aircraftman.

In India, ground crew were not assigned to a specific RAF squadron but to 'maintenance units.' Roy's first posting from 21/03/1942 – 16/11/1943, 20 months in total was No. 303 Maintenance Unit, No. 303 Maintenance Unit was unit originally No.3 (India) Maintenance Unit but was renumbered by the Air Ministry on 18th March 1942. The unit began as an Aircraft Repair Depot for the overhaul and maintenance of Harts and Audaxes aircraft. Squadrons and units operating throughout India were under the control of Air India Command up until the end of 1943, when it came under the Air Command South-East Asia (ACSEA). Formed on 16th November 1943 as 'South East Asia Command,' under Air Chief Marshal Sir Richard Peirse, as a combined RAF/USAAF operational command, it covered India, Ceylon, Burma, Siam, Malaya and Sumatra. The title changed to 'Air Command South-East Asia' on 30th December 1943. *(Personal Communication, Liz Deery, 10th November 2020/Air Historical Branch, RAF, Ministry of Defence).*

During the war, No.1 Servicing Flying Training School was stationed at Ambala, consisting of six flights 'A to F'. The school ran two flying courses, Intermediate Training School and Advanced Training School, each lasting for three months. Aircraft operating during the period were Harvards, Hurricanes and Oxfords *(Personal Communication 24th October 2019 Office of Pro (Air Force,), Directorate of Public Relation, Ministry of Defence, New Delhi, India).*

The Hawker Audax was a tropicalised variant of the Hawker Hart, a two-seat light bomber which was an early design attributed to Sydney Camm. The Audax represented a significant step forward in performance compared with the types that were serving with the Royal Air Force in the inter-war years... The type was very similar in appearance to the Hart but featured longer exhausts and a message pick-up hook, attached to the undercarriage spreader bar that could be lowered as required.

Roy working on a Hawker Audax

Of concern was the well-being and health of personnel as sickness could affect productivity: During the month of May the unit worked under a shift routine. The men worked six days a week with Sunday off. The working week consisted of 52 hours less 1 hour deducted from the 10 minute break taken each morning, resulting in the actual working hours being 51 hours per week. On 31st June 1942 it was decided that working hours of the unit would be slightly reduced on the advice of the Station Medical Officer, it was considered the reduction of man hours would not seriously affect the output as the fall off in sickness would more than offset the loss. But on 1st September 1942 the hours were increased to 52 hours. 20 mins, altered to suit the Indian daylight saving scheme and the continued cool spell of weather, with a view to giving the airmen more time for recreation. On 14th October 1942 machine shop personnel went on a two-shift routine in order to obtain maximum output from machinery available. The following day, 15th September 1942 a party of 17 men arrived aimed at increasing production

In addition to the above measures, regular requests for blood donors were made. On 19th July 1943, 'A lecture was held by a medical officer calling for blood donors, 63 volunteered from this Unit.' As a result, on 17th and 18th November 1943, 78 personnel donated blood. Barely a month following Roy's departure there was a smallpox outbreak, which resulted in an increase in vaccinations for the disease, and on 29th November, smallpox vaccinations were allocated to personnel and their families.

For obvious reasons, safety and security were under constant review at the unit. Throughout 1942 and 1943 'batches' of RAF personnel were instructed on aerodrome defence, '30th January 1943 Station Combatant Course. 'Backers Up.' To date a total of 100 airmen completed and passed course.' Monthly air raid precaution practices took place with exercises where personnel wore respirators whilst at work. 'All personnel of the unit saw the Security film 'Next of Kin' a good picture which gets home it's message.' *Next of Kin* was a propaganda movie produced by Ealing Studios about the importance of discretion with regards to military movements or matters, as the consequences of inadvertently giving away this sensitive information could be catastrophic for the allies.

During November of 1942 there was little airframe production due to the lack of 'Red Dope'; a plasticised lacquer applied to fabric-covered aircraft. By tightening and stiffening the fabric, it stretched over the airframes, rendering them airtight and weatherproof. Supplies of tools and parts were obtained from Lahore, 264 km away. On 1st February 1943, a propeller repair shop was reopened at the Forest Research Institute at Dehra Dun, which was responsible for personnel and equipment matters only. The strength at the time of opening was a Flying Officer, a sergeant, a corporal and a Leading Aircraftman.

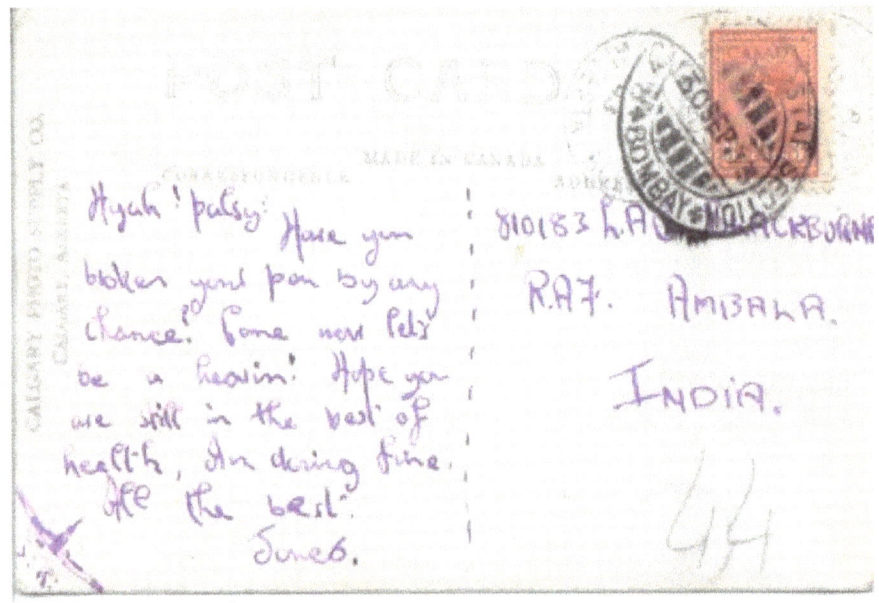

'Hiyah palsy, have you broken your pen by any chance! Come now let's be hearing! Hope you are still in the best of health, I'm doing fine. All the best, Jones.'

Monthly output/production of major and minor repairs and overhauls of airframes and engines varied month to month due to equipment problems, availability of parts and supply of labour. In 1943 the standard working week was increased to 58 ½ hours on a two-shift routine. As the unit continued to expand, more personnel were brought in to support the increase in productivity, and monthly production records/output were noted in the ORBs.

An aircraft on fire at RAF Ambala, no mention of the blaze in operation record books during the time of Roy's posting

Near the bathing pool, Ambala, India

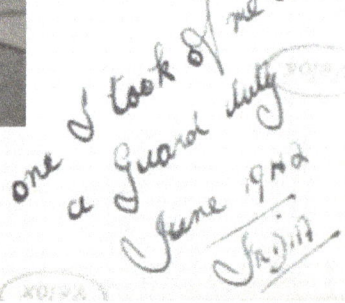

one I took of me on
a Guard duty
June 1942
India

As a young man from the industrial town of Ellesmere Port, away from the ravages of war back home, Roy took the opportunity to go to places he had only ever read about. Just a fortnight after arriving in Ambala on 5th April 1942, he spent ten days leave visiting sights in New Delhi, a five hour drive away. Ten weeks later he spent further leave visiting the sights of Punjab province, a four hour drive from Ambala. He found India a fascinating place, having the greatest respect for its people and an appreciation of its culture and history. The work of an aircraft mechanic was often hard and tedious, but even so, his time in India became an experience of a lifetime.

Above, Gandhi pictured wearing his dhoti (or loin cloth), with which he identified himself with the poor

During his visit to New Delhi in April 1942, Roy witnessed Mahatma Gandhi, the leader of the independence movement against British rule, during one of his campaigns for independence. Gandhi preached satyagraha, non-violent civil disobedience.

Typical India.
Bazaar Ambala

Oct. 1943

Two native pottery makers.
They look fierce but
there harmless.

Punjab. 1943

A Venereal Disease Clinic

Opium Shop

On the 5th April 1942, five days after Roy arrived at Ambala, Air Officer Commander-in-Chief, India General Wavell and Air Chief Marshal Sir Richard Peirse, below, inspected the unit.

General Wavell, Commander in Chief of India and a member of the Governor's Executive Council, became Governor General and Viceroy of India in September of 1943. Air Chief Marshal Sir Richard Edmund Charles Peirse, KCB, DSO, AFC (30th December 1892 - 5th August 1970), was a senior Royal Air Force Commander. In 1943 Peirse was appointed Air Officer Commander in Chief RAF India and in November 1943 he was made Allied Air Commander in Chief, South East Asia.

The ONLOOKER
...sees most of the game

Vol. IV   SEPTEMBER 1942   No. 9

A pleasant and natural photograph of His Excellency General Sir Archibald Wavell, G.C.B., C.M.G., M.C., A.D.C. It is just about 14 months since he first came to India as Commander-in-chief. Recently he visited our armies in the Middle East and later went to Moscow where he took part in the historic conferences held on the occasion of the visit to Russia of Britain's great Prime Minister, the Hon. Winston Churchill.

'Onlooker' newsletter found amongst personal effects

Quetta Arsenal

Amongst the paperwork was this photograph (below) of Quetta Arsenal. Quetta (fort), town is the capital of Beluchistan Province, one of the four provinces of now Pakistan, located in the southwestern region of the country and bordering on Iran and Afghanistan it is one of the most important military locations in Pakistan. *(www.warlinks.com/WW11 Memories, The Great Quetta, John Ernest Brown).*

During WW II Quetta Arsenal was a fort and arsenal. Quetta had a 'Staff College', with the surrounding hilly terrain used for Jungle Training by the armed forces.

The following pages are of a letter from Roy's father Jack to his sister Mim. Of interest is how the war affected their family life, and it also mentions Roy and Singapore prior to the Japanese invasion on 15th February 1942.

72 Princes Road

Ellesmere Port

25-11-42

My Dearest Sister Mim,

At last I am making time to write to you. I believe some our letters have gone to Davy Jones for him to read. Well Mim old dear, I hope you get this one and in time for Christmas. Well Mim about yourself and the girls how are you all keeping, well, I hope, do remember Uncle Jack to them all. I believe Marita is quite a good girl and helps you. Well Mim about your family here. Alice is just the same and as good as ever, no ... there is only the three of us here at present as Jackie has been in hospital since May but he is going alright. The two girls May and Millicent are alright, May is at home and Millicent is in a new home two miles from here, her husband is a motor cycle dispatch driver. May's husband is still in Libya, now for nearly the last two years in the R.A.F. but up to the present time he is alright. I don't know if you got any letters telling you about Roy. He got away from Singapore at the beginning of the year and he got to India and is now against the Japs not the Jerries he had plenty of them while in England in the Battle of Britain, we heard from him lately and he said he was alright and it was fine flying over the Himalayan Mountains the highest in the world. He gets plenty of food. Well Mim about myself things are not too good in health and trade is bad in the furniture line as it is so dear and there is to be no more made utility furniture, which is not yet in the shops. There is plenty of work in munitions and money but I am too old and in bad health. Millicent is on a machine in a government factory, nearly all the women in the country are now working on one thing or another or in the army or

R.A.F. and the Navy arm, well Mim the old country is doing splendid as I always did think that they would as I never once thought we would lose even when we stood by ourselves, things are now just about beginning to turn, there is a good chance of the war being over about next summer but the boys will not get home for about two years after except a few in key positions. I expect Mim you are as pleased as us at the way things are going now. The Jerries are in for a bad winter where ever they are and just think what losses they have had I don't think what the German people are doing to let Hitler and co. gel all them men ... slaughtered. They know now about the might of the R.A.F. now night and day they are getting it heavy and they don't like it. It was alright when they were so strong and were so weak and they were ... us but now the boot is on the other foot they don't like it. They can't take it like we had to do. Thank goodness it is quiet here in this country with no air raids but I expect we will still get some yet, but get a surprise when he comes from over defenses and the R.A.F. fighters, we are not doing so badly for food we get enough to eat it is not fancy food nearly everything is nutritional, it is quite a business looking after the ration books from shop to shop, sweets are rationed 3/4 per month up to the present we are getting enough coal to keep us warm. People in Britain have learned to make food and things go a long way, the girls go without baking or they cut out coupons to have for them. Now that the cold weather is here they taken to wearing slacks that is flannel trousers it will soon seem strange to see a woman in frocks here they all work in trousers or overalls. Well Mim I must about be closing this letter as I am tired it is after 10pm. Alice, May and Millicent wish to send heaps of love to you and your girls and of course, dear Mim I now wish you myself the old old wish, A Very Merry Christmas and a Happy and Prosperous New Year. So, goodbye for the present I will try and write again soon, no more now from your ever-loving brother Jack. xxxxxxxx

Roy's service record for the Far East from January 1942 until departure from BHQ Karachi 1st November 1945

NEDERLANDSCHE TELEGRAAF MAATSCHAPPIJ "RADIOHOLLAND"

DE OCEAANPOST.

Tuesday, January 20 1942.

WASHINGTON - Japanese forces have sent skirmishing parties against General Mac Arthurs Bataan lines, the War Department reported yesterday, possibly in an attempt to find a opening for a big attack. There was a lull in major operations and fighting was of a desultory nature reflecting the defenders success in beating off the largescale and infiltration efforts which the Japanese have launched in the past week.
The Japanese airforce was relatively inactive confining itself to reconnaissance flights.
It was reported that native farmers have been rounded up and formed into labour groups by the Japanese while Filipinos in the occupied areas have been disposed of their means of transportation and harvested crops and food stores have been seized by the invaders.

RANGOON - Japanese troops have occupied Tavoy seacoast town of Burma adjoining Thailand, a communique announced yesterday.

TOKYO - Newspaper reports say that the Sultan and other dignitaries of British Borneo had offered cooperation to the Japanese and had asked their people to stop resisting.
From Batavia it was reported that everything useful to the Japanese including shipping was destroyed at Kuching, capital of Sarawak Borneo, before the small garrison fell back to Dutch Borneo, a Sarawak European officer, who was among the last to leave, told the United Press on arriving there.

LONDON - An Admiralty Communique issued late Monday night said that in view of axis allegations that allied naval forces have been active against axis shipping on the Spanish island Fernando Po no British or allied warship was in the vicinity of this island at the time of the alleged incident. The British commander in chief has despatched reconnaissance patrols to cover the area and a report has been received that a large unidentified vessel has been sighted and British naval vessels are proceeding to the spot to make investigations.

RIO DE JANEIRO - A war of nerves developed at the conference of American foreign ministers yesterday after rumours circulated here that the axis nations had warned South American countries that a joint diplomatic break would bring war with Germany, Italy and Japan. Some of the rumours were traced to Argentine and Chile and some quarters believed that they may have been floated to support Argentines opposition to the resolution calling for full diplomatic, economic and financial breaks with the axis powers. An unconfirmed report was that the Japanese ambassador in Santiago has warned Chile that Japan would declare war following a severing of relations.
Argentine Foreign Minister Ruiz, who opposes an open break conferred at length yesterday with Brazilian President Vargas, who is emerging, with United States Under Secretary of State Sumner Welles and Brazilian Foreign Minister Aranha as strong man of the conference.

DEAL - Thousand of Kent coalminers on strike have been served with summones for breach of their contracts.

WASHINGTON - President Roosevelt agreed to rush plans for the expenditure of 400 to 600 million dollars for the compensation and defense training of four million industrial workers faced with temporary unemployment during the change-over of the nations produc-

Tuesday, January 20 1942.
===

LONDON - A single enemy aircraft harmlessly bombed a place in Southwest England last night.

CAIRO - The GHQ communique says that operations in Libya again were greatly curtailed by continued bad weather.
During previous nights bombers of the RAF raided enemy transports on the roads East and West of Sirte.
Objectives at Tripoli were also attacked.
Naval aircraft made a highly successful attack in the Central Mediterranean on a large enemy tanker and two escorting destroyers. The tanker was torpedoed and one of the destroyers received a direct hit.
The number of prisoners captured in the Libyan campaign now number almost 15.000 and Italy with the latest capture of Halfaya hast lost her 79th general.
In the occupation of Bardia, Sollum and Halfaya less than 100 imperial troops were killed and 400 wounded, Headquarters said.

MALTA - Enemy aircraft raided the island yesterday. Some damage was done to civilian property.

MOSCOW - The Soviet Communique reported that during the 19th the enemy was fought on all fronts. Breaking the resistance of the enemy our troops continued their advance. Our bombers and fighters supporting ground operations were active.
London reported that the bitter struggle for the Crimea was continuing.
Berlin in a broadcast yesterday claimed that the Black Sea port of Feodosia had been recaptured but it appeared that the Russians still were on the offensive elsewhere on the southern peninsula.
The German broadcast also said that Mozhaisk, Orel and Kursk which with Kharkov constitute the four anchor points of the 600 mile German line north of the Sea of Azov had not been captured by the Russians. This was believed in certain circles to indicate that those towns were in grave danger since the Russians have not officially claimed these towns.
London said, commenting on the military convention signed by Germany, Italy and Japan, that the significance of the agreement was not clear but was probably an attempt by the axis to match the allied agreement for a unified command in the Far East.

SINGAPORE - Japanese troops attacked heavily yesterday at the opposite ends of a forty mile line on the West Malaya front and forced a British withdrawal below the mouth of the Muar river 90 mi from Singapore. Strong imperial plane forces rushed to the aid of the ground troops and made a heavy bombing and machinegun attack on Japanese transports along the road and the river.
A communique said that it is known that three Japanese planes were destroyed during the last heavy raids on Singapore. The casualty list was put at 56 killed and 135 wounded, mainly civilians bringing the total to 186 killed and 235 wounded.
Despite the admission of further withdrawals it was understood that the situation at the front continued to be more encouraging. Australian commander Bennett stated that everything was going according to plan and that the Japanese still seemed to avoid major action. He added that the situation especially on the West coast is still grave.
From Australia it was learned that War Minister Forde cabled Singapore yesterday that the Government was taking emergency steps to strengthen the imperial airforce there. Reinforcements of men and planes were arriving in Malaya in such force that we may soon equal or surpass the Japanese airstrength in Malaya.

REUTER COPYRIGHT

'De Oceaanpost' was a newsletter issued by Radio Holland that was sent by Morse code to the vessels. The radio operator on board received the message, typed it and then it was shared among the crew and passengers on board the vessel. *(personal communication, Erwin Bik, RH Marine Group, Radio Holland. 3rd August 2020)*. This copy likely obtained on the MS Christiaan Huygens when Roy was en route from Durban to his intended destination of Singapore.

A Sunday in December 1943. Looking at the Pishat talking films, language Urdu. With Kane and Carter. Roy in the centre.

'a native film poster' good camera snapshot don't you think.

Nishat Talkies
Ambala native Sudar
Bazaar.
Simla Dec 43.

The Hindi means
'Saint Cauri'

RAF Hill Stations

Naini Tal

Whilst stationed at RAF Ambala Pradesh, Roy and other weary servicemen, with no opportunity to return home in the foreseeable future, were sent to RAF Hill Stations for rest and recuperation, one such Hill Station was Naini Tal, situated in the outer foothills of the Himalayas, 6.837ft above sea level, where the climate was cooler and more equitable than the hot plains below.

Football match – Roy 3rd on right, back row

Local children 'standing to attention'

Lakeside at Naini Tal

Solan

Solan another minor Hill Station which was situated 100 kms away from Ambala and 345 kms from Delhi in the foothills of the Himalayas between Dehra Dun and Simla. Operation Record Books of RAF Ambala detail how the 'Hill Parties' departed on regular basis, staying a month at a time in the picturesque area. During the 18 months Roy was stationed at Ambala, 14 Hill Parties departed overall - as one returned from Solan, another departed. *(TNA, ORBS, No. 303 Maintenance Unit, Ambala, Air/29/1073/3)*

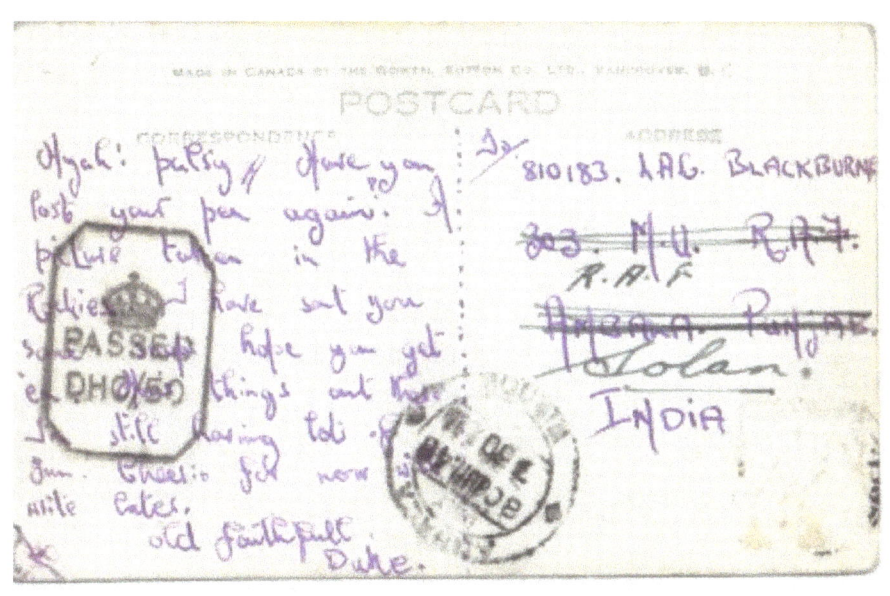

810183 LAC Blackburne R

RAF India Command

18.07.43

My Dear Milly and Tom,

I do hope this letter finds you in the best of health and spirits, (non-alcoholic) as it leaves me at present. Really, I was greatly surprised hearing from you nevertheless it doesn't alter the fact I do know that you could not have previously written to me working those long hours at the R.O.F.

The mail situation has considerably improved somewhat lately. I regularly receive the letters from Mother, she tells me of her recent outings in the bath chair, I hope she keeps it up, at least a regular outing weekly might do wonders. I hear very little news from John these days how he is faring in hospital, the last word I had of him he was improving fast, any more news since then I would like to hear.

This past summer has been very cool in comparison with last year the temperature has been remarkably low hence I have been making the best of it, going to various places during the weekend passes I have. So far, I have patronised Lahore as the controlling element. There is however an interest there, a girl, we have been having great fun together and she dances superbly.

A short while back I had a spell at a rest camp in the Himalayan mountains, fourteen days to be precise, I had a lovely time, cool fresh air the temperature in those mountains being considerably less than on the plains here, gave me ample scope to indulge in plenty of sports, as football, tennis etc., I had two-day spell at Sinla, reckoned to be no.1 hill station or the best: I enjoyed myself by all means but in comparison with Naini-tal as it was last year it will take a lot of beating.

Here again I did a bit more dancing even though the respective dance halls were full of brass hats, Dukes, Lords, etc., not forgetting the high-class Indians, I felt no inferior complex but just barged in and had an A1 time, needless to say, I have since found out that pure Indian of high class are educated in the European manner; are extremely polite and friendly some passes a sort of shy or reserved manner.

Travel is a great education. Since I have been abroad I have tried to travel as extensive as possible, I have learnt a lot and my views have changed considerably, particularly in the political world. You asked me is there anything I could send for your house would you like a silk set like mother in any colour you like. I could send bed spreads anyway; the next time I go to the local native bazaar I will have a good scout around.

Give my love to May and Mother next time you go home, I am still feeling ok and doing alright, I cannot say much about work not supposed to etc. Cheerio for now all the best and good luck to you both,

Your loving brother,

Roy

General Working Conditions of Ground Crew in India

Once enlisted, an airman's 'terms of service' during the war were relatively vague, beyond the certain knowledge he was unlikely to be released from the service until the close of the war unless for medical reasons, or other individual possibilities. He automatically became subject to all and every rule and regulation found in the Kings Regulations and ACIs, was bound in disciplinary matters by the imposing volume Manual of Air Force Law (MAFL), apart from a host of temporary wartime impositions placed upon all Servicemen and civilians. He could be (and often was) posted at the shortest of notices to far-flung corners of the globe, with no redress. If such a posting was to an overseas theatre of operations, his stay outside his homeland was undefined in the context of specific length of sojourn, i.e. there were no laid-down, set parameters to an overseas tour of duty. This might be months or more likely two, three or four years away from family with no known date for repatriation home until only weeks before actually leaving with his unit abroad.

Working hours depended on whichever unit, station or command he might be with or in, the hours were varied, but generally depended on the airman's trade and whether he was with a front-line operation or not. The usual working week for 'Erks', on operational stations was six and a half days a week with a forty-eight-hour pass once a month, and very occasionally a few days leave. For the ground crew directly concerned with the aircraft, they worked whenever work was necessary, even if this meant staying on the job until the task was completed, day and/or night. (*The Royal Air Force, 1939-1945, Chaz Bowyer / Bison books Ltd 1977/page 10*).

During wartime, a telegram was usually the bearer of bad news, Roy's was no exception. As the day dawned on the 25th May, Roy, aged just 24, received a telegram from his mother informing him his father had died just days earlier on the 18th May 1943. This was a terrible shock in itself, made worse by the fact he was unable to make the journey home to console his disabled and now widowed mother, nor even contact her. It must have been a devastating time for him, and being wartime, it must have crossed his mind he may never make it home at all. Thankfully, she had two loving daughters and a son who helped as much as they could, but they too had their own wartime commitments and young children. Roy's sister Millie worked in a munition's factory at nearby Helsby and his sister May was a cashier at the local 'Queen's Cinema,' who after a day's work would stand on the roof of the cinema on fire watch duty, looking out across the night sky for any fires caused by incendiary bombs. Roy's brother Jack was a bricklayer, a 'reserved occupation' and suffered from health issues, which lead to hospitalisation on several occasions. This meant Jack was unable to reliably support his mother financially. Following their father's death, that role fell to Roy and his sisters.

Prior to the war there was little in the way of government welfare support for those in need, this proceeded post-war in 1945 with a change of government, initially with the introduction of the Family Allowances Act.

During the war correspondence between loved ones took many weeks, sometimes months, to reach its destination, if it arrived at all. However, receiving post raised morale both home and abroad. Telegrams were the quickest form of communication during wartime, but rarely sent unless in times of crisis or to deliver the devastating news that a loved one was 'missing in action'. Charges were by 'per word' an average cost being nine words for 6d.

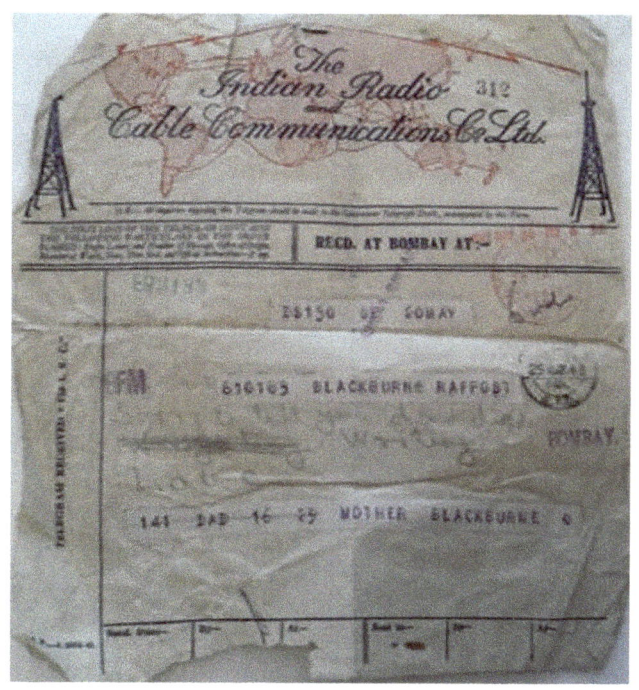

Written over the red stamp on Roy's telegram, '6 wds'

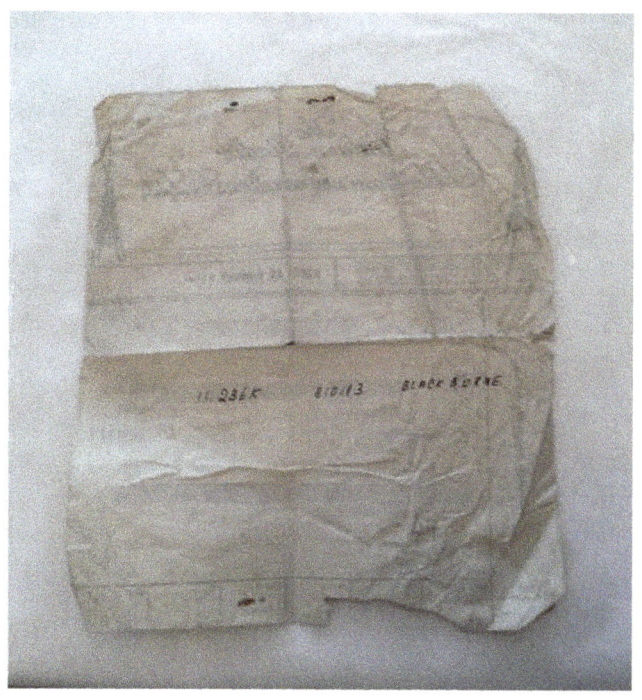

It is doubtful if word of bombings back home reached Roy in India. Unfortunately, his home town of Ellesmere Port suffered its share of bomb damage during the war. As an industrial town situated on the River Mersey with the Manchester Ship Canal running alongside, it was a prime target. The shipyards of nearby Birkenhead sustained extensive bomb damage. On the Wirral there were two RAF sites, RAF West Kirkby was a camp with no airfield, and RAF Hooton. There were also a number of anti-aircraft sites to protect the docks of Birkenhead and Liverpool. Liverpool, just over 27 miles from Ellesmere Port and visible across the River Mersey, was bombed extensively from August 1940 – January 1942 in the Liverpool Blitz. Residents of Ellesmere Port, many whom had relatives in Liverpool, would have watched with absolute horror as night after night the bombings continued.

> 'The city was a lifeline for Britain's maritime trade, being the main point of entry for imported fuel, food and raw materials. It also served as the strategic hub of the longest campaign of the war, the Battle of the Atlantic... Liverpool was defended by RAF fighters, who were based at Speke as well as sites in Cheshire, Shropshire, Wales and Blackpool'.

As the Luftwaffe made their way back to Germany, remaining bombs were jettisoned en route. Little Sutton suffered several major hits. A house opposite Peggy's (Roy's then future wife) in Dudleston Road was destroyed, killing all the occupants. Surprisingly, the huge oil storage tanks at the Shell and Burmah refineries in Ellesmere Port were never located nor bombed. Cleverly, the huge structures had been completely covered in turf making them extremely hard to see from the air particularly at night.

Cawnpore

On 8th April 1942, Mr. C.W. Casse M.I.C.E. the chief mechanical engineer, U.P. Government visited Ambala with a view to the formation of C.R.O. Cawnpore.

A posting followed from Ambala to 322 Maintenance Unit, Cawnpore. The nucleus of this unit formed on the 21st May 1943, as a service manned Base Repair Depot, in No. 226 Group. The unit was initially posted at No. 29 Personal Training Transit Camp,

RAF Drigh Road (Karachi), but moved to RAF Cawnpore (Northern India) on 1st July 1943.

The British erected protective bamboo scaffolding over the Dome of the Taj Mahal

    322 Maintenance Unit was formed to support air operations in the Far East in 1940 at the 21 TATA hangars at Cawnpore (now Kanpur). The function of the unit included the arming of bomber and fighter aircraft such as Liberators, Lancaster, Hurricane, Tempest and Dakota. The unit was further expanded to include aircraft storage and servicing activities while the logistics, support and aero engine storage functions operated at Armapur Estate 25 km away from Chakeri. In August 1945 after Japan surrendered to the Allied Forces and hostilities came to an end, this number

322 Maintenance Unit was disbanded and Royal Air Force Station Kanpur came into formal existence. *(WW2talk.com/Dave B. very senior member/ Maintenance Command/Maintenance Units)*. No. 322 Maintenance Unit, Cawnpore, became the largest service-based repair depot in India, ultimately capable of undertaking major repairs to 55 large aircraft and a monthly engine overhaul capacity approaching 500 units.

Every trade of aircraftsman was assembled and a large hangar was built to keep the men out of the blazing hot sun which could heat the metal of the aircraft to a temperature so high it could burn flesh on contact. The large hangar is still there today.

India Command was renamed South East Asia Air Command on 16th November 1943. It was a combined RAF/USAAF operational command covering India, Ceylon (Sri Lanka), Burma (Myanmar), Siam (Thailand), Malaya (Malaysia) and Sumatra. The title changed to Air Command South East Asia on 30th December 1943.

1943 Roy in uniform showing arm insignia of a propeller i.e. Leading Aircraftman, above that the RAF arm Eagle shoulder flash. The Eagles were worn in all ranks underneath Warrant Officer, from Aircraftman 2nd class, Aircraftman 1st Class, Leading Aircraftman, Corporal, Sergeant and finally Flight Sergeant and were worn in pairs, one on each shoulder and facing rearwards.

The unofficial translation of the RAF Eagle Motto is; 'We have eyes everywhere.' Reflecting how the wearer's eyes face forward whilst the Eagles face backwards. The official translation is 'Through struggle to the stars'

As 322 Maintenance Unit was centrally located, Roy was able to travel to 'nearby' cities such as Agra and Lucknow through the 'Golden Triangle'. During the later years of the war he traversed across India to a posting at Ranchi, Eastern India. His means of transport is unknown, but it is likely to have been by train, although he does mention in a letter to his father, 'How fine it was flying over the Himalayas'.

K.R. & A.C.I. 2139. CARE AND AWARDING ASSESSMENTS OF CHARACTER.

1. When assessing character the C.O. will always bear in mind that its value to the individual and the service depends on the care and deliberation with which this important duty is performed; that the future prospects of the airman may largely depend on the character awarded; and that the certificate of service is often an airmans passport through life. The effect of character assessments on awards of G.C. Badges and long service medal must carefully be borne in mind.

2. In assessing the character of an airman the C.O. will consult the Adjutant, the airmans subordinate commander and any officer who may have special knowledge of his character; he will consider fully intermediate assessments that have been entered on his miscellanious record sheet and all the entries against him on the conduct sheets for the period covered by the assessments, and also his general character, so that this duty may be performed justly with proper deliberation.

3. In all questions relative to or dependant upon, an airmen's character the notations made upon his certificate of service will be considered as conclusive subject only to revision under the authority of the Air Ministry. Should the Certificate appear to have been tampered with the C.O. will immediatley report the particulars in the manner laid down in para 2133.

K.R. & A.C.I. 2140. CHARACTER - HOW ASSESSED AND RECORDED.

1. The following rules will be observed in the assessment of character, but the C.O. may always exercise his descretion within the limits prescribed, viz:-
  (a) "Good" Except as provided in clause 2 a higher character than "Good" will not be given to an airman if during the period for which his character is being assessed, he has been sentenced to be punished in any of the following ways.:-
     (i) Reverted, reduced in rank or deprived of seniority for misconduct.
     (ii) Deprived of Long Service and Good Conduct Medal or Good Conduct Badge.
     (iii) Sentenced to field punishment by court Martial, imprisionment or detention, for periods up to but not exceeding twenty days aggreate.

  (b) "Fair" A higher character than "Fair" will not be given to an airman if, during the period for which his character is being assessed he has been sentenced to field punishment by court martial, imprisionment, or detention, or any two or more of these punishments for 21 days or more up to but not exceeding 60 days aggregate.

  (c) "Indifferent". A higher character than Indif is not to be given to an airman if, during the period for which his character is being assessed, he has been sentenced to field punishment by court martial impisionment, or detention, or any two or more of these punishments, for 61 days or more in aggregate.

2. The C.O. may assess an airmans character as "V.G" once during his career, although he may have been puniƨned and such punishment has rendered him eligible for "V.G." but not ineligible for "GOOD" under clause 1. This priviliage is granted in order that ab airman may not by one slip forfeit the rewards due to an unblemished record. It will not therefore be allowed unless the C.O. is entirley satisfied with the behaviour, conduct, and work of the airman for the year, apart from the offence in question an air man who has previously received character below V.G. is not eligible for the conession. V.G. will be regarded equivelent to and for all purposes, the asterisk being placed against the award only in order to ensure that the airman dose recive such special consideration more than once during his service.

3 Imprisonment by the civil power will be taken into consideration in the assessment of character when the offence is one that has been brought disgrace or discredit on the uniform, the service on the possesion which the offender holds, and character inferior to that which might he have been otherwise have been given under Clause 1 may be awarded in this account if approved by the air or other officer commanding

Winter in the Murree Hills

13th November 1944 – 9th December 1944

The permanent town of Murree was constructed in 1853. Murree became a popular tourist station for the British within British India.

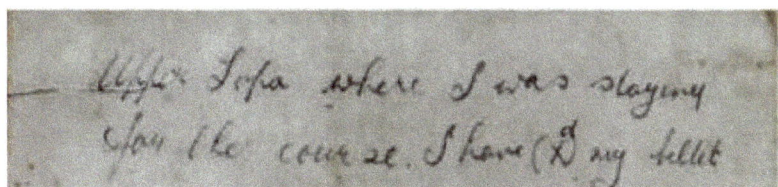

Junior Non-Commissioned Officer Course

One of the most interesting items found in Roy's kitbag was a notebook written whilst attending a Junior N.C.O course in Upper Topa, Murree Hills, a beautiful mountain resort town founded in 1941 as a sanatorium for British Troops in what was then India, now Pakistan, (1947). The hills are 7,000 ft above sea level lying at the foothills of the Himalayas. The climate there being very cold in the winter but pleasant during the summer months, the complex is still a military training facility to this day, Military College Murree, Pakistan (MCM).

Roy's handwritten notebook contains a wealth of information outlining the complexity of the work ground crew were expected to do such as, reporting, guarding and salvage of crashed aircraft, casualty procedures in war, stores procedure, petrol and oil issues, Air Council, inspection schedule Hurricane, major jobs on aircraft and more. A full transcript of the notebook is included in this book.

Roy became a non-Commissioned officer in 1944, later becoming 'Acting Sergeant.' Non-commissioned officers are enlisted members of the RAF who have been delegated leadership or command authority by a commissioned officer. They are the junior management of the Service. Experienced NCOs are a very important part of many armed forces; in many cases NCOs are credited as being the metaphorical 'backbone' of their service, and their individual units. Non-commissioned ranks are split into three groups; airmen (Aircraftsman up to Junior Technician), non-commissioned officers (or NCOs; Corporal to Flight Sergeant) and Warrant Officers, Warrant officers have many years of experience and are respected by both rank structures. *(www.thestudentroom.co.uk/employers/royalairforce/Raf-nco-vs officer - The Student Room).*

Corporal Roy Blackburne

RAF Ranchi

RAF Ranchi, now called Birsa Munda Airport, was considered a good posting as the sub-tropical climate was pleasant with an annual rainfall of about 1,100 mm. The surrounding area is hilly with dense tropical rainforests. It was in those rainforests the military did their 'Jungle Training' in preparation for Burma. (wiki.fibis.org/families in British India Society/Ranchi)

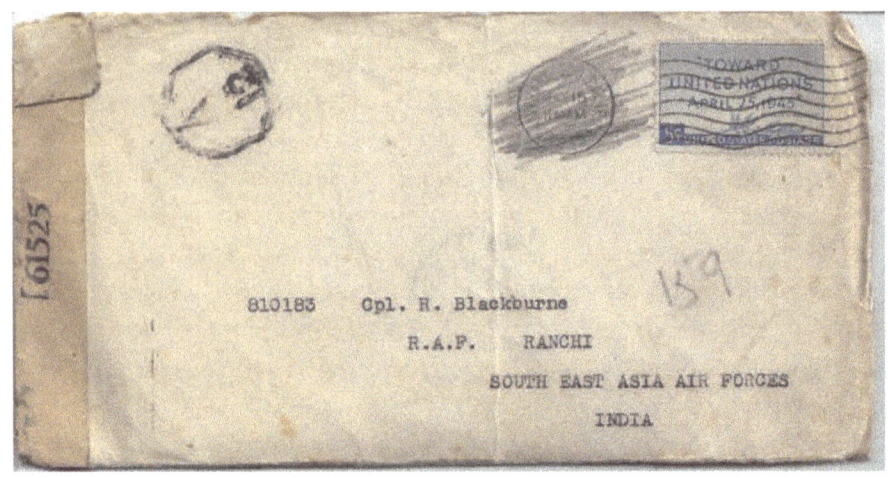

This postcard was posted February 1945 from Roy's cousin Miriam Blackburne in San Francisco

'Thank you, Roy for all the letters. The view on the card will give you an idea of what to expect when you arrive here!!! I do hope you can. It will be so different to India, always cool here.

Love to you and all the R.A.F'ers, from a Lancashire Lass M.B.

R.A.F. Ranchi

South East Asia Air Forces

Good Friday (30th March 1945)

Dear Mother,

I received a letter from you yesterday the letter was dated 20.3.45 it took nine days to reach me. You say Tom brought back the money well I have previously told you that the Shell have given me a rise of 145 a year now making a total of 250 a year plus 20% increase as well for cost of living. I am now getting approximately 6 a week less Provident Fund so am not doing too badly. So, from now on there is no need to send any money.

Well the present I sent Micky Hope was six brass egg cups like I sent you. I will be getting more money now so I will be sending some things home. It seems as though Fred Hall is pretty well certain that he is coming home in August. I am expecting to be home myself about that time though. I cannot give you any definite date yet. Nowadays it is getting warmer I am once again becoming brown working in the open all day long soon fatigues one, believe me after working hard on aero engines from 7am to 5.30pm in this heat one feels the heat pretty bad. A lot of boys have just come out from England with them a boy named Stanley Hornby from Oldfield Road. I am trying to find out the old Pioneers for him, he moans incessantly about the hot sun and forever wishes he was back home.

Think you will have to forgive this bad paper but it is Indian made so it smudges badly.

Tonight, it is really lovely a full tropical moon peeping through the trees, the atmosphere is humid, mosquitoes and crickets are bugging and chirping, all the night life of the tropics seem to venture forth on such nights. I could almost

> *read by the brilliant light of the moon.*
>
> *I am quite well these days mum, I am still feeling A.1. my weight is still 11 stone 6 1lbs so for a hot season I reckon I am doing ok,*
>
> *Well goodbye for now I hope we get better paper next time, love to May, Arthur, Milly, Tom and John, all the babies too,*
>
> *Yours Roy*

Whilst at Ranchi, Roy worked as ground crew at a Specialised Low Attack Instructors School, this being one of the main 25 units located there along with seven other detachments. What date Roy left Ranchi for Burma is not mentioned on his service record, possibly a clerical error.

As documented in Roy's service record, he was admitted to a British Military Hospital between 14th March 1944 and 24th March 1944. The reason is unknown, but one of the main reasons for hospitalisation in the area was due to malaria, dengue fever or dysentery. Up until mid-1943 the RAF was largely dependent on the army hospitals, as the RAF became increasingly worried about what was happening to its aircrew and skilled tradesmen, who when sick were simply flown to distant base hospitals which resulted in a long time away from duty. During 1943, approximately 200,000 service days were lost in Air Command due to malaria, of which 18,000 were lost by aircrews. To enable such men to be treated and returned to duty as quickly as possible, a system of mobile field hospitals were built and linked to an RAF hospital in Calcutta. The field hospitals conditions were far from ideal, but met the need for more localised treatment areas. *(The Forgotten Air Force/The Royal Air Force in the War Against Japan 1941-1945/ Air Commodore Henry Probert/Victory Beckons/ page 241/recollections of Mr. J R Taylor)*

An unknown tropical barrack room, note the mosquito nets. The standard of accommodation would vary depending on the posting, whether it was at home or overseas, from very basic to relative comfort

Calcutta

Roy's condition must have been quite serious for him to be admitted to the British Military Hospital in Calcutta (now known as Kolkata), 250 miles away from where he was based with the 322 MU, Ranchi. Despite being hospitalised, he never ever spoke of such a major event in his life. Had it been malaria, he possibly would have had relapses upon coming home, but none were ever witnessed nor mentioned. The likelihood of him being 'wounded in action' is doubtful as he bore no physical scars of such a traumatic occurrence. The ground crews working in India worked in incredibly difficult conditions, occasionally whilst under attack. Exhaustion and dehydration may well have played a part in his admission, or it may have been due to a workplace injury.

Following his hospitalisation, he was relocated to Calcutta M/E (maintenance engines), where he was stationed for six months. Thirty-eight units were based in Calcutta at the time of Roy's posting as it was seen as an important location for the execution of military operations, consequently Calcutta was under curfew and blacked out. Whilst here, it is very likely he would have witnessed the Japanese bombing raids which continued until December 1944, when the Japanese bombed the densely populated city night after night.

Despite Calcutta having a good air defence system, previous bombing raids, particularly in 1942, had damaged much of the infrastructure and dockland. Calcutta's proximity to Burma, already overrun with Japanese, who were stopped at the border, bombed Calcutta with a view to invading India. In August of 1943, the British brought in Spitfires and because of their speed and manoeuvrability they brought down many Japanese aircraft turning WW II into the Allies favour.

Roy's promotions to Corporal and Sergeant were probably local, acting promotions, notification of which were not added to his records in the UK. As a fitter he would have been working on the engines of the various aircraft used by the units he was serving with. He was qualified to work on the Audax (Kestrel), Wellington (Pegasus and Hercules), Hurricane, Spitfire (Merlin). As a corporal he would have been supervising other fitters and been in charge of small sections within the Engineering setup. *(Personal Communication Malcom Barras 9th October 2020/'Air of Authority'/ www.rafweb.org/airbritain 18070/RAF Historical society)*

Burma

Unfortunately, this is where the paper trail runs cold, there is very little documentation indicating what Roy's role could have been in Burma. There is no mention of it in his service record, but a role he likely played there was retrieving serviceable crashed aircraft. During the Junior NCO course which Roy undertook in the Murree Hills, he was instructed in great detail about such eventualities.

Ground crew would operate with their squadrons wherever they were located. Roy was not assigned to a squadron, but to 322 Maintenance Unit operating behind the frontline. Salvage teams from the MUs would need to go close to the frontline to recover aircraft from forward airfields, or even crash sites, when the repairs required were beyond the resources of the squadrons.

In November 1943, an Airborne Salvage Section was formed, which flew to crash scenes in a specially adapted transport aircraft capable of carrying spares, tools and engines. On reaching the crash site damaged aircraft would be patched up and flown to the nearest repair depot. The Airborne Salvage section operated a C47 Dakota – which it had previously salvaged – in which the main planes of large aircraft, and even complete Spitfires, were on occasion carried. Maintenance units had different functions, some were Aircraft Repair Depots, whilst others could be Equipment or Storage Depots. 322 was an ARD so would have operated teams of personnel to travel out to airfields to carry out repairs and/or modifications and to salvage crashed aircraft for repairs or parts retrieval. The main Maintenance Unit at Cawnpore would have carried out the major repair and major maintenance tasks at Cawnpore. Therefore, it is quite likely Roy was with or in charge of a Salvage team from No. 322 MU, tasked with recovering aircraft from Burma or other qualifying areas, making him eligible for the medal. *(Malcom Barrass/ personal communication9thOctober2020, 'Air of Authority'/www.rafweb.org/airbritain 18070/RAF Historical society.)*

It is possible, therefore, that he was detached to units operating from locations nearer Burma (to the east and south of Calcutta). Travelling by road, in order to be able to recover aircraft or alternately they may have been flown into a landing ground to strip parts from a crashed aircraft that could not be recovered for repair. Surrounding these vacated landing strips was the ever- present threat of Japanese snipers . Roy once recalled to his wife Peggy that whilst in Burma he had horrifically witnessed a fellow airman who, whilst walking ahead of him, was shot dead by such a sniper, obviously fearing for his own life.

To qualify for the Burma Star medal, a serviceman did not have to actually serve in Burma. Army personnel and Air Force ground crew serving ashore must have served between 11th December 1941 and 2nd September 1945. The Burma Star was awarded for service in Burma from 11th December 1941 and included service in Assam/Bengal east of the Brahmaputra River from 1st May 1942. Airborne troops of the Armies who took part in airborne operations in a qualifying area for land operations qualified by entry into operational service. Air crew who flew over the qualifying land and sea areas within the specified dates qualified by an operational sortie, while air crew on transport or ferrying duties qualified by at least three landings in any of the qualifying land areas.

The Burma Campaign was a series of battles fought in the British colony of Burma, South-East Asian theatre of World War II, primarily between the forces of the British Empire and China, with support from the United States, against the invading forces of Imperial Japan, Thailand, and the Indian National Army. British Empire forces peaked at around 1,000,000 land and air forces, and were drawn primarily from British India, with British Army forces (equivalent to 8 regular infantry divisions and 6 tank regiments),100,000 East and West African colonial troops, and smaller numbers of land and air forces from several other Dominions and Colonies.The geographical characteristics of the region meant that weather, disease and terrain had a major effect on operations.The lack of transport infrastructure placed an emphasis on military engineering and air transport to move and supply troops, and evacuate wounded.

In August 1943, the Allies created the South-East Asia Command (SEAC). Roy was part of the South-East Asia Air Force. After the Singapore debacle and the loss of Burma in 1942, the British were bound to defend India at all costs, as a successful invasion by the Japanese would be disastrous.

'The British depended on strategic air defence, as it had in 1940 over England, before the forces could be built up for a combined attack on the Japanese positions in Burma and southern China. Because of this concentration on the strategic use of aircraft the winning of air supremacy was regarded as an essential prelude to the fulfilment of more general strategic ambitions. The allied determination to build up massive and diversified air power before resources for invasion could be diverted from the European theatre, led to the final defeat of Japan through blockade and destruction from the air.' Roy and his fellow mechanics played a major role in supporting this strategy. One of the major stations where he was based was RAF Station Ranchi (Northern India), Air Headquarters Bengal, Air Command South East Asia. Ranchi was geographically not far from Burma and therefore ideally located as a forward airfield for Burma.

The ground crews deserved a tremendous share of the credit for the fine performance of the squadron. They got up before dawn every day to ready the planes for the morning missions. They performed their arduous task late into the night in all kinds of weather to keep their charges in top shape. They refuelled the fighters from 55-gallon drums with hand pumps and strained the fuel through chamois to filter out the water, rust and other sediment and they did it in the boiling sun in the short periods between mission'. At the same time the armourers clambered on and under the hot wings, manhandling the heavy bombs and ammunition belts and changing gun barrels when necessary. Every night the guns were carefully cleaned and lubricated and the airplanes were inspected for damage, where plugs, (twenty-four per engine) were changed if necessary, new magnetos were installed and carburettors were adjusted. This work was done day in day out without relief of days off, which the pilots got regularly… Their living conditions were very basic and they were constantly tormented by hordes of rats, snakes were also a problem, on top of that they had poor food and washing facilities. Its sentiment can be applied to all of the allied ground crew.

In the official history of the Fourteenth Air Force it states, 'Mechanics worked all night in the steamy heat to repair damage from missions, replace worn parts, and have a full complement of airplanes ready for a dawn take off. Whilst working, the men would be eaten alive by malaria carrying mosquitoes. Credit to the efficiency of this system was down to the non-commissioned officers' (NCO's such as Roy). Lieutenant Lopez, a decorated American pilot who flew in the China Burma India Theatre said, 'The ground crews were the unsung heroes of not only the China Burma India Theatre but also of the entire allied war effort during World War II.'

The pocket guide below was issued by the War and Navy Department, United States, as a guide for those serving in Burma. It details the climate, the language, the food, diseases, local customs and people. It states how despite the locals being very friendly, the servicemen were not to discuss military matters with them or even within earshot, as they may well be active enemy agents.

The conflict was only part of the challenge in Burma. The terrible heat and tropical weather, poor food, poor accommodation, plus jungle illnesses and debilitating tropical diseases such as malaria and dysentery were much cause for concern.

During the monsoon season between May and October, the crews would have to contend with mud, in the summer, dust. When flying sorties, pilots often had to navigate through the monsoonal weather in extremely hilly terrain, when massive rain clouds resulted in limited vision they could easily lose communication with each other. The consequences of this could be dire, if they were lost over enemy territory they may never be seen again. The Japanese made numerous attempts to break into India, but the contribution the RAF played in supporting the Fourteenth Army prevented this happening.

Very often the history of the Burma campaign, when compiled by the army, gave little credit to the RAF's part, but in his book Defeat into Victory, Field Marshal Sir William Slim noted his appreciation for the work by the RAF. He said, 'Rarely can so small an air force have battled so gallantly and so effectively against a comparable force'.

The Circumstances of the War in Burma

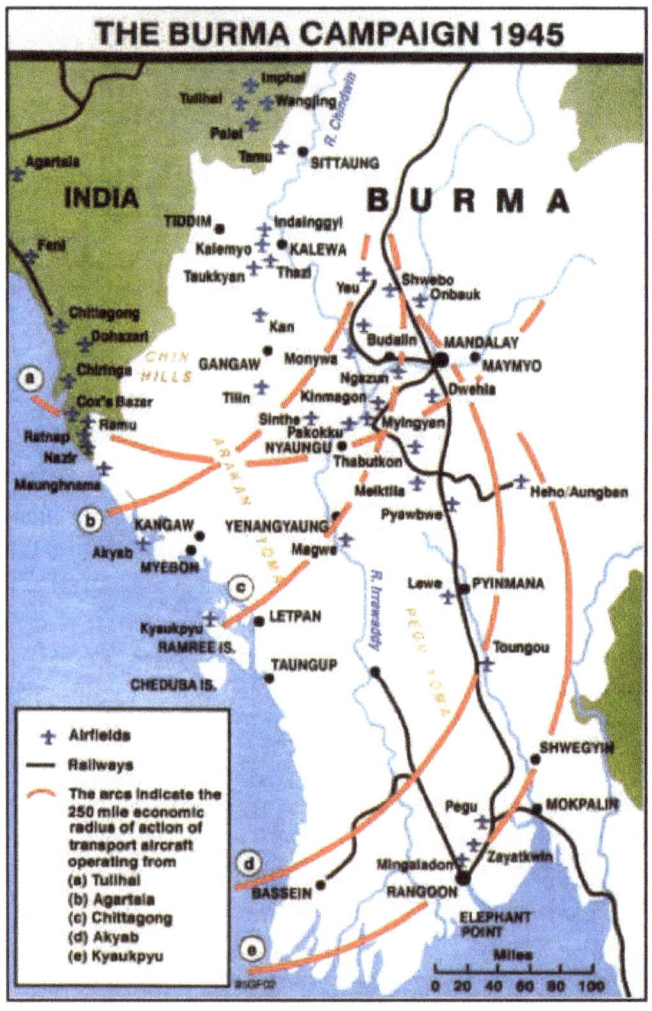

The Burma Campaign 1945 map courtesy of the RAF Historical Society reproduced from 'The RAF and the War in the Far East 1941-1945/personal ommunication, Jeff Jefford, Editor, RAF Historical Society Publications.

The war in the Far East started in December 1941, simultaneously with the bombing of Pearl Harbour. The Japanese captured Hong Kong on Christmas Day and moved into the Malay Peninsula, the Philippines and the Dutch East Indies. Malaya was overrun and Singapore fell on 15th February 1942. The Japanese army advanced into Burma, involving the defending British and Indian troops in a long and demoralising fighting retreat through thick jungle terrain over a distance equivalent to that from Istanbul to London. Rangoon fell on 8th March 1942 and by mid-June the Japanese advance had reached the hills on the North East frontier of India.

In December 1942, British and Indian troops mounted their first offensive in the malaria ridden coastal Arakan region. It was unsuccessful, although much was learned. During 1943, Chindit columns under Brigadier Orde Wingate, supported by the Royal Air Force, penetrated deep behind Japanese lines in central Burma. In March 1943, a further determined attempt to invade India was repulsed after fierce fighting. In August 1943, the South East Asia Command was formed under Lord Louis Mountbatten and in October that year General William Slim was appointed as Commander of the Fourteenth Army.

In March 1944, the Japanese launched an offensive across the Chindwin River, cutting the Imphal-Kohima road. There followed the ferocious battles of the 'Admin Box', Kohima (with its famous tennis court) and Imphal, at the end of which the defeated Japanese withdrew. Further Chindit columns operated deep behind enemy lines during 1944 and at the beginning of 1945 the Fourteenth Army launched a successful offensive down the Arakan Coast, followed by a major advance deep into central Burma. Mandalay was retaken on 20th March after a twelve-day battle, and the Fourteenth Army continued on to Rangoon which was reoccupied in an amphibious operation on 3rd May.

The role of the RAF South East Asia Command in Burma was to support the Fourteenth Army as they chased the Japanese out of Burma. Fighter combat became rare, but they attacked the enemy on the ground. The Allies had prevailed during ground battles, due to a large extent, to the RAF's supply dropping missions, while the Japanese suffered greatly due to a lack of food and water as well as armaments with which to fight. *RAF Fighter Pilots Over Burma/ chapter 9/finale/page143*

Ground crews worked tirelessly servicing the aircraft at the many airfields around Imphal during the main offensive to reoccupy Burma in 1945. The airfields being Imphal (main), Kangla, Tulhal, Sapam, Wang Jing and Palel some of which were more like landing strips than airfields. Another major airfield was at Mingalandon in Rangoon.

In an effort to keep cool in the searing relentless heat of the Indian and Burmese summers, ground crew wore shorts, light shirt, shoes or suede jungle boots, a pith helmet or sloppy hat. Below, Roy is wearing such attire working on an engine supported by a test cell. As a fitter (engines) Roy would have stripped down the engine into its component parts before it was rebuilt and tested. *(airfix/ Aerodromemagazine,' Keep 'em flying'2015)*

The Fourteenth Army, known to many as the 'Forgotten Army', numbered over one million men under arms, the largest Commonwealth army ever assembled. Air lines of communication were crucial; some 615,000 tons of supplies and 315,000 of reinforcements were airlifted to and from the front line, frequently by parachuted air drops, and 210,000 casualties were evacuated. The Royal Air Force and the Indian Air Force, supported by carrier-borne Fleet Air Arm aircraft, provided constant offensive bombing sorties, together with fighter cover and essential photo-reconnaissance in support of the Army. Towards the end of the War, RAF Liberator aircraft carried out some of the longest operations ever flown to drop mines into the Pacific. At sea, the Royal Navy and the Royal Indian Navy provided the landing craft, the minesweeping operations and the combined operations necessary for the coastal offensive in the Arakan, as well as providing gunfire support from seaward. The Royal Marine Commando, as well as Royal Marines from the units of the Fleet, took part in the Arakan operations.

The Japanese surrendered on 15th August 1945, now known as VJ Day.

Found amongst paperwork in the kitbag, a Japanese newsletter of Western propaganda origin dropped during the Battle of Imphal.

Indian Field Broadcasting Unit in Burma: Details about the Indian Field Broadcasting Unit in Burma have long been secret, but it is now revealed that the unit uses loudspeakers and fires leaflets and newspapers from mortars. During the battle for Imphal, the Burmese news sheet, 'The Spirit of the Air,' was dropped for the civilian population along with the Japanese language Gunjin Shimbun ('Battle Newspaper'). Edited for the Japanese soldiers. IFBU's Japanese newspaper was favourably received by the enemy. A Gurkha patrol came upon four Japanese soldiers so engrossed in the current issue of the 'Battle Newspaper' that they had lost all interest in the battle itself. *(From a British source). (Ref: Command and General Staff School, Military Review, Number 3, Volume XXIV June 1944, Issues 3-12 – page 80, Editor Colonel Frederick M. Barrows, F.A.)*

Grateful thanks to my Japanese friend Ota Noboru for kindly translating the paper.

GUNJIN SHIMBUN No.59 17.2.44.

日本の宣傳法

政府は戦の状相を国民に発表して居るや否や、厚生省の代表者村田五郎氏は次の如く云ふ。…

日本軍部と俘虜

捕虜に對する取扱方は近代戦争の一方式として野蛮なるものとして極めて重要なる問題であり…

聯合國軍のニューギニヤ基地

モレスビイ港は五月以來一度も空襲を受けて居らず、其港には大型の…

聯合國の日本語放送 (毎 關東キロ放送局)

日本時間	波長	
八・三〇	一九・五	三一・三二
八・四五	一三・九五	四一・九九
六・〇〇	二五・三五	三九・二五
六・三〇	一九・六七	三六・七六
八・〇〇	九・五五	二五・三六
九・三〇	一九・八	三一・一五
九・四五	一九・六七	四九・四二
三・三〇	二五・三二	四一・四八

軍陣新聞

第五十九號

昭和十九年二月十七日

日本軍緬甸に攻勢

〔通戦況は計畫中〕

本十七日大本營發表
去四日金曜日本軍
は四日攻撃を開始する
その退避隊は日下アラカン
ダウン後方ブツダウンデン
を突破し遙にアラカン
本十七日大本營に於ては
右の方面作戦の状況に
就いて大略次の如く
報告があった

〔ヘーダウン〕

日下関東軍に於ては日
六日我軍はチャゴン
ヒルマ前線同胞八日
の中に日本軍の三方から
攻撃に依ってマユ山脈
の状況の機動を突破し同
六日にはマユ河口まで
進出我軍は作戦中二月
十日の本陣地を占領した

東京十日發

マーシャル群島の占領

日本軍の徹底なる抵
抗だに撼く米國軍は
シギルバート諸島を突破し中
央太平洋に進出した一
九四二年八月二十
日米國軍は百武中將の
少數の海軍部隊より日
本軍の死守するガダルカナル
島を奪回し決定的勝利
を博してより六十
ヶ月以後には決して
米國軍の手中にはならず更に
アッツの日本軍をさらに
マキン、タラワの二十
五ケ国に占領された一九
四三年二月には今や米
軍はマーシャル群島の一
部を占領すべくクェゼリン
環礁の攻撃を強行中
であり、要するに米軍
の今回の作戦は大成功
であると言わねばならない

これに対し日本軍の
反撃は如何にあるか
この問題は実に重大で
ある、日本軍は一年内
に機能の新鋭を尽く
した千五百機以上の航空
機を以って此の大洋を
中心に機動的作戦を主と
し何なる事も必勝する
に於いてはマーシャル群
島の全米軍を殲滅しアメリカ
に対する決定的勝敗を
決し得る形である
また日本軍の海軍も決
して沈没したとは思は
ざり日本海軍は必ずや
必勝する日本の必勝を
期する事を我々は信じて
居る

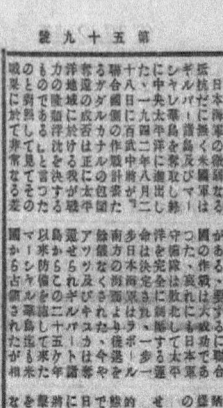

太平洋作戦

米國軍は目下マーシャ
ル群島中のマーシャル
ケレイン、アトール
の各島々は現に日本軍
守備隊の手中にあり同
島に於ける日本軍の
海兵守備隊は何處にある
のか一見して何故かに
あらざれば皆日本守
備軍の大部分は他の島
に移動してしまったと
の説もある、併しこれ
は全く敵側の日本軍
に対する虚言である
実に今日本守備軍は
マーシャル群島に於て
各島々殊にクェゼリン
環礁の島々並びに
ウォッチェ、ヤルート等
に於いて頑強に抵抗し
つつあり日本海軍は全力
を挙げて敵の侵入艦隊
を阻止する為にこの
戦に向ひ刻下真に太平
洋上の大作戦を展開
しているのである
軍事評論家の述べる
處によれば此の太平洋
上に於ける日米両軍の
戦斗は今や未曾有の
大規模なるものであり
何れが勝利を博するか
は速断を許さざるもの
であるが併し近日中に
必ずその勝敗の結着を
見るに至るであろう
軍の豫定によれば目下
の太平洋上の戦局は
どうしても日米両軍
艦隊の大海戦の決行を
必至とする程に追ひ
つめられつつあり早
晩米國海軍は主力を以て
日本海軍に挑戦するを
余儀なくされるに至ら
ん、その結果米英は一
大痛撃を受け日本の一
大勝利を招来するに至る
であろうと予測されている

新式兵器の研究

日本の兵器が相当品
質優秀なる事は今度
本邦バーネス陸軍兵
器部大佐が研究して
日本の兵器と戦に
ついて述べて居り兵器
の性能に関する少く
もの多くの点に於て
歩兵用兵器は敵の兵器
より数段に優秀である
しかも生産が非常に
多く、米國の如き
多量に生産し得ざる
日本の兵器は簡易
しかも大量生産に適
する如く工夫されて
居る、特に歩兵用の
武器、小銃、機関銃
等の火器は米國軍の
兵器よりも一段優秀
である

〔長距離P三八型〕

米國陸軍機P三八型
は改良によって一層
其の性能を発揮せり
と云ひ今回は遠距離
にも耐へうる長距離
式の新型を発表す

〔フィンランドの立場〕

リスボン發同盟
フランス、スペインの外交機関
によって英米フランスが
正式にスペインの国
交を断絶したのは
フランコ将軍の独裁政策
によるものである
フィンランド國は今日
まで無条件降伏を固
く拒絶して居るが今後
はそれが可能かどうか
はまた十分なる考慮を
要するものである

〔海封鎖〕

琉球封鎖船舶三隻撃沈
サザーランド号外
十八時セエラント号
其他十万屯撃沈

17 February 1944

Japanese method of publication

Answering the question whether or not the government is disclosing true information on war, Mr Goro Murata said representing the Information Agency, 'It is the government's policy to present information on every move of the war to the people. It is because the people understand the war situation that they exert themselves with high morale.' It is true that the answer is completely the same as what the democracy maintains. However, in fact, the totalitarian governments of the axis powers have a policy not to disclose true information on war situation to the people.

Especially, the Japanese people know less about the war situation as well as the state of the world than any other peoples in the world do. We cannot help feeling that the Japanese people are indifferent about the freedom of speech. Even in peace time, the Japanese government takes a heavy-handed measure using brutal police forces against news which it thinks to be inconvenient at all for itself. It is well-known to all Japanese.

Since before the current war broke out, or since Manchurian Incident, newspapers have been prohibited from carrying diplomatic correspondences to Japanese government from Western countries. Sometimes, summaries of the replies by Japanese government to these correspondences are published. But they are bolts out of the blue, and people are surprised to know what is happening to external affairs. It, for sure, evidences that the military leaders are afraid of people's knowing true facts. It is no exaggeration to say that it is Japanese government's policy to make fools out of the people.

The facts of defeats from the complete destruction

of the expeditionary force at Port Moresby to the recent fall of Marshall Islands are being kept secret. Inauthentic wins have been reported to the people.

Before the war, the government did not let the people know news which conflict with its antidemocratic ideas, news which take on anti-war ideas, or news which is unfavourable for its policy. As before, it cracks down on any public criticism about its administrative policy. It is evidenced from Japanese way to object to 'Complaint about treatment of prisoners' made by the allies. In a press conference with foreign journalists, Mr Iguchi and other top staff argued against the complaint. But their answers to the question about the cruel treatment of prisoners were vague. Japanese people are not let know the true fact of the conflicts between Japanese government and allies. Which do Japanese people think to be correct? If Japanese people know the true fact of the issue about the treatment of prisoners, if they are human, they will think what the allies insist on to be right. The Japanese military is afraid of it.

However skilfully the military leaders try to deceive the people by propaganda full of deceit, there is one thing which they cannot overcome. That is people's sharp sense to the situation getting worse. It may be because Japanese government is implementing a policy of concealing the true facts from the people and because the people are not satisfied with the government's administrative policy that parliament debates such as the one mentioned above occur. We would answer to the question that a weakness in boosting morale of the people toward the war can be found in the point where the Japanese military leaders' dislike for telling the truth. We think that the time has already come when true facts cannot be hidden from the people.

Japanese Military and Prisoners

The axis powers introduced barbarous system into modern war, which became more barbarous. In medieval times, especially in Britain, belligerent countries had chivalrous spirit. Today, there is a rule about treatment of prisoners of war, which is provided by The Hague Convention. Japan does not follow the rule and treats prisoners very cruelly. Information given to the allies have been revealing a lot of cases of assault against prisoners.

It may be too early to talk about Japan's assaults. In the future, as a civilised country, Japan itself may say that it was an uncivilised country which mistreated prisoners with uncivilised measures. It cannot say now because of the military clique which is dominating Japan.

The Japanese military clique treats even Japanese soldiers barbarously. Soldiers are only 'tools' for them. When Japanese soldiers are taken as prisoners, they are 'used-up tools'. Because the clique treats soldiers of its own country like this, it is natural that it treats foreign prisoners even more cruelly. They do not care about international laws at all. They do not have humanity. They are cruel and brutal.

The Japanese military clique rejected inspections of prison camps by the Red Cross, and refused to submit a list of prisoners. They not only mistreat prisoners physically, but also mentally. British and Indian prisoners are forced to say over the air that Japanese treatment of prisoners is very good. The military clique is shouting 'bushido' (Japanese chivalry) as a slogan. But what is chivalry? The military clique is good at doing violence to people who cannot make resistance. It is completely opposite of bushido.

It is a disgraceful behaviour for a human to condemn prisoners to do what they do not want to do by utilising their miserable situations where they cannot make resistance. The military clique is bringing reproach on Japanese country and people by doing such a mean act.

Bases of Allies in New Guinea

Port Moresby has not been aerially attacked since May last year. There has not been even any sign of air raid. The military capacity of the allies has been enhanced. Large troops from the allies occupied the bases which were regained from Japan between April and December last year, and are preparing massive attacks. Air bases and military roads are being constructed all around. Massive attacks are being prepared surprisingly fast.

The war situation in New Guinea is generally calm at the moment. Only air force of the allies are acting. The positions of the Japanese army are aerially being attacked without cease.

An Australian army is advancing along the Ramu Valley. The war situation there is not so fierce. Another Australian army has marched from Sio to the north coast of New Guinea. In this area, the large army has crossed Sari River, and already advanced 7.5 miles after it passed Race Point. It is no more than 30 miles away from American Army in Saidor. The Japanese armies around there have been completely destroyed. There are bodies and arms abandoned by Japanese armies scattered around.

Spanish neutrality guaranteed

President Roosevelt stated that the US and the UK would act in union to support Spain's taking a neutral stance.

Time (Japanese Mean Time)	Wavelength (m)	Frequency (kHz)	Station
3:30	41.15 48.47 49.30 60.48 85.84	7290 6190 6085 4960 3495	Delhi
9:45 9:30	19.54 19.54	15355 15355	San Francisco
14:15	25.27 41.15	11870 7290	Delhi
14:15 and 16:15	41.39 31.50	7250 9490	San Francisco
16:33	25.62	11710	Australia
17:00	25.27 41.15	11870 7290	Delhi
18:30	25.47 19.46 19.42	11780 15420 15450	London
19:30	25.27 41.15	11870 7290	Delhi
19:30	41.39 31.50	7250 9490	San Francisco
20:05	19.76	15180	Chongqing
20:45 and 21:15	41.39 31.50	7250 9490	San Francisco
21:20	31.08	9650	Chongqing
22:15	41.61 49.30	7210 6085	Delhi
22:30	41.39 33.59 31.50	7250 8930 9490	San Francisco

Domei News Agency from Tokyo

Dr Aikitsu Tanakadate talked about a new surprising invention at the House of Peers saying, 'Japan successfully performed an experiment using element including energy strong enough to destroy all the British naval forces in a flash at a minimum cost.'

It is amazing that Japan's science is making a rapid progress.

Degradation of German Air Power

Marshal of the Royal Air Force, Viscount Trenchard, at a press conference during his visit to the US, said, 'The German air power has been degraded, and is losing a balance. For recent air raids of London, Germany used 5 different types of aircrafts. I believe Germany is suffering from lack of aircrafts.'

German propaganda reporting fictional victory (cartoon)

The German man in uniform says, 'Russian military is facing destruction.'

Japanese broadcast by the Allies.

Thursday 17 February 1944

Japanese Army's Campaign in Burma

On Friday 4th February, Japanese Army began a campaign in Burma. The volunteer corps is capturing Taung Bazaar behind Buthidaung. Domei News Agency reported that the campaign was large.

The first goal is Chittagong. (Domei News Agency dispatch from Rangoon on 7 February 1944)

The spokesman of the Japanese Army in the Burma

area said, 'Our army began a new campaign on 4 February. The first goal is an occupation of Chittagong. And then, we will march into the Indian Territory, in cooperation with Indian National Army.'

The war situation is going according to the initial plan.

Domei News Agency reported the war situation in Arakan. Please compare the report with the real situation.

Domei News Agency dispatch from Burmese front on 8 February 1944:

'Due to fierce attacks by Japanese 30000-man army, the British Army and the Indian Army around the Mayu Range between Naf River and Mayu are getting stranded by degrees. Till the sunset of 6 February, the Japanese Army on operation around the Ngakyedauk Region destroyed all the enemies, and now chasing them. At the same time, residuals of the enemy army troops, which are withdrawing from Rettoadetudo Region (?) to Ngakyedauk, are being sniped.'

From Tokyo on 10 February 1944:

'The Imperial Headquarters announced at 5 PM today, 'The Japanese Army are making a daring attack on the main force of the enemy army in the eastern district of the Mayu Range, after cornering it from the west and the south.' Besides, a troop of the Japanese Army intercepted the retreat of the enemy army withdrawing from the Mounkdauk (?) District, and gained the ground in the whole area around Ngakyedauk. The details of the war situation in the Buthidaung and Mounkdauk (?) Regions are:'

'(1) The Japanese army, which crossed the Mayu River near Taung Bazaar, is now going southward along the right bank of the Mayu River. An army which broke through an enemy line in Buthidaung *is now going northward. These army troops which began operations at the same time have surrounded the main unit of the enemy in the eastern district of the Mayu Range, and are making a fierce attack.'*

'(2) Powerful Japanese army troops went over the Mayu Range at Taung Bazaar, and destroyed a bridge on 6 February in order to intercept the retreat of the enemy army from the Mounkdauk Region (?). As a result, the Japanese army has gained control of the Ngakyedauk Region and the surrounding area.'

Occupation of the Marshall Islands

Without any resistance of the Japanese Navy, the US Navy captured the Gilbert and Marshall Islands, and advanced at last to the Central Pacific. Vice-admiral Hyakutake said on 28 August 1942, 'The rise and fall of the Japanese forces in the Pacific depend on whether the siege of Guadalcanal by Allied forces can be ended or not.' Compared with the Japanese military success at that time, the one at this time is very different. In short, the campaign by Allied forces was a great success. The Japanese garrison were miserably defeated, which frustrated their plan to gain control of the whole Pacific. The Japanese Navy was forced into gradual retreat from the southern waters of Rabaul. They lost Attu and Kiska Islands. Not only Gilbert Island but also Marshall Islands

Japanese Weapons are of Low Quality.

Major Barnes of the Army Weapon Department inspected weapons seized from the Japanese Army, and said, 'We compared Japanese weapons with our weapons. Japanese weapons seem to be for battles in jungles. Weapons carried by infantry soldiers are generally light and portable. However, their firepower is low.'

'Japanese and the Allies' weapons are making a progress in accordance with the transition of the war. However, when all the power of the Allies is concentrated on the Pacific, they will maximise the ability of heavy weapons to contain the Japanese resisting power.'

Improved Long-Range P38 Attack Bomber

The US War Department said that improved long-range P38 attack bomber had been flung into some battles. It was improved mainly in-flight range to infiltrate deep into enemy territory to complete missions such as escorting bombers and return home. It was also improved in power and rate of ascent.

Domei News Agency dispatch from Lisbon:

About the issue on the Spanish neutrality, the UK newspapers went for the tone that General Francisco Franco should take a drastic measure to keep 'strict neutrality'.

Diplomatic sources in Spain say a plan against this problem will be concreted in two weeks.

Three Blockade Runners were sunk in the Atlantic

Gazette of the Department of the Navy

Fleets of the Allies sank three German blockade runners for 48 hours.

The blockade runners were transporting cargoes of war supplies from Japan, laden with gum, tin, cooking oil, and iron ore for use in manufacture of weapons.

Finnish Crisis

German Foreign News Agency dispatch: When the Finnish Parliament was opened, the Finnish president Risto Ryti said, 'Facing a crisis, we need cautiousness, courage, calmness, and strong will. If Germany collapses, the Finnish people will have to consider a separate peace with Russia or unconditional surrender.'

Correspondence

Roy was stationed in St. Athan, Wales on his 21st birthday

Roy, aged 24 yrs was stationed in Ambala, India 1942

★ OFFICIAL SLOGAN: "Well, I *Should* Go Home, But Just *One* More Hand." ★ OFFICIAL ALIBI: "I *Wanted* to Go Home, But I Was a Little Ahead."

THE GRAND SUPREME INTERNATIONAL ORDER OF A-FEW-HANDS-WITH-THE-BOYS

AFFILIATED WITH THE IDLE HOUR KIBITIZERS' AUXILIARY

OFFICE OF THE
Magnificent Grand Master and
Supreme Exalted Ruler
(Only 53 Offices Higher)

ORGANIZED TO
UPHOLD SEVERAL THINGS
INCLUDING
BEER STEINS

Edith

January 25, 1945

My Dear Roy:

I'd be willing to bet you nearly tossed this in the waste basket thinking it to be some sort of advertising, am I right?--(come to think of it though, you may still feel like tossing it out). Marita gave it to me for a Christmas gift--I think her sense of humor suddenly went berserk or something. It's a little thicker than ordinary stationery so I decided to exhibit my minus-x typing ability in order to get more said on less paper (it's the Scotch coming out on me).

"SERVE US"
Is Our Motto--
The Oftener, The Better.

I don't think I've thanked you yet for that fine snap of yourself you sent in your last letter--I was pleased as punch to get it and it's with a good deal of pride I show it to our friends. You're certainly right about the English channel being worth it's weight in gold--if it hadn't been for that channel and the gallant boys who fought over and around it to hold the hun back our nice safe world would have been no more. We owe a lot to you English for all you went through until we were ready to lend a hand. Maybe I feel this way because I'm half English for I know there are people (the isolationists for one group) who don't agree with my point of view at all, but thank God my side is in the majority. Oh dear, here I go off on another lecture again--sooner or later I invariably get wound up in politics, did I put you to sleep with my ranting? To get back to the snaps again--you're going to think I'm a pest and never satisfied, I know, but I haven't received the other pictures you were going to send--I believe you said there were four. I hope you haven't forgotten you promised them to me--send them real soon, won't you? I'll thank you in advance for them. I wish I had some to send of us but we haven't been able to buy film here for song now. So photography is your hobby--I know it's fascinating as Lillian's husband, George, is an amateur photographer--developes his own pictures and enlarges, he's very good at it too. Those I sent you last were some of his work. Are you able to

Our Oath:

Attend the

BIG ANNUAL
STAG PARTY

Every Thursday
Night

WE STAND TOGETHER AND TOGETHER WE FALL UNDER THE TABLE

(over)

get equipment there and fix up a dark room and all? I don't think I've
ever asked you, Roy, but what type of building do you live in?--a tent
or a barracks? (I know what you're thinking now--something like this,
no doubt: "these fool women!") I haven't the faintest idea though and
curiosity killed the cat you know. You know, you've certainly shattered
all my romantic illusions about India and the far east--all the exotic
stories of that country omit the unpleasant realities such as the dust
and dirt, the ignorance of the natives, the smells, the heat and so on.
It's refreshing to hear the truth for a change. Gosh, you've been away
from home for a good many years now, haven't you! Don't you rate a furlough by now? One boy came back to Antioch the other day after 32 months
in the South Pacific and all of us thought that was a very long drag.
Thank goodness, Earl hasn't had to go off to the wars yet, but our home
isn't out of the shadow of war by any means. His deferment is up Feb.
8 and I'm biting my nails down to the quick worrying about what the draft
board will decide he's to do in the future. He's a war worker, works 7
days a week and sometimes 12 hours a day--he had a day off this last Christmas and we thought ourselves very lucky he got that. They need him pretty
badly at the factory so I'm in hopes he'll be deferred again. About the
only males we see around here anymore are vitally needed plant (factory)
workers, lads under 17, and men around 50--all the stores have women clerks
now. Our little town came into the spotlight last week all over the nation,
and even around the world I hear, when a sailor boy from here was put off
a plane along with 2 other servicemen down in Tennessee in order that a
dog might have their seats! The dog belonged to one of the President's
sons (Elliot, who is in England now) and he was sending it to his new wife,
a movie star (Faye Emerson). The dog was given a priority for the plane
seats (he took up 3) ahead of the serviceman! Everyone has been mad as
blazes about it. This sailor from Antioch was rushing home to see his
mother who was ill (and had been recently widowed, his dad was our chief
of police). The story ran on the nations front pages for 3 or 4 days
and is still going strong. It's a heck of a note when a serviceman who's
been risking his all for his country is left in the lurch for a dog, eh?

(It's about time I was making a new paragraph!) There's a
phrase here in your letter I particularly like--where you say: "the trip
was hot, dusty-with the chances of a bad berth and remote as a second Pearl
Harbor"--boy, you've really caught the spirit of the American people in
that sentence, believe me! For there very definitely never will be a
second Pearl Harbor incident again. The japs (small j) are paying for
that piece of infamy too--and they're going to pay more and more until
it really hurts. Wait till we have the Philippines all in our hands
once more--we'll make them very sorry they ever drove those American
prisoners in that "March of Death". Have you ever heard of that? You
can bet your life we'll never forget it! Did you know those little
yellow so and so's beat one lad with a 2 by 4 timber in the head and
face until his nose was a bloody pulp and one of his ears torn off and hanging by a string??? Any Filipino who was so unfortunate as to chance by
the scene was forced to grasp the timber and smack the Americans a few
times too. It's a long gruesome tale and I get mad as the dickens when
I think about it so before my blood starts boiling I'd better look
around for another topic. Mavis is an active church worker and thinks
all men should be brothers--but though I think I'm a reasonably good
Christian I've developed too strong a hatred for the japs to consider
them anything but savages and sadistic fiends.

Are you wishing fervently that I'd find a more amiable subject?
I always turn bitter when the jap war comes up. Gosh, you're lucky only
paying 20¢ for airmail letters--I (groan) have to shell out the magnificent
sum of 75¢. Think I'll write my Congressman or something--growl!

Page 2.

OUR MEMBERSHIP INCLUDES
THE UGLIEST MONSTERS IN
THE BUSINESS.

You Are Invited to Join.

OFFICIAL SLOGAN:
"O-O-O-O-O-O-O-O"

"LET US DIG UP A GIRL
FIEND FOR YOU"

OFFICIAL THEME SONG
"A Haunting We Will Go"

The Supernatural Association of House Haunters, Demons, Witches and Gremlins
Affiliated with the Nat. Chamber of Horrors

HEADQUARTERS:
HAUNTED MANSE,
CEMETERY DRIVE,
DEAD MAN'S GULCH

—o-O-o—

BRANCHES IN ALL
PRINCIPAL
GRAVEYARDS

—o-O-o—

Dealers in Good Used
Shrouds — Second-hand
Coffins as Good as New.

—o-O-o—

Choice Real Estate
A Typical Rock-Bottom
Bargain

"THE MOLDY
DUNGEON"

A cosy, dank country place
— just the spot to retire
—permanently.

A Stone's Throw from the
Morgue.

75 ROOMS WITH
ADJOINING RAILS

Required in ADVANCE
Payable in advance or out
of your Life Insurance

—o-O-o—

Retail and Wholesale
Dealers in
UNDERGROUND
NOVELTIES

Ghosts 24.00
Ghosts, extra pale .. 2.25
Specters, ordinary .. 1.50
Specters, sheet 2.00
Spooks 1.75
Spooks, hot spooks .. 1.85
Vampires 1.90
Hobgoblins 2.15
Skeletons, walking .. 2.00
Skeletons, blood
  curdling 2.04

—o-O-o—

ATTENTION,
MEDICAL STUDENTS:
Get Our Interesting
Pre-proposition!

FROM THE CAVE OF
THE CHIEF WITCHES
BREWER AND
CAULDRON WASHER.

—oOo—

From the way those amazing Russians are pushing ahead on the eastern front this war (the European one at least) may be over by the time you get this letter (takes about 3 months to reach you, doesn't it?). But there I go getting overoptimistic again--our government has been berating us for that. We were all considerably deflated when the Germans went on the offensive and drove that bulge into Belgium--but thank goodness, they've been pushed back where they came from now. If we don't hurry the Russians are going to be marching down--what is it now? Unter Den Linten? (quit laughing--I know I messed that up)before we get there. We haven't any relatives in that fight--you probably know that Billy is here in the States again in a hospital with a tropical disease and Louis is honorably discharged (heart ailment)--our cousin Charlie, Jr. is a Lieutenant and I think he's in San Francisco--you know Hilda's husband is a Lieutenant-Commander, don't you? He's practicing dentistry on the Treasure Island Naval Base. My cousin (on my dad's side) in New York State is training in a Naval Station and Earl's youngest brother is in Texas now in an overseas training camp so it looks as though it won't be long before he's shipped over. So it looks as though you're the only member of (that must be one of my favorite expressions or something: "so it looks as though"...) the group of relatives who's right in there pitching--up in the front lines so to speak.

Roy and Grace are well and growing so fast I'm afraid if I turn my back for a minute and look again they'll have reached the voting age--Roy will be 9 in March (St. Patrick's Day to be exact) and Grace will be 5 in July....and I'll be ---oops, nearly slipped up on myself there. Roy stood up in class and told all the kids he has a cousin with the same name as his in India--but he forgot to say you were with the R.A.F.--so the next day he got up and told them, by golly! I didn't have any idea he was going to stand up and make a speech about you--I think it was right after

★ PUREBRED WEREWOLF PUPPIES FOR SALE CHEAP ★

(over)

Christmas when we got your nice card and he just had to tell everyone about it. Your mail is the only foreign mail we get now since Earl's brother was transferred from Cuba to Texas so he considers it an exciting event (as do we all).

For the past week practically all I've done is sit around and feel sorry for myself--I took the bus over to Pittsburg (5 miles west) last Friday (Jan. 19) and caught a severe chest cold when I walked in a sharp, piercing wind--now I can scarcely make myself sound intelligible to anyone--my voice breaks and growls, and misses words, have to talk in a whisper most of the time. (isn't this a sad tale?) I'm afraid Earl is going to have to do the shopping for groceries for me this week and does he love that? He DOES NOT!

Our weather has been very nice up until today when we had a heavy mist (bend your ear while I whisper that it was really rain--we Californians are not supposed to use that word, you know). Earl has been busy putting our vegetable garden in and we're looking forward to a nice "harvest" this summer. Earl's folks back in snow-bound Michigan can hardly believe we're putting in a garden at this time of the year. Yessir, don't let anyone tell you California isn't the best state in the union!

You mentioned once that you saw a cinema (movie to us) but you didn't say what picture you'd seen--are they showing any late Hollywood films over there? Or are they 1930 vintage? Some of our troops have been complaining that they're showing pictures they saw in the states when they were kids.

My eyes are beginning to feel abused so I think I'll call a halt to this document along here somewhere. Don't you hate being about that, eh? I surely hope we'll be hearing from you real soon--keep sending by airmail so I won't have to wait too long for a reply (listen to who's talking--I've been owing you a letter for some time then I tell you to speed up your answers--but I'll do better from now on, honest Injun!)

Keep well and write very soon and oh yes, you won't forget those snaps, will you?

Much love and the best of everything to you,

Edith and family

(I imagine you're thankful I used the typewriter this time so you wouldn't have to decipher my handwriting!)

January 25, 1945

My Dear Roy,

I'd be willing to bet you nearly tossed this in the waste basket thinking it to be some sort of advertising, am I right? (come to think of it though, you may still feel like tossing it out). Marita gave it to me for a Christmas gift. I think her sense of humor suddenly went berserk or something. It's a little thicker than ordinary stationary so I decided to exhibit my minus – x typing ability in order to get more said on less paper (It's the Scotch coming out on me).

I don't think I have thanked you yet for that fine snap of yourself you sent in your last letter. I was pleased as punch to get it and it's with a good deal of pride I show it to our friends. You're certainly right about the English Channel being worth its weight in gold, if it hadn't been for that channel and the gallant boys who fought over and around it to hold the hun back our nice safe world would have been no more. We owe a lot to the English for all you went to until we were ready to lend a hand. Maybe I feel this way because I'm half English for I know there are people (the isolationists for one group) who don't agree with my point of view at all, but thank God, my side is in the majority. Oh, dear here I go on another lecture again – sooner or later I invariably get wound up in politics, did I put you to sleep with my ranting? To get back to the snaps again – you're going to think I am a pest and never satisfied, I know, but I haven't received the other pictures you were going to send – I believe you said there were four. I hope you haven't forgotten you promised them to me – send them real soon, won't you? I'll thank you in advance for them. I wish I had some to send of us but we haven't been able to buy film here for eons now. So, photography is your hobby – I know it's fascinating as Lillian's husband George, is an amateur photographer – develops his own pictures and enlarges, he's very good at it too. Those I sent you last were some of his work.

Are you able to get equipment there and fix up a dark room and all? I don't' think I've ever asked you Roy but what type of building do you live in? – a tent or a barracks? (I know you're thinking now – something like this, no doubt 'these fool women') I haven't the faintest idea though and curiosity killed the cat you know. You know you have certainly shattered all my romantic illusions about India and the far east – all the exotic stories of that country omits the unpleasant realities such as the dust and dirt, the ignorance of the natives, the smells, the heat and so on. It's refreshing to hear the truth for a change. Gosh, you've been away from home for a good many years now, haven't' you? Don't you rate a furlough by now? One boy came back to Antioch the other day and 32 months in the South Pacific and all of us thought that was a very long drag. Thank goodness Earl hasn't had to go off to the wars yet, but our home isnt' out of the shadow of war by any means. His deferment is up Feb. 8 and I'm biting my nails down to the quick worrying about what the draft board will decide he's to do in the future. He's a war worker, works 7 days a week and sometimes 12 hours a day – he had a day off this last Christmas and we thought ourselves very lucky he got that. They need him pretty badly at the factory so I'm in hopes he'll be deferred again. About the only males we see around here anymore are vitally needed plant (factory) workers, lads under 17, and men around 50 – all the stores have women clerks now. Our little town came into the spotlight last week all over the nation, and even around the world I hear, when a sailor boy form here was put off a plane along with 2 other servicemen down in Tennessee in order that a dog might have their seats! The dog belonged to one of the Presidents sons (Elliot who is in England now) and he was sending it to his new wife, a movie star (Faye Emerson). The dog was given a priority for the plane seats (he took up 3) ahead of the servicemen! Everyone has been mad as blazes about it. This sailor from Antioch was rushing home to see his mother who was ill and had been recently widowed, (his dad was our chief of police). The story ran on the nation's front pages for 3 or 4 days and is still going strong. It's a heck of a note when a serviceman who's been risking his all for his country is left in the lurch for a dog eh?

(It's about time I was making a new paragraph!) There is a phrase here in your letter I particularly like – where you say' the trip was hot, dusty – with the chances of a bed berth as remote as a second Pearl Harbour' – boy you've really caught the spirit of the American people in that sentence, believe me! For there very definitely never will be a second Pearl Harbour incident again. The japs (small j) are paying for that piece of infamy too- and they're going to pay more and more until once more – we'll make them very sorry they ever drove those American prisoners in that 'March of Death'. Have you ever heard of that? You can bet your life we'll never forget it! Did you know those little yellow so and so's beat one lad with a 2 by 4 timber in the head and face until his nose was a bloody pulp and one ear was torn off and handing by a string??? Any Filipino who was so unfortunate as to chance by the scene was forced to grasp the timber and smash the American a few times too. It's a long gruesome tale and I get mad as the dickens when I think about it before my blood starts boiling I'd better look around for another topic. Marita is an active church worker and thinks all men should be brothers – but though I think I 'm reasonably good Christian I've developed too strong a hatred for the japs to consider them anything but savages and sadistic fiends. Are you wishing fervently that I'd find a more amiable subject? I always turn bitter when the jap war comes up. Gosh you're lucky only paying 20c for airmail letters – I (groan) have to shell out the magnificent sum of 75%. Think I'll write my Congressman or something – growl!

From the way those amazing Russians are pushing ahead on the eastern front this war (the European one at least) may be over by the time you get this letter (takes about 3 months to reach you, doesn't it?). But there I go getting overoptimistic again – our government has been berating us for that. We were all considerably deflated when the Germans went on the offensive and drove that bulge into Belgium – but thank goodness, they've been pushed back where they came from now. If we don't' hurry the Russians are going to be marching down – what is it next 'Under Dar Linten? (quit laughing – I know I messed that up) before we get there. We haven't any relatives in that fight – you probably know that Billy is here in the States again in a hospital with a tropical disease and Louis is honourably discharged (heart ailment) – our cousin Charlie, Jr. is a Lieutenant and I think he's in San Francisco – you know Hilda's husband is a Lieutenant –Commander, don't you? He's practicing dentistry on the Treasure Island Naval Base. My cousin (on my dad's side in New York State is training in a Naval Station and Earl's youngest brother is in Texas now in an overseas training camp so it looks as though it won't be long before he is shipped over. So it looks as though you're the only member of (that must be one of my favourite expressions or something, 'so it looks as though' …) the group of relatives who's right in there pitching- up in the front lines so to speak.

Roy and Grace are well and growing so fast I'm afraid if I turn my back for a minute and look again they'll have reached the voting age- Roy will be 9 in March (St. Patrick's Day to be exact) and Grace will be 3 in July.,.. and I'll be …oops, nearly slipped up on myself there. Roy stood up in class and told all the kids he has a cousin with the same name as his in India – but he forgot to say you were with the RAF- so the next day he got up and told them, by golly! I didn't have any idea he was going to stand up and make a speech about you—I think it was right after Christmas when we got your nice card and he just had to tell everyone about it. Your mail is the only foreign mail we get now since Earl's brother was transferred from Cuba to Texas so he considers it an exciting even (as do we all).

For the past week, practically all I've done is sit around and feel sorry for myself – I took the bus over Pittsburgh (5 miles west) last Friday (Jan. 19) and caught a severe chest cold when I walked in a sharp, piercing wind – now I can scarcely make myself sound intelligible to anyone – my voice breaks and growls and misses' words, have to talk in a whisper most of the time. (isn't this a sad tale?) I'm afraid Earl is going to have to do the shopping for groceries for me this week and does he love that? HE DOES NOT!

Our weather has been very nice up until today when we had a heavy mist (ben our ear while I whisper that is was really rain – we Californians are not supposed to use that word, you know). Earl has been busy putting our vegetable garden in and we're looking forward to a nice Harvest' this summer. Earl's folks back in snow-bound Michigan can hardly believe we're putting in a garden at this time of the year. Yes sir, don't let anyone tell you California isn't the best state in the union!

You mentioned once that you saw a cinema (movie to us) but you didn't say what picture you'd seen – are they showing any late Hollywood films over there? Or are they 1930 vintage! Some of our troops have been complaining that they're showing pictures they saw in the states when they were kids.

My eyes are beginning to feel abused so I think I'll call a halt to this document along here somewhere. I bet your happy about that, eh? I surely hope we'll be hearing from you real soon—keep sending by airmail so I won't have to wait too long for a reply (listen to who's talking- I've been owing you a letter for some time then I tell you to speed up your answers – but I'll do better from now on, honest Injun!)

Keep well and write very soon and oh yes,

You won't forget those snaps, will you?

Much love and the best of everything to you

Edith and family

(I imagine you're thankful I used the typewriter this time as you wouldn't have to decipher my handwriting!)

A letter from Georgie Black: a childhood friend of Roy's.

'Yorkville',

Chester Road

Whitby

Ellesmere Port

Wirral Cheshire

31st January 1943

Dear Roy,

I am rather ashamed that I have taken so long to answer your long and most interesting letter, and all the airgraphs you have sent me. But I would ask you to believe that they were very much appreciated. Doubtless you will have received the airgraph from me ere this arrives. The most irksome part of your service overseas will possibly be the long and unavoidable delay in receiving our mail. When you are at a field station this no doubt arrives very regularly, and remembering the distance, and the perils of the oceans in time of war, the

regularity is probably amazing, but in the very nature of things the period between writing and receipt of mail, which I realize must be eagerly looked forward to.

    I hope this finds you in the very best of health, and that the country, despite the great

heat agrees with you. Although normally one would not expect such a thing to happen. I know many who have served in tropical countries and have put on weight. How has it affected you? You mustn't come home like a barrel you know, otherwise that might mean increasing the officer accommodation, you know.

    I am pleased to say that I am very well, yes in spite of rationing, which the enemy would like to believe is not sufficient for us to live upon. Well, all I can say is that if we fare no worse in the future we will have fared very well indeed.

The winter has been and unusually mild one, and I have had wallflowers growing in my garden all winter. As I had a stroll today I saw some primulas, as pretty as you like, as if spring was here already.

I am kept very busy at work, for you see we old hands have to carry on while the younger generation shoulders the more intimate responsibilities of war. And a great job they are doing, for the news is most heartening.

Well Roy I will draw to a close with the best of good wishes to you, and let's hope the efforts of all those overseas will shortly enable the Victory to be won, and our lads soon be home once more,

Yours sincerely

G. Black

12th August 1945

Dear Roy,

     The war is now almost over, I expect you know almost as quick as we did, all are now waiting for the final word tomorrow, then I expect everywhere will go gay, very gay this time. Last Monday we went to Rhyl, it was just like winter but there were thousands there, you could see all the people staying inside the cars, but I enjoyed the drive very much it was lovely going through the countryside, we were back about eight o'clock so you can see we did not stay there long. Last Thursday Uncle Bill and Auntie Gertie came to see us in a friend's car, they wished to be remembered to you, they hear plenty of news of you from Auntie Minnie they went on to Uncle Alfred, they have gone to Blackpool for a fortnight. Harold Rowley and Louis Jeff are home from Italy, they really do look well fine and well. I don't think they are going back again. Yesterday May met Johnny Grimes, he was in Germany but has to go back again, he has now married some girl from Bristol. I would not bother to send any more tea as we are sure to get a few extra things, now it is all over in the Far East. I can hardly believe it, really is true, they will be getting you all home as quick as they can.

Yesterday we had a drive through the country and stayed a few hours at Moreton again. I got out and sat on the grass, the side car isn't new but is doing excellent work and carrying me around a lot. We are going to Delamere and around today.

Good bye for now, love from all of us here a quick letter,

all the best

from

your loving mother.

October 4th 1945

Dear Roy,

I have now received another 1 lb. of tea from you, any sign yet of coming home again. I hear of several boys who have got home again, and some have not been three years out there. I heard from the Shell again today, ok you have had an increase in your pay, it is all taken off even income tax, but I have all the papers for you to see, they also sent a slip of paper I know it is no use so I will write it out.

Important Notices

If for any reason you are released under the class 'B' scheme and directed to other industry you must inform us immediately

I expect they have been pulling some of the men in that class as nobody seems to want to go, the photographs of Maureen have come out lovely, Millicent is going to take Sylvia to have hers taken again, that is if she will sit for him, kiddies have funny little ways and can get black. Sylvia is trotting around and Maureen crawls all-round the place. Fred Stall has not got here yet and he gets demobbed this month. I believe they are fuming over there. I am sure they could have speeded up a bit quicker than they have done. The weather has taken a new turn for the better, warm in the day time, chilly at night and morning. I do hope it keeps like this for a time for you, or will be frozen and we cannot have fires as big as we like now, 3 bags every few weeks is our allowance but we did manage to get 20 bags of coke a while back. Things here are not all honey, I don't think there ought to have been an election until everything was over. Well Roy goodbye for now, hoping it won't be very long before we see you walking in. We all send our love, lots of luck and a fine trip home,

Cheerio, all the best from your loving mother.

Part 3
Post War

Demobilisation

The Holy Land

Homeward Bound via Jerusalem, Palestine and Gibraltar

In November 1945, with the war barely a month over, Roy, along with other RAF personnel, started their much-awaited journey home. For those who departed from one of the RAF stations near Karachi, Maripar or Drigh Road, ahead was a five-week journey by ship via the Indian Ocean, the Arabian Sea, Red Sea, Suez Canal and Port Said. Then it was onwards through the Mediterranean, the Straits of Gibraltar, across the Bay of Biscay and finally to English shores.

However, it would appear that rather than sail the whole way home from India as some servicemen did, Roy's journey home took him via Jerusalem, Palestine, from there flying from one of the many RAF airfields near Palestine such as, Ein Shemir, Qastina, Aqir or Petah Tiqva, stopping en route at Gibraltar, as he mentioned to Peggy in later years. His documentation clearly states he was in Palestine until January 1946 and just a week later was demobbed at Hednesford, Staffordshire 8th January 1946, almost four years after he sailed from Liverpool on the 7th February1942. Roy was released under 'Class A', the order of which was determined by age and length of service. Class 'A' included the majority of servicemen and women who were given eight weeks full pay on release. Roy's papers show he was of 'very good character' and had an above average ability in all his RAF duties and was 'superior' in his trade.

In later years, Roy recalled, as his fascinated young family listened, how he and his fellow servicemen had swum and floated in the nearby Dead Sea. This was about the only comment he made to his children about his time away. The sense of relief they must have felt would have been indescribable, after six long years the war was over at last and they had survived it. The relief was visible on their faces in the following photograph. For those RAF servicemen left behind in India awaiting their demobilisation, eager to get home to loved ones they hadn't seen or spoken to for many years, the mood must have been more akin to despair at the painfully slow process.

The Dome of the Rock, Qubbat As-Sakhrah: an Islamic Shrine and a UNESCO World Heritage Site. A very fit and tanned Roy 2nd from rt. first row at Temple Mount, Jerusalem

Unfortunately, not all RAF personnel were lucky enough to get away within weeks of the war ending. In January 1946, due to the slow demobilization and repatriation at many RAF stations in India and South-East Asia, thousands of RAF servicemen went on strike, which resulted in The RAF Mutiny of 1946. War weary servicemen not only wanted to go home but also complained about poor living conditions, particularly in Cawnpore 322 Unit where excessive heat had resulted in deaths. The mutiny involved over 50,000 men in 60 RAF stations, from its onset in Karachi to as far away as posts in Singapore. It took 11 days for it to be fully resolved. It has gone down in the history of the RAF as the one and only time the RAF went on strike. Prime Minister Clement Attlee was presented with a petition by India stationed servicemen, it stated, 'We have done the job we joined up to do. Now we want to get back home, both for personal reasons and because we think it is by work that we can best help Britain. No indication has been given of when we will see our families again. Is it because the government wishes to talk tough to other powers?' (*wikia.org/Post-World War 11 demobilization strikes*)

The logistics of returning over five million service men and women back home from abroad was enormous. Nine out of ten service personnel were men all eager to get home now the war was over. The repatriation fell to the shoulders of the wartime minister of Labour and National Service, Ernest Bevin, chief architect of the plan. A week after the German surrender he announced his demobilisation plan would commence on June 18th 1945, most of the men and women were to be released depending on their age and service number i.e. release was calculated from their age and how long they had served in uniform. Those whose pre-war occupational skills such as builders, miners, engineers who were urgently needed to rebuild post-war Britain were released ahead of their turn and were identified as class 'B'. Married women and men aged over fifty were also given priority. All other personnel were in class A. The release process started in June of 1945. *(The Peoples War, Britain 1939-1945, Angus Calder, page 569-570)*

At least going home was quicker and safer than coming out and the journey to a UK port was now under two weeks, though the Medloc (Mediterranean Lines of communication) route was used for a time. Most travelled by rail to Egypt and then by sea from Port Said. There was a shortage of ships, however, and transit in Egypt could mean an impatient wait.

The war over and hostilities ceased, it was no longer necessary for returning ships to sail in convoy.

Whilst awaiting demobilisation servicemen took the opportunity to visit the many places of interest in the Holy Land.

The Wailing Wall Jerusalem

Holy Sepulchre, Jerusalem, November 1945

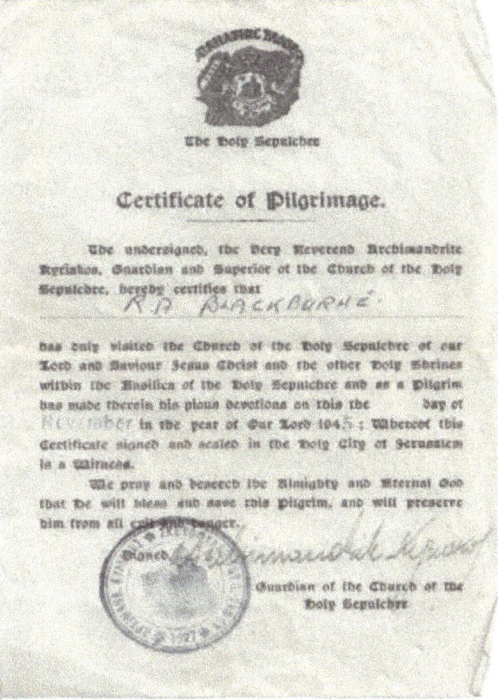

Palestine, December 1945 to January 1946, awaiting transportation home

Roy's Medals

Front   Reverse

The Burma Star 	The metal is yellow copper zinc alloy. The colours of the ribbon are dark blue, overlaid with a central red stripe to represent the Commonwealth Forces, and orange stripes to represent the sun. The Burma Star is a military campaign medal instituted by the United Kingdom in May 1945 as an award to subjects of the British Commonwealth who served in the WW II, specifically in the Burma Campaign from 1941 - 1945.
The Campaign Star 	The metal is yellow copper zinc alloy. The colours of the ribbon are stripes of dark blue to signify the Royal and Merchant Navies, red to signify the Armies and pale blue to signify the Royal Air Force. The 1939 - 1945 Campaign Star covered the full duration of the WW II from its outbreak on September 1939 to the victory over Japan on 2nd September 1945
Air Efficiency Award 	Made of silver, The Air Efficiency Award was instituted by Royal Warrant on 17th August 1942 as a long service award for part time auxiliary and Voluntary Air Force Officers, airmen and airwomen in the United Kingdom, the Indian Empire, Burma, the British Colonies and Protectorates and those British dominions whose governments desired to make use of the award. At the time, the award was unique being a decoration that could be conferred on officers.

The Defence Medal 	Those who qualified for any one of the Campaign Stars could be awarded the Defence Medal in addition.
The War Medal 1939 - 1945 	The metal is cupronickel. On the obverse is an effigy of King George VI and on the reverse, a lion standing on a fallen dragon. This was awarded to members of the British Commonwealth who had served at least 28 days full time service in the armed forces or Merchant Navy between 3rd September 1939 and 2nd September 1945. The red, white and blue colours of the ribbon represent the Union Flag.

Homecoming

October 1st 1945

Welcome home, whenever you get there. Hope it will be soon! This is your old firm 'The Shell' Love to all, ' ......M.

'Originally built in 1938 and sold for demolition in 1958, Hednesford was originally an RAF Technical Training Facility situated 7.5 miles South East of Hednesford, Staffordshire. When the war came to an end, Hednesford became a personnel dispatch centre for the demobilisaton of returning RAF servicemen and women'. (Rafcommands.com/forumposts/Royal Air Force Commands/Malcolm - raf/25th May 2018) Other centres handled different categories of personnel based in the UK. *(Personal communication 18th October 2020, Malcolm Barrass/Air of Authority/www. rafweb. org)*

All RAF contingents returning from overseas were demobilized through No. 104 Personnel Dispersal Centre, Hednesford (personal communication 15th December 2020, Alan Thomas/Air Historical Branch (RAF) Ministry of Defence.)

Prior to the start of the war, Roy, aged 20 yrs. had sensibly secured a staff position in the revenue offices at Shell Refinery, Stanlow, in his home town of Ellesmere Port, as per his pay slips. With already holding this position at the start of the war he was granted a monthly Ex Gratia payment. Consequentially, on his return to home after the end of hostilities his position remained open and he was guaranteed continuation of employment. Unfortunately for many men who had fought for King and country, they came home to long term unemployment, many of those who too had secured jobs on departure came home to find the positions had been filled during their absence.

Whilst away, times must have been very hard for Roy's widowed and disabled mother who would have required more financial assistance than most. Roy happily supported her throughout, but unfortunately on his return home much of his wartime salary had gone. His home coming bittersweet. Thrilled to be coming home and seeing his family again although sadly his father was no longer alive, but after working so hard for six years, and at times putting his life on the line, the nest egg he had hoped for was non-existent. This was not an unusual situation for many returning servicemen, whose families found their needs greater than the wartime rations allowed. Men came home to towns and villages barely recognizable after six years of German bombings, friends and neighbours dead or displaced, consequentially there would be a long period of readjustment ahead.

The majority of industries in Ellesmere Port had good social clubs for its employees, Shell was no exception. For many years 'The Shell Club' held ballroom dances, Roy and Peggy were both excellent dancers, coach trips, Christmas parties for the children of the employees and many other social occasions held on a regular basis. Roy was a regularly attendee of the rifle range at the club and studied German at night classes; did he think there was going to be another war? These activities gave him the opportunity to socialize and reminisce with other local ex-servicemen, some who had also served with 610 (County of Chester) Squadron and worked for Shell.

SC/V/2 Ens
-0 NOV 1947
N.W.73

R.A.F. Form 2520A
AIRMAN

ROYAL AIR FORCE
SERVICE AND RELEASE BOOK

Rank ...... ACT SGT ...... PERM. RANK CPL.

Service Number 810183

Surname ...... BLACKBURNE

Initials ...... R. A.

Class of Release ...... A

Age and Service Group No. 25

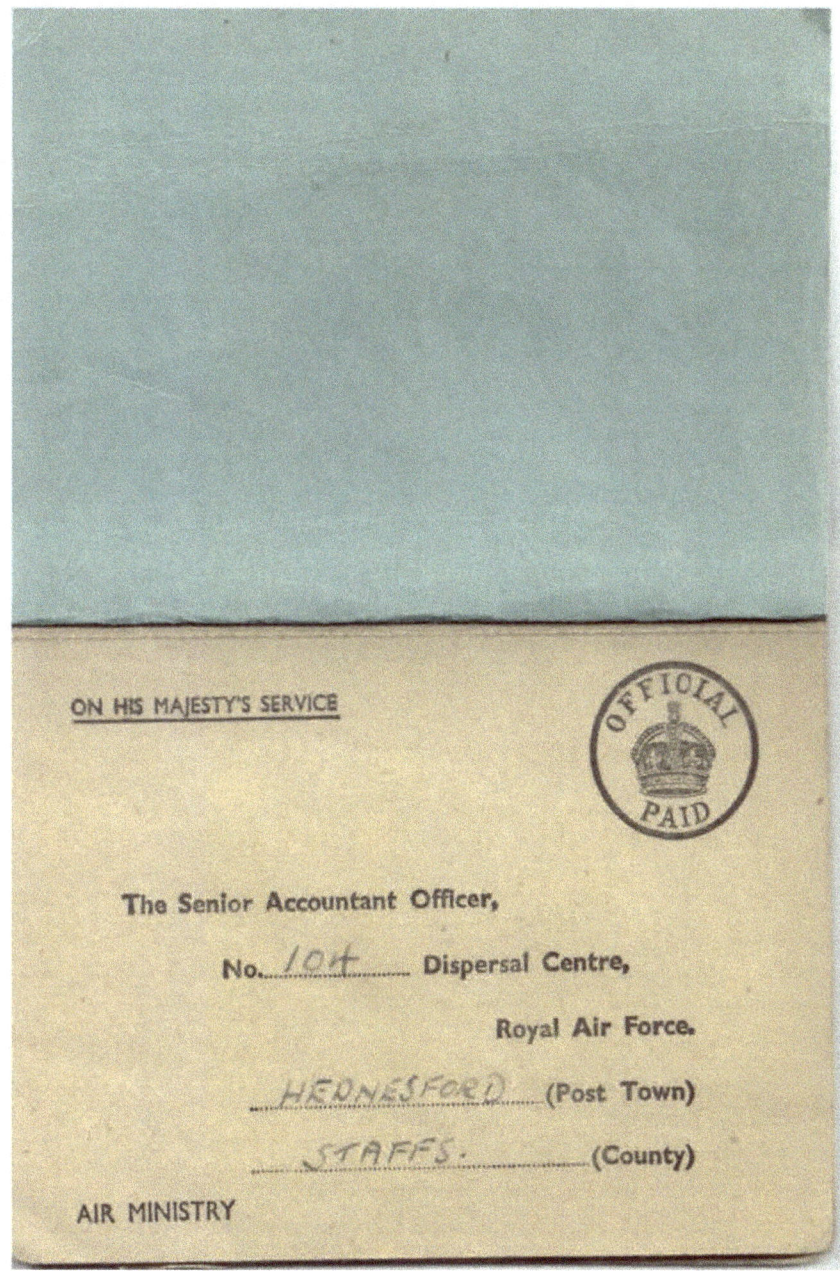

ON HIS MAJESTY'S SERVICE

OFFICIAL PAID

The Senior Accountant Officer,

No. _104_ Dispersal Centre,

Royal Air Force.

HEDNESFORD (Post Town)

STAFFS. (County)

AIR MINISTRY

Roy, still in India, was not released until January 1946 as per the following release papers.

R.A.F. Form 2520/20

NOTIFICATION OF CHANGE OF ADDRESS FOR FINAL PAYMENT OF PAY AND RELEASE BENEFITS

Note to Airman

Final payment will be made to the address which you gave at the time of your release. If, however, you change this address before you receive final payment, you should complete this card and send it to the Dispersal Centre from which you were released, about one week before the dates indicated in the Notes on Pay and Emoluments for which see Form 2520/26.

Airman's No. 810183   Surname BLACKBURNE
(Block Letters)

Date as shown on Form 2520/26.

Initials R.A.

Class of Release A

I desire to inform you that I have changed my address from that given on my release, and I now request that all further payments to be made to me be sent to the following address:—

_____

_____ (Post Town)

_____ (County)

Nearest Post Office
(if known)

_____

Signature of airman

Date_____

R.A.F. Form 2520/25

CONDITIONS OF RELEASE AND AUTHORISATION

Under the provisions of the Armed Forces (Conditions of Service) Act, 1939, YOU ARE HEREBY RELEASED FROM AIR FORCE SERVICE, or if a member of the Auxiliary Air Force, released from the obligations to which you are subject by reason of embodiment.

This release is subject to and on the following conditions :—

1. You are relegated to a Reserve of the Royal Air Force unless you are a member of the A.A.F. in which case you remain in the A.A.F.

2. You have not by this release been discharged from the Service. You remain liable to recall to Air Force Service until the Emergency is declared ended by Order in Council, when you will be discharged unless you are on an engagement extending beyond that date.

3. If you are recalled by Special Notice full instructions will be given you as to where and when you are to report. If any general notice or proclamation is issued revoking releases or recalling the reserve to which you belong, you must immediately follow the Remobilisation Instructions in this Book.

4. You must notify Air Officer i/c Records (K Division), Gloucester, of any change in your permanent address both for Service reasons and to ensure that any communications in regard to any medals reach you.

5. If you become medically unfit through any sickness, injury or other disability which renders you unfit for further service and which is not temporary only, you must write to the A.O. i/c Records (K Division), Gloucester, enclosing a medical certificate.

R.A.F.—Form 2520/25
(*continued*)

CONDITIONS OF RELEASE AND AUTHORISATION
(*continued*)

6. Until final discharge you may not enter or enlist in any other branch of H.M. Forces or the service of any other country, or depart from the U.K. without permission from the Air Officer i/c Records. If you desire to do so, write to him for his consent.

7. After the effective date of your release (i.e. at the expiration of any leave granted or if no leave is granted the day of departure from the Dispersal Centre) you may not wear uniform except on any specially authorised occasions, unless you are recalled for service.

8. You should preserve the uniform which you retain on your release in good condition in case of recall.

9. If you handed any Medals to your Commanding Officer for safe keeping apply to Air Officer i/c Records (C.I.M. Section), Gloucester, for their return, giving full particulars.

10. Your pay and allowances cease on the effective date of your release unless the release is revoked and you are recalled to service. No reserve pay is issuable in respect of the liability to recall referred to in para. 2 attaching to your release.

11. **The following conditions apply to Class A (Age and Service) releases only.**
Any reinstatement rights you may have under the Reinstatement in Civil Employment Act, 1944, arise on the commencement of your leave.

12. **The following conditions apply to Class B (National Reconstruction) releases only.**
You have been released at the request of the Ministry of Labour and National Service. You will be directed by that Ministry to your reconstruction employment for the purposes to which you

R.A.F. Form 2520/25
(continued)

CONDITIONS OF RELEASE AND AUTHORISATION
(continued)

have been released. Instructions setting out the Employment Exchange or Employer to which and the date by which you are to report are set out below. You must comply with these instructions. If at any time you discontinue such employment, save for reasons of ill-health, your release will be revoked and you will be recalled to Service.

13. **The following conditions apply to Class C releases only.**

You have been released on extreme compassionate grounds. Any reinstatement rights you may have under the Reinstatement in Civil Employment Act, 1944, arise on departure from the Dispersal Centre.

R.A.F. Form 2520/25

RELEASE AUTHORISATION

PART I
To be completed in Unit except when marked**.

Rank ...CPLY../.A/ST... Number ...810183.

Initials ...R. A........... Surname ...BLACKBURNE...
(Block Letters)

To be completed at the Dispersal Centre

Release of the above-named airman is hereby authorised as a Class A release, ~~and he is relegated to Class G.I of the Reserve.~~
The effective date of release (i.e. last day of service) is

...30-4-46.......**.

It is hereby certified that the above airman served in the R.A.F. on whole-time service during the following periods:

From	To
26/2/39	
26. 8. 39	8-1-46 **

(*Date of departure from Dispersal Centre*)

He is granted [102] days' leave on release commencing the day following the date of departure from the Dispersal Centre

R.A.F. Form 2520/25
(*continued*)

RELEASE AUTHORISATION
(*continued*)

PART II

Instructions to Class B releases to report for Employment

You have been released to take up employment

Delete one of these
{
as a ....
(Industry Group Letters;
Occupational Classification Number......................)
and are to report within seven days from your departure from this Dispersal Centre to the following Employment Exchange
....
}

OR

{
with Messrs. ....
of ....to whom you are to report within seven days from your departure from this Dispersal Centre.
}

You will ordinarily be required to commence work on the expiration of your leave, but you may if you desire commence at any earlier time.

PART III

Date ....**

....**
for A.O. i/c Records

Dispersal Centre Stamp.

R.A.F. Form 2520/26

NOTES ON PAY AND EMOLUMENTS

1. FOR CLASS A RELEASE

You will have received at the Dispersal Centre a payment in cash and postal drafts on account of your leave pay and allowances. Postal drafts for the final balance of your pay account and notification of amounts due to you for War Gratuity and Post-War Credit will be forwarded by the Senior Accountant Officer of the Dispersal Centre on or about the 42nd day after your departure from the Dispersal Centre. Amounts due in respect of War Gratuity and Post-War Credits will be made in the form of a deposit in the Post Office Savings Bank on the 57th day after you left the Dispersal Centre. A Post Office Savings Bank Book will then be forwarded to you by the Head Office of the Post Office Savings Bank.

2. FOR CLASS B RELEASE

You will have received at the Dispersal Centre a payment in cash on account of your leave pay and allowances. The balance of pay and allowances will be forwarded to you by the Senior Accountant Officer of the Dispersal Centre on or soon after the 14th day after your departure from the Centre. If, however, you were sent home from overseas for immediate release, delay in making the final payment will in some cases be unavoidable. Any payment to which you may be entitled in respect of your service overseas or for War Gratuity and Post-War Credit, will be made in the form of a deposit in the Post Office Savings Bank at the end of the emergency. A Post Office Savings Bank Book will then be forwarded to you by the Head Office of the Post Office Savings Bank.

3. FOR CLASS C RELEASE

You will have received at the Dispersal Centre a payment in cash on account of the balance of pay due to you. If, however, you are entitled to overseas leave the cash advances to be made at the Dispersal Centre will be increased. Postal drafts for the balance of your pay and overseas leave entitlements, and notification of amounts due to you for War Gratuity and Post-War Credits will be issued from the Dispersal Centre on or soon after the 14th day after your departure. If, however, you were

R.A.F. Form 2520/26
(*continued*)

NOTES ON PAY AND EMOLUMENTS
(*continued*)

sent home from overseas for immediate release, delay in making the final payment will, in some cases, be unavoidable. Any payments to which you may be entitled in respect of your service for War Gratuity and Post-War Credit will be made in the form of a deposit in the Post Office Savings Bank on the 57th day after you left the Dispersal Centre. A Post Office Savings Bank Book will then be forwarded to you by the Head Office of the Post Office Savings Bank.

FOR ALL RELEASES

4. You will have given on release an address at which you desire the final payment of your account made. If you change this address before you receive the final payment of your account and desire the payment made to any other address you should, in order to prevent loss or misappropriation, notify the Senior Accountant Officer of the Dispersal Centre from which you were released. A card (Form 2520/20) is provided in this book for the purpose.

5. Payment will be made to the address given on release unless notification of any change is received before payment; the Air Ministry will not be responsible for any loss or misappropriation resulting from your failure to notify a change of address.

6. The balance of pay forwarded to you by the Senior Accountant Officer of the Dispersal Centre does not preclude any adjustment of income tax liability which the Department of Inland Revenue may require to make subsequent to your release.

7A. The entitlement of wives, dependants and allottees to R.A.F. allowances and allotments ceases at the end of the allowance week (Thursday to Wednesday inclusive) in which leave expires (or if no leave is granted, at the end of the allowance week in which the airman/airwoman departed from the Dispersal Centre). Instructions will be issued to payees at the last known addresses for them to return the allowance books to

R.A.F. Form 2520/26
(*continued*)

NOTES ON PAY AND EMOLUMENTS
(*continued*)

the Director of Accounts, Whittington Road, Worcester, after the books have been cashed for that week. *Airmen and Airwomen are required to ensure,* irrespective of whether the official notice has been received, *that payees return the books at the time stated.*

7B. In certain cases however (e.g. Class A releases,) a form will be sent to payees from the Air Ministry which, on presentation to the Post Office, will enable them to draw allowances and allotments due for the last four weeks in one lump sum. When payment is made in this manner, the allowance books will be retained by the Post Office for return direct to the Air Ministry. If bulk payment is not authorised the procedure in paragraph 7A is to be followed.

7C. If the book is improperly encashed with your connivance or owing to your negligence, you may be liable to be prosecuted.

8. Any queries on your final payment, or War Gratuity entitlement or Post-War Credit arising after receipt of final payment are to be addressed to the Senior Accountant Officer of the Dispersal Centre at which release was effected quoting the following particulars:—

(*a*) Class of release (A, B or C).
(*b*) Date as Stamped below.

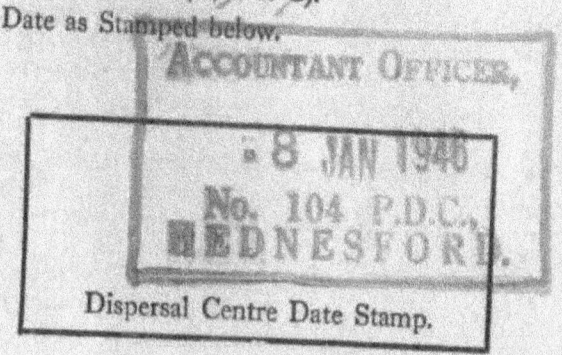

Dispersal Centre Date Stamp.

R.A.F. Form 2520/24.

REMOBILISATION INSTRUCTIONS

1. Although released you have NOT BEEN DISCHARGED.

2. Until you are finally discharged when the Emergency is declared ended by Order in Council you still remain liable to recall to service by public notice or proclamation or by a notice addressed to you personally.

3. If you receive an individual notice you will be sent a travelling warrant with full instructions as to what you are to do and where you are to report.

4. If a public general notice or proclamation is issued revoking releases and recalling the reserve of which you are a member, you should immediately prepare yourself to return to duty and watch the Press or Public Notice Boards for further instructions as to when you are to report.

5. You should report at your Remobilisation Station as shown below, in Uniform, bringing with you all service clothing and necessaries left in your possession when you were released.

6. You should also bring with you (1) this Book containing your Certificate of Service (2) your National Health and Pensions Insurance Contribution Card (3) your Unemployment Insurance Book (4) your Civilian Identity Card (5) your Service Identity discs. If you cannot get these at once do NOT delay but arrange for them to be sent on after you. If you are sick when due to report, you must immediately inform the Officer Commanding the station at which you are to report enclosing a medical certificate. You should report immediately you are fit for duty.

Please read overleaf.

R.A.F. Form 2520/14

To be detached only by Booking Clerk and exchanged for Ticket.

RECALL TO SERVICE OF AN AIRMAN ON REMOBILISATION

(*To be completed in Unit except where marked***)

TRAVEL WARRANT

Charges payable by Air Ministry (F3c)   R.A.F. 3rd Class

The Directors of the Railway Company or Shipping Company concerned are hereby requested to provide conveyance for one airman by the recognised direct route to.. **

N.B.—The airman concerned may only use this warrant if and when public notice of proclamation has been issued calling out the Reserve.

Airman's Number __810183__

Surname __BLACKBURNE__
(Block Letters)

Initials __R. A.__

Stamp of Dispersal Centre **

[Stamp: HEDNESFORD 1940]

Particulars of Ticket issued, to be filled in by Railway/Shipping Co.

R.A.F Form 2520/24.
(continued)

REMOBILISATION INSTRUCTIONS
(continued)

7. Do NOT bring any medals or decorations with you unless you are unable to leave them in safe custody.

8. If you have to travel by rail, use the Travel Warrant in this Book and complete the name of the Railway Station as necessary. If you do not require it, leave it in this Book which must be handed in when you report for duty.

9. If you need money for the journey the money order for 5s. in this Book may be used; present it for payment at any Post Office and produce your Identity Card and you will be paid 5s. which will be adjusted later in your account. (If you do not need the money, hand in the money order on reporting or you will be charged the 5s.).

NOTE: This money order and Warrant can only be used after a Public Notice or Proclamation has been issued; they are not valid till then.

REMOBILISATION STATIONS

10. If remobilisation or return to duty is ordered by general notice, or proclamation revoking releases or recalling the Reserve of which you are a member, a list of R.A.F. remobilisation stations will be published in the press and by public notice, shewing the particular stations under code letters. Your code letter is shewn below, and you should report to the station to which the code letter applies.

Your remobilisation station code letter is:—

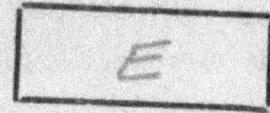

R.A.F FORM 2520/13

To be completed at Unit.
To be retained by Post Office.

ROYAL AIR FORCE

AVAILABLE ONLY ON REMOBILISATION BY PUBLIC NOTICE OR PROCLAMATION

To H.M. Postmaster General.

Please pay the sum of 5s. on production of his Identity Card to the airman mentioned below, if and when by Public Notice or Proclamation the R.A.F. Reserve has been called out for further Active Service before the present Emergency is declared ended. The receipt overleaf must be signed by him.

Surname __BLACKBURNE__
(Block Letters)

Christian Name(s) __ROY ALBERT__

Service No. __810183.__

Signature of Airman __R Blackburne.__

Stamp of Paying Post Office.

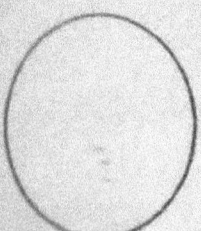

Stamp of Issuing Unit and Date.

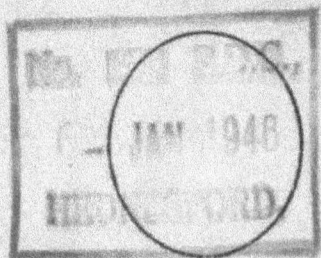

Please read overleaf.

Receipt to be signed if and when the Order is cashed. I hereby acknowledge receipt of the sum of 5/- (five shillings), being advance of pay, issued to me on rejoining.

....

Date..

NOTICE TO AIRMAN
If this Order is not used, it must be delivered to your Accountant Officer on joining your Unit, otherwise the five shillings will be charged against your pay account.

NOTICE TO POSTMASTER
After payment, this Order must be treated as a Postal Draft and claimed accordingly.

ROYAL A
CERTIFICATE OF SE

SERVICE PARTICULARS

Service Number: 810183   Rank: ACT. SGT.

Air Crew Category and/or R.A.F. trade: FITR II E.

Air Crew Badges awarded (if any): —

Overseas Service: 5. 1. 42: 7. 11. 45. (SEAC) 4 YEARS.

R.A.F. Character: V.G.   (see notes on back of certificate on opposite page)

Proficiency A: SUPR.   (" ")

" B: —   (" ")

Decorations, Medals, Clasps, Mention in Despatches, Commendations, etc.: BURMA. DEFENCE
WAR MEDAL 39/45.

Educational and Vocational Training Courses and Results: N.C.O. 1944
M.   J.C.T.A.

DESCRIPTION

Date of Birth: 20/11/1918   Height: 5' 10"

Marks and Scars: NR.

Specimen Signature of Airman: B Blackburne.

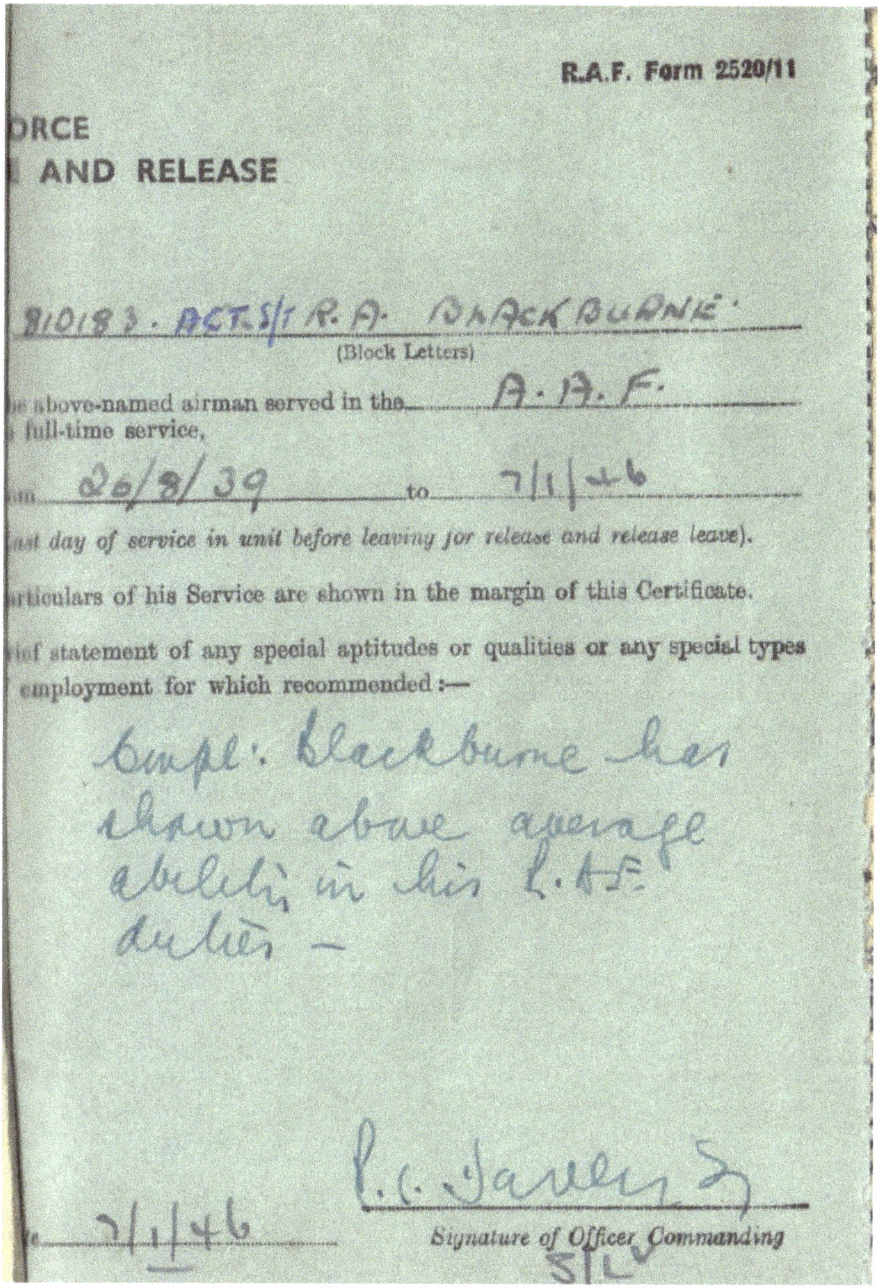

R.A.F. Form 2520/11

...RCE
...AND RELEASE

810183 · ACT.S/T R.A. BLACKBURNE ·
(Block Letters)

...above-named airman served in the R.A.F.
...full-time service,

...26/8/39 to 7/1/46

...day of service in unit before leaving for release and release leave).

...particulars of his Service are shown in the margin of this Certificate.

...statement of any special aptitudes or qualities or any special types
...employment for which recommended :—

Cpl. Blackburne has shown above average ability in his R.A.F. duties —

7/1/46

[signature]
Signature of Officer Commanding
S/L

Demobilization records show Roy had an excellent service record: 'Corporal Blackburne has shown above average abilities in his R.A.F. duties.'

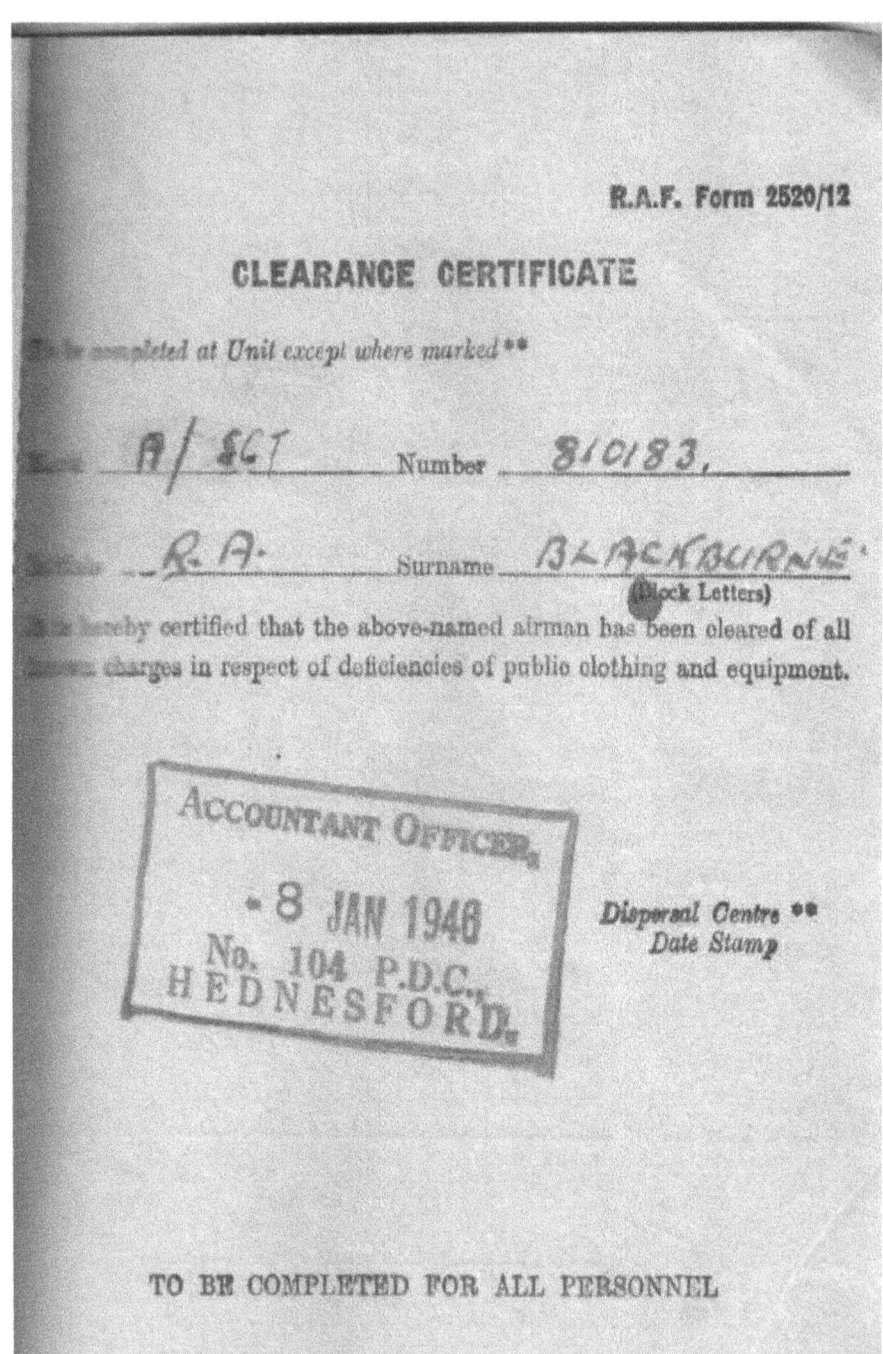

Up until the time of demoblisation, as an Acting Sergeant Roy would have become a Senior Non-Commissioned Officer.

Notes :—

R.A.F. trade—For air crew with a basic trade, show the trade in brack[ets] after the air crew category, e.g., Pilot (Armourer).

R.A.F. Character during Service :

V.G. is the highest character which can be awarded in the Royal Air For[ce]. The character assessment reflects the airman's conduct throughout [the] whole of his service.

Proficiency :

The trade proficiency headings A and B signify :—

TRADESMEN

A. Skill in his trade (applicable to airmen up to the rank of Corpo[ral] inclusive).

B. Ability as technical Warrant Officer or Non-commissioned officer, i.[e.] as foreman manager, foreman or supervisor in his trade.

AIR CREW PERSONNEL

A. Proficiency as pilot, navigator, air bomber, air gunner, etc.

B. Ability as a Warrant Officer or Non-commissioned officer.

Proficiency will be shown as

Ex.	for exceptional	
Supr.	for superior	
Sat.	for satisfactory	No higher or other assessment is permissible.
Mod.	for moderate	
Inf.	for inferior	

The date to be inserted as the date of commencement of service is the da[te] on which the airman reported for service, was called up from deferr[ed] service, called out or embodied as applicable.

R.A.F. Form 2520/10

THIRD CLASS RAILWAY TICKET

To be detached only by Ticket Collector.

NOT TRANSFERABLE

R.A.F.

3

Airman on leave on release.

Valid for single journey for one person only within **3** days of date of issue, by any recognised route.

Valid only within 3 days of date of issue

From *Rugeley* Railway Station
To be inserted by Dispersal Centre

Dispersal Centre Stamp and date of issue

[Stamp: No. 104 D.C. 8 JAN 1946 HEDNESFORD]

To *ELESMERE PORT* Railway Station
To be inserted by Unit

CONDITIONS.

This ticket is issued subject to the General Notices, Regulations and Conditions of the respective Companies over whose system it is available. It must be shown on demand and given up to the Railway or Shipping Company concerned at destination or on demand.

Any alteration to this ticket will render it invalid unless such alteration is signed and stamped at the Dispersal Centre or by an R.T.O.

P.T.O.

R.A.F. Form 2520/14

To be detached only by Booking Clerk and exchanged for Ticket.
RECALL TO SERVICE OF AN AIRMAN ON REMOBILISATION
(*To be completed in Unit except where marked***)

TRAVEL WARRANT

Charges payable by Air Ministry (F3c)   R.A.F. 3rd Class

The Directors of the Railway Company or Shipping Company concerned are hereby requested to provide conveyance for one airman by the recognised direct route to................................ **

N.B.—The airman concerned may only use this warrant if and when public notice of proclamation has been issued calling out the Reserve.

Airman's Number __810183__

Surname __BLACKBURNE__
(Block Letters)

Initials __R. A.__

Stamp of Dispersal Centre ** — HEDNESFORD

Particulars of Ticket issued, to be filled in by Railway/Shipping Co.

Notes on R.A.F. Form 2520/18
MPB 281

CLAIM FOR DISABILITY PENSION—(AIRMAN)

THE ATTACHED FORM is to be used only if you claim to be suffering from a disability attributable to or aggravated by WAR SERVICE. You may complete it at any time WITHIN 6 MONTHS after the date you ceased to draw service pay.

When completed the form should be sent to the Air Officer i/c R.A.F. Record Office, Gloucester.

If there is insufficient space on the form further explanations or answers can be written on a plain sheet of paper which you must SIGN and attach firmly to the form.

Any pension granted on this application will commence on the day following cessation of service pay.

After 6 months from the cessation of service pay, any claim to pension must be made on a different form to be obtained from the nearest office of the MINISTRY OF PENSIONS, the address of which can be obtained at the local Post Office.

(b) Wife's present address

R.A.F. Form 2520/18
MPB 281

CLAIM FOR DISABILITY PENSION—AIRMAN

1. Surname BLACKBURNE   2. Service No. 2/0/83
   (BLOCK LETTERS)
3. Christian Names ROY   ALBERT
   DEMOB
4. Rank CPL   5. Unit/Group 184 PDC/2.T
6. Date of Release
7. Have you served in the Armed Forces before the present War and been discharged?
   ("Yes" or "No") _____ If "Yes" give particulars below:—

Former Regt. Corps or Ship, etc.	Army or Official Number	Date of Discharge	Cause of Discharge	Particulars of Pension (if any) for disablement or service

8. Give particulars of your wife and children now under 16 years of age for whom you received family allowances at any time during service:—
   (a) Wife—full Christian Names and name before marriage.
   (b) Wife's present address
   (c) Date of marriage
   (d) CHILDREN:—
       Full Christian Names (and surnames where different from your own) and dates of birth
       1. _____ Date of birth _____
       2. _____ Date of birth _____
       3. _____ Date of birth _____

9. Give particulars of any child born after release
   Name/s _____
   Date/s of birth _____

PARTICULARS OF CLAIM

The following questions should be answered with care. The answers will assist in the enquiries to be made of official records. Incomplete answers may delay the consideration of your claim.

QUESTION	ANSWER
10. What is the disability for which you claim pension? If a wound or injury state when and where received and part of body injured.	
11. Give the names of the hospitals or other places at which you received treatment during service for the disability and the dates as nearly as you can.	

(continued overleaf)

R.A.F. Form 2520/18
MPB 281
(continued)

CLAIM FOR DISABILITY PENSION—AIRMAN
(continued)

12. IF YOU CLAIM SOLELY IN RESPECT OF A WOUND OR INJURY, YOU NEED NOT ANSWER ANY OF THE FOLLOWING QUESTIONS—but this claim form must be signed and dated.

QUESTION	ANSWER
13. (a) When did you first suffer from the disability ? (a)	
(b) If before your war service when did you first notice the effects of war service on it ? (b)	
14. State what particular incidents or conditions of service you consider caused or worsened the disability.	
15. (a) In which Unit were you then serving ? (a)	
(b) Where were you stationed ? (b)	
(c) What was the precise nature of your duties at the time ? (c)	
16. If you suffered from the disability before joining the Forces, give the name and address of any doctor, hospital, etc., from whom you received treatment. Give approximate dates.	
17. Have you been treated for the above or any other complaint since Release ? If so, state nature of complaint and name and address of doctor or hospital with first and last dates of attendance.	

Signature .... Date ....

Any person knowingly making a false statement will be liable to prosecution.

Address ....

....

....

Address (if different from above) to which you desire the result of your claim to be sent ....

Witness to signature .... Date ....
(Any householder)

Address of Witness ....

....

Second signature of applicant
(for record purposes) ....

R.A.F. Form 2520/13

Part II to be completed at Unit.
Part III to be completed at Dispersal Centre.

PART I.
Instructions to Released Person.

MEDICAL TREATMENT AFTER LEAVING DISPERSAL CENTRE

You are now entitled to medical benefit under the National Health Insurance Acts, and a medical card telling you how to get treatment will be sent to you as soon as possible. Medical benefit includes free treatment from an insurance doctor at his surgery, or if your condition requires it, at your home, and free medicine.

If you go back to live in your old district and had an insurance doctor before you joined up you will be restored to his list if he is still in practice himself or by deputy.

If you fall ill before the medical card comes, fill in the application below and hand this book to your previous insurance doctor (or, if absent, his deputy). If you did not have an insurance doctor before you joined up or if you go to live in another part of the country, apply to any insurance doctor. You can see a list of insurance doctors at the local Post Office.
Do not detach the form from the book. The doctor will do this.
Turn over for information about hospital treatment.

Form Med. 50A

PART II to be completed at Unit.

Rank _CPL_ Number _810183_

Initials _R.A._ Surname _BLACKBURNE_
 (Block letters)

Date of birth _20/11/1918_ Sex _MALE_

PART III to be completed at Dispersal Centre.
(Dispersal Centre Date Stamp)

The above-named person departed
from this Dispersal Centre on _____

PART IV
Available for three months from date of leaving Dispersal Centre

To be completed by released person ONLY if needing medical treatment before a medical card is received.

I have NOT received a medical card since leaving the Dispersal Centre and I hereby apply for a medical card to be issued to me.

Delete as may be necessary
- I was on the list of Dr. _____ immediately before I was mobilised or called up for service.
- I was not on the list of a doctor in the district where I am now, and I desire to be placed on the list of _____
 (Insert name of doctor or approved institution)

My present address is _____

Do you intend to leave this district within three months from the date hereof?

If so, when? _____

(Continued overleaf)

_____

_____

_____

Membership number _____

_____
(Signature of Released Person)

Date _____

* If you were a member of an Approved Society before you were mobilised or called up for service, or if you joined an Approved Society during service, your membership is still effective.

PART V

HOSPITAL TREATMENT DURING RELEASE LEAVE

If you need hospital treatment before the end of your leave you should show this book to your doctor and if he is of opinion that such treatment is necessary he will advise you as to the steps to be taken to obtain that treatment. You should show this Release Book to the hospital authorities when admitted to or attending hospital for treatment.

For the information of the doctor.

In-patient treatment would normally be given at the nearest service or civil Emergency Medical Scheme hospital where the treatment required can be given. If you are in doubt as to the location of the nearest suitable hospital the Hospital Officer for the district in which the patient resides can give you the required information, and he will also be in a position to advise as to the nearest military or E.M.S. hospital where any massage, X-ray examination or other out-patient treatment can be obtained.

PART VI to be completed by Doctor providing treatment who should also detach the form and send it to the Insurance Committee (in Northern Ireland) to the Ministry of Labour, Palace Grounds, Armagh, Northern Ireland), for the area in which the insured person is staying.

_____

* The person named overleaf who was not on my list immediately before serving in H.M. Forces is accepted as from to-day as a temporary*/permanent* resident.

* The person named overleaf who states that he was on my list immediately before serving in H.M. Forces has to-day applied to me for treatment.

Date _____   Signature _____
* Delete where not applicable.

If doctor is to supply drugs he should enter DR here _____	If doctor claims mileage he should enter mileage distance here _____

FOR ALL AIRMEN

Take the utmost care of this book which contains your Certificate of Service. The Certificate cannot be replaced when loss is due to any action or negligence on your part. You should not part with your Certificate of Service, but if you desire to give anyone full particulars of your service, make a copy.

WARNING.—You are reminded that the unauthorised communication by you to any person at any time of any information you may have acquired while in H.M. Service which might be useful to an enemy renders you liable to prosecution under Official Secrets Acts 1911 and 1920.

In case of death, next-of-kin are requested immediately to inform A.O. i/c Records, K Division, Gloucester.

R.A.F. Form 2520/21

NOTIFICATION OF CHANGE OF ADDRESS AFTER RELEASE

Rank _Act·S/S/_ Number _810183._

Initials _R. A._ Surname _BLACKBURNE._
(IN BLOCK LETTERS)

I have to inform you that I have changed my permanent address which now is :—

Insert Full Postal Address in Block Capitals
{
_____
_____ (Post Town)
_____ (County)
}

Date_____ Signature_____

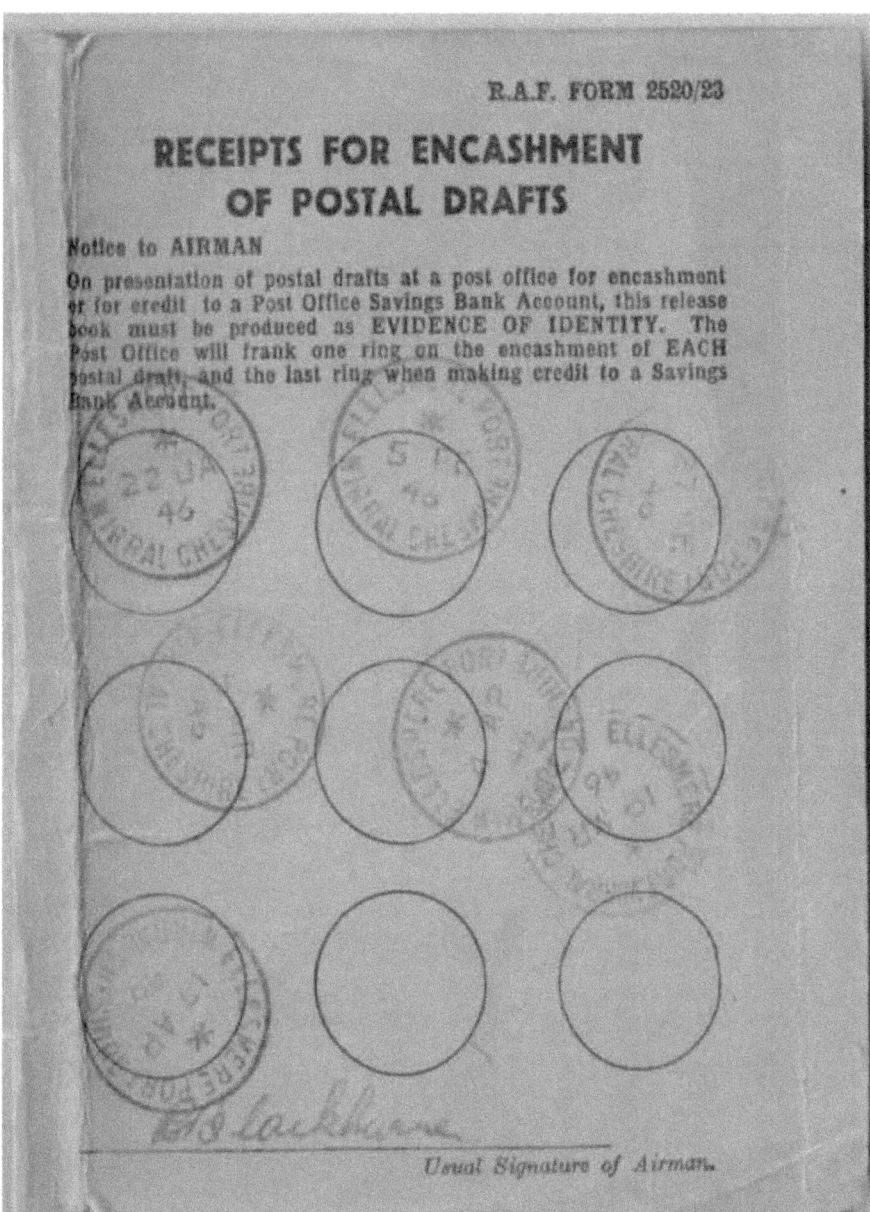

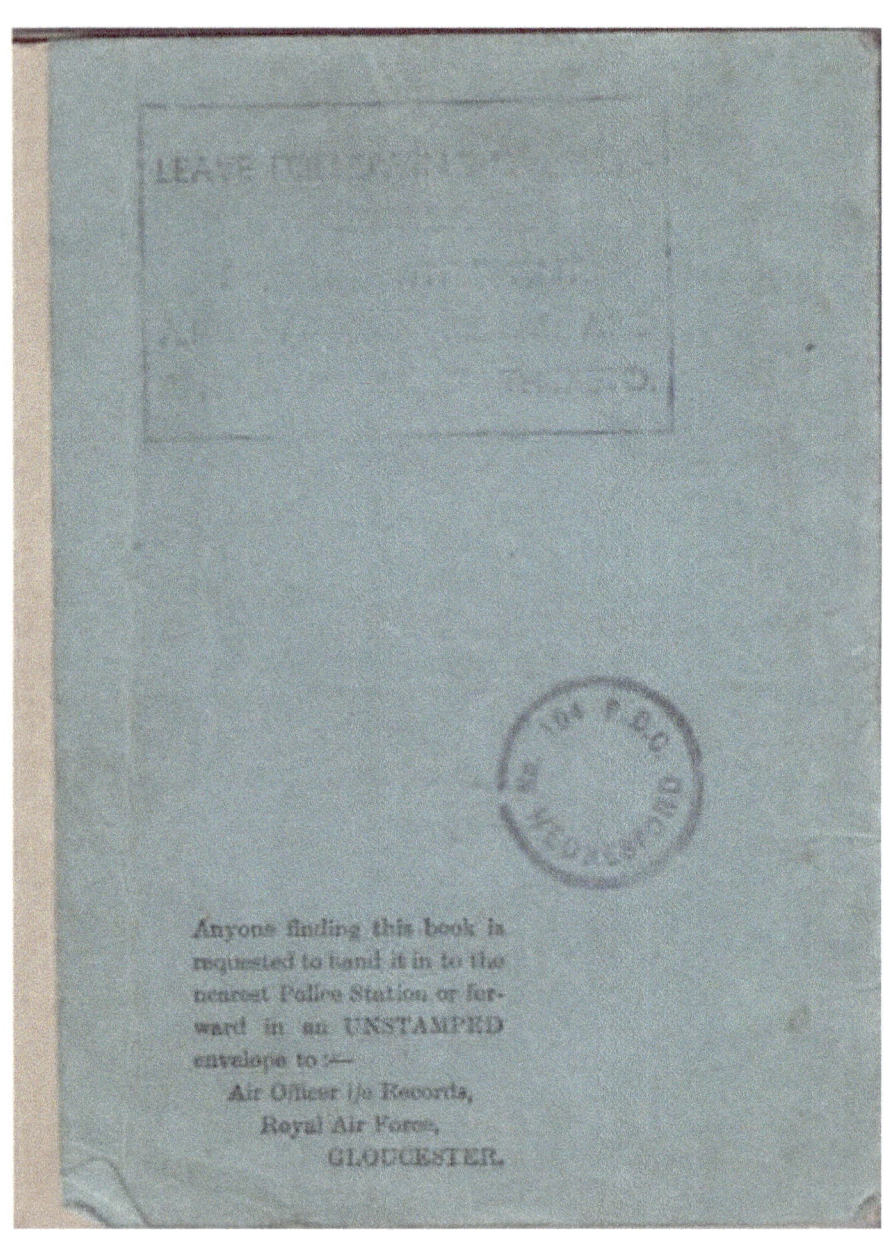

Anyone finding this book is requested to hand it in to the nearest Police Station or forward in an UNSTAMPED envelope to :—
　　Air Officer i/c Records,
　　Royal Air Force,
　　　　GLOUCESTER.

FORM A.14

"SHELL" REFINING & MARKETING COMPANY LTD.

EX GRATIA PAYMENT (APPLICABLE TO MEN SERVING IN H.M.FORCES)
FOR FOUR WEEKS ENDING 28 November 1943.

EMPLOYEES NAME Blackburne R   CHECK NO _____

PAYABLE TO Mrs A Blackburne

CIVIL PAY.. £19 4 8
WAR ALLOWANCE...   3 17 0
                                                            23 1 8
DEDUCT:
  SERVICE PAY.................................. £17 10 2
  ALLOWANCE FOR WIFE & CHILD/CHILDREN
                                                            14 17 6
                                                             8 4 2

DEDUCT:
  INCOME TAX................................... £1 0 0
  SAVINGS......................................
  HOSPITAL CONTRIBUTIONS.......................
  PROVIDENT FUND...............................   2 7 4
  AMOUNT RETAINED AGAINST EXISTING
    OVERPAYMENT OF £_____ ....
                                                             3 7 4

BALANCE DUE)/PAID INTO YOUR BANK ACCOUNT
)/ENCLOSED IN FORM OF MONEY/POSTAL ORDER   £ 4 16 10

RECEIVED BY: _____   ) TO BE FILLED
              (Signature)   ) IN IN INK
FOR AND ON BEHALF OF: _____
                       (Employee's Name)
(NOTE: THE ABOVE NEED ONLY BE FILLED IN WHERE A MONEY ORDER OR
        POSTAL ORDER IS ENCLOSED)

REMARKS:_____
        _____
        _____

IG.

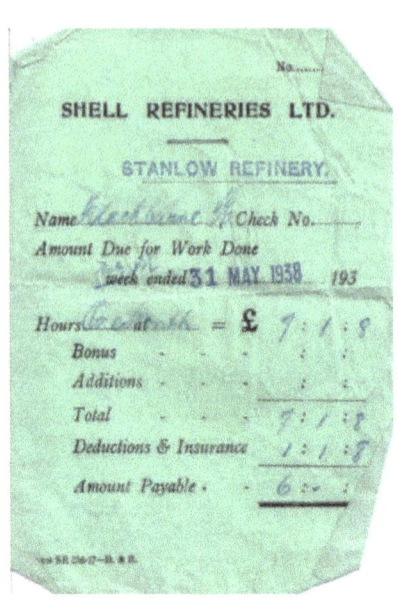

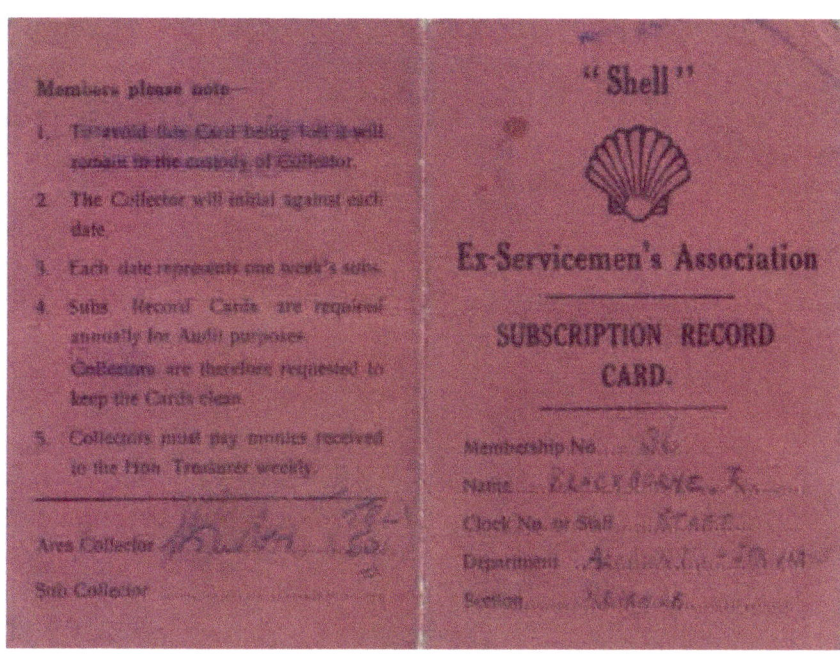

Roy in his demob suit

On returning home, Roy was a changed man. No longer the shy young boy who had enrolled in the Auxiliary Air Force in 1939, now an experienced ex-serviceman with a wealth of skills behind him and a greater knowledge of the world. A bright future lay ahead and he grasped it with both hands.

After years of being apart, not knowing if the other would survive the war, Roy and Peggy finally married on 21st June 1948. The reception was held at the Carlton Cafe, Little Sutton.

We still have Peggy's wedding dress!

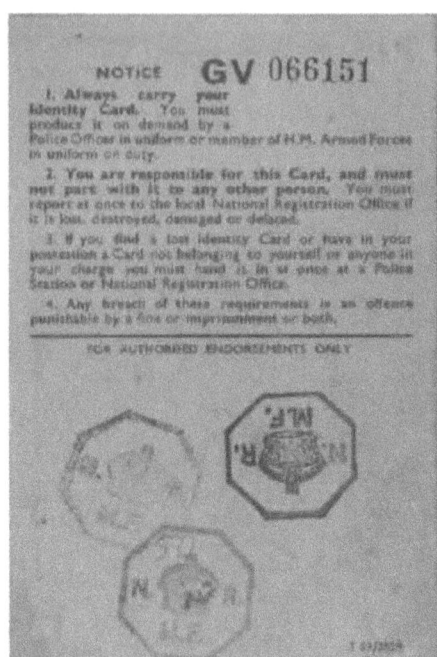

Peggy's ID card dated from 1948 at the time of her marriage to Roy and their changes of address in 1949 and 1950. It was no longer compulsorily to carry ID cards after 21st February 1952

National Registration Identity Cards

The National Registration Act of 1939 was implemented at the start of the WW II. The Act included enumeration of households to compile a National Register to assist with identifying civilians during wartime, issuing rations and control the call-up for the forces.

Wartime Rationale. Three main reasons were put forward by the government for passing the law in September 1939. The first was the major dislocation of the population caused by mobilization and mass evacuation and the wartime need for complete manpower control and planning to maximise the efficiency of the war economy. It may or may not have been necessary, that is a matter of dispute but it was seen as emergency, temporary legislation to cope with special circumstances. The second reason why the Act was passed was the likelihood of rationing. It was felt that the imminence of rationing (introduced from January 1940 onwards) entailed the need for an up to date system of standardised registration, so rationing could be introduced as easily as possible. The third reason was the government needed recent statistics about the population, as the last census had been held in 1931 and the next was not due until 1941, there was little accurate data on which to base vital planning decisions.

The National Register was in fact an instant census. The whole process of registration was carried through in three weeks and would form the basis for proper wartime planning. *(Statewatch, monitoring the state and civil liberties in Europe. Statewatch new online: Identity cards in the UK – a Lesson from History/28th March 2012).* The particulars of each citizen throughout the United Kingdom entered on the register included; names, sex, age, occupation, profession, trade or employment, residence, condition as to marriage and whether they were a member of Naval, Military or Air Force Reserves, or Auxiliary Forces or of Civil Defence Services or Reserves. It was the responsibility of the holder to carry the card at all times and produce the card on request to the police. The card had to be surrendered when a person died, and in such cases as may be prescribed should a person go overseas. Identity cards were necessary for wartime efficiency and planning. *(freepages. rootHweb.com)*

General Register Office: National Registration: Correspondence and Papers', *The National Archives*, access from https://discovery.nationalarchives.gov.uk/details/r/C13353 on 15th October, 2020.

Despite the war being over, rationing continued until nine years later, on 4th July 1954. Amongst the paperwork in the family home, Peggy and Roy had kept some cuttings from the local newspaper, the Ellesmere Port Pioneer, which ran an advertisement on how to get new ration books, and another from the Merseyside and North Wales Electricity Board advertising a cookery demonstration.

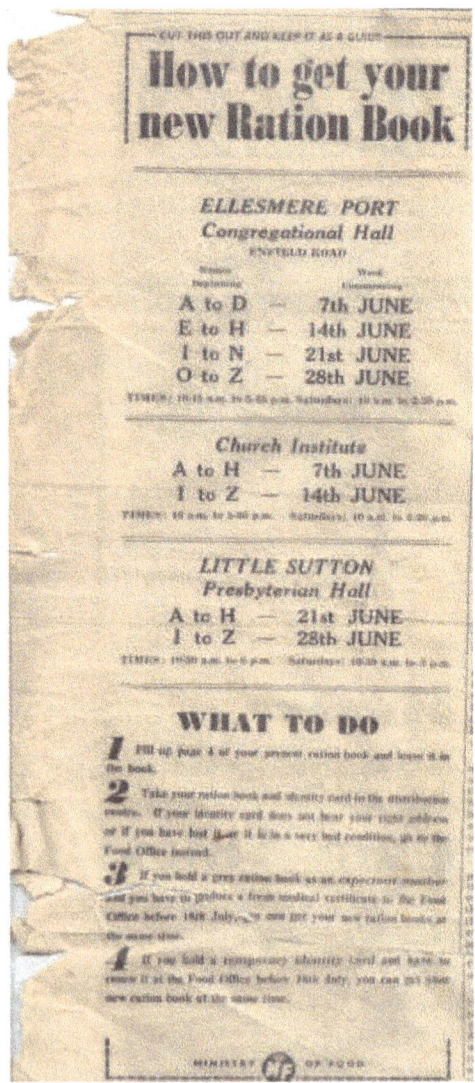

What to Do

1 Fill up page four of your present ration book and leave it in the book.

2 Take your ration book and identity card to the distribution centre. If your identity card does not bear your right address or if you have lost it or it is in a very bad condition, go to the food office instead.

3 If you hold a grey ration book as an expectant mother and you have to produce a fresh medical certificate to the Food office before 18th July you can get your new ration books at the same time.

4 If you hold a temporary identity card and have to renew it at the food office before 18th July, you can get your new ration book at the same time.

Ellesmere Port's local cinema The Hippodrome and the Gaumont in nearby Chester were showing popular film stars of the day, Alan Ladd and Veronica Lake in 'Saigon' and Bing Crosby and Fred Astaire in the much acclaimed 'Blue Skies.

According to Peggy, in the first few months following his demobilisation to England, Roy would react nervously at the sound of or sight of airplanes flying overhead, instinctively heading for cover. Funded by the sale of Peggy's hairdressing shop, they built a large family home in Little Sutton. There at last they could move forward and try and forget about the horrors witnessed and start to enjoy the life they could only have dreamt of just months before. It would appear Roy could not forget his time with the RAF. By secreting his kitbag under the eaves of the loft of their house, he must have felt the need to hold onto such a momentous part of his past.

Roy worked for over forty, very happy years in the accounts department at Thornton Research Centre, Shell, Ellesmere Port. He retired aged 55. Being a very active man, he soon became bored and returned to work, this time for the accounts department at the local council. Disillusioned 'with the slapdash' way the council ran things (in his words), he moved on to work for a finance company, (from where he lectured his children on *not* what to do with their money), before reluctantly retiring for good in his late sixties. Roy and Peggy were married for almost sixty years.

Where Roy was at his happiest

Even in retirement Roy was never idle, spending hundreds of hours over the years tending to his huge 90ft square garden. He grew fruit and vegetables, his crops so bountiful his family thrived on them, and neighbours benefited from Roy's hard work. His trusty mechanic who kept his car going for many a year, was the recipient of the windfalls from the numerous fruit trees. Roy audited books for local societies, enjoyed playing golf and was a good amateur photographer, some of his photographs appearing in local exhibitions. Philately was also a great hobby of his. As an avid DIYer, he built his own conservatory and numerous sheds and greenhouses. Roy was the ultimate recycler, very little was thrown out that could be used again or for another purpose.

Peace at last. How he must have dreamt of days like this whilst away at war

Roy was reliable, well intentioned and a fiercely independent man. He flatly refused any form of help until he was well into his eighties, choosing not to rely on others. He came from a generation of resourceful fighting men who had experienced dreadful times, who would ask for nothing from anyone and soldier on regardless. Despite his own physical infirmities, his determination and strength of character served him well as he cared for Peggy in the best way he could when sadly the ravages of old age took its toll and she became physically infirm.

He appreciated what he had fought for and was very happy to have survived a brutal war unlike many of his fellow airmen. Roy died on October 18th 2005 surrounded by his family. He had lived a good, honest, eventful life.

His family mattered above all else. A father to be proud of indeed.

Following Roy's death, Peggy, like Roy, was fiercely independent. She managed with help to remain in the family home until her death two years later on 9th March 2007. She too rarely spoke of her war years, only occasionally to her brother Tom over the loss of their brother Billy. The war was not forgotten but laid to rest. Both Roy and Peggy are buried at St. Paul's Church Hooton where they married.

Over but Not Forgotten

A letter found amongst the correspondence in the kitbag, an invitation to re-join as a member of the Auxiliary Squadron, an undated letter but likely to be 1946.

'The squadron was reformed at Hooton Park in June 1946, first with Spitfire MK XIV'S and then with Spitfire MK XX11'S, in 1951 the squadron received its first fast jets the Gloster Meteors MK 1V's and then in 1952 Gloster Meteors MK V111, 610 Squadron was disbanded again in 1957. (610 Squadron (County of Chester), Compiled by Mark Oliver, Oliver Aviation Collection/pg 15.)

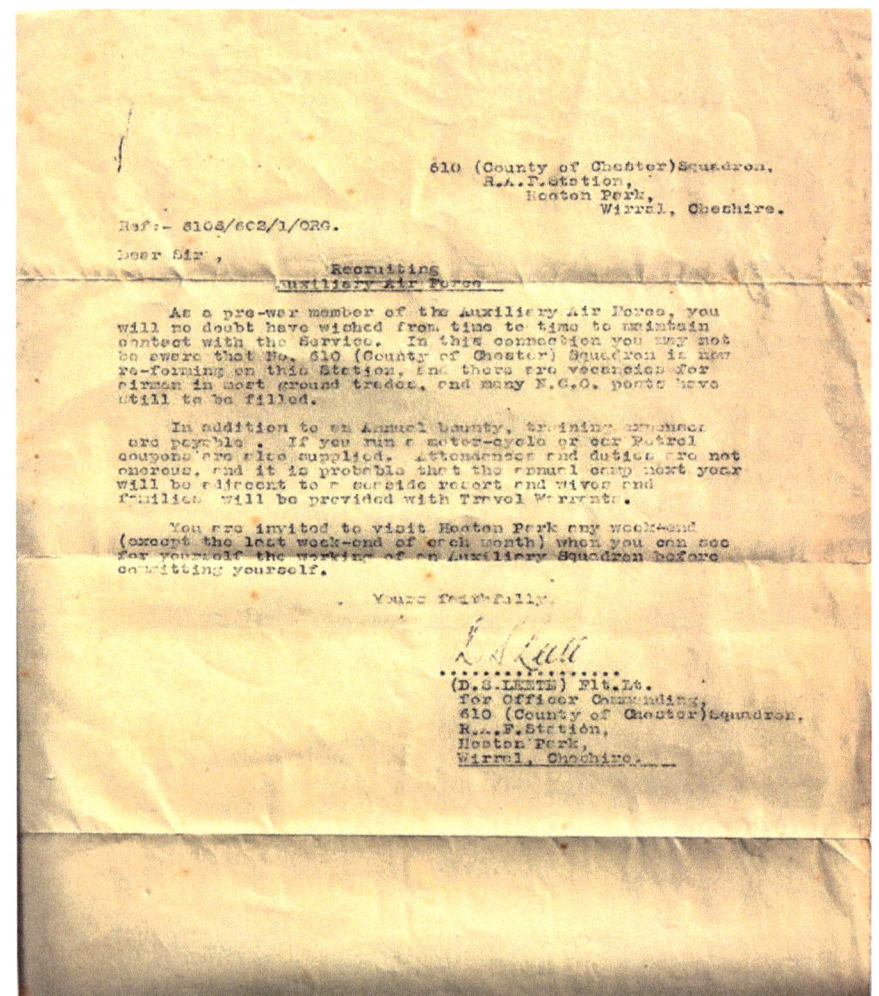

610 (County of Chester) Squadron
R.A.F Station
Hooton Park
Wirral, Cheshire
Ref: - 610S/6C21/ORG

Dear Sir,

Recruiting Auxiliary Air Force

As a pre-war member of the Auxiliary Air Force, you will no doubt have wished from time to time to maintain contact with the Service. In this connection, you may not be aware that No. 610 (County of Chester) Squadron is now re-forming on this Station, and there are vacancies for airmen in most ground trades, and many N.C.O. posts have still to be filled.

In addition to an annual bounty, training expenses are payable. If you run a motorcycle or car petrol coupons are also supplied. Attendances and duties are not onerous and it is probable that the annual camp next year will be adjacent to a seaside resort and wives and families will be provided with Travel Warrants.

You are invited to visit Hooton Park any weekend (except the last week-end of each month) when you can see for yourself the working Auxiliary Squadron before committing yourself.

Yours faithfully,

D.S. LEETE Flt. Lt.

for Officer Commanding 610 (County of Chester) Squadron

R.A.F Station Hooton Park

Wirral,

Cheshire.

THANKS A LOT

A year ago there were many in this country ready to jeer at Britain's "week-end flyers," the young men who dashed from shops and offices to learn to fly, to bomb, to shoot.

Today the B.E.F. says "Thank God" for these young men. Their record in the fierce fighting of the past three days is unequalled in the glorious history of the R.A.F. One squadron of these "auxiliaries" brought down seven German bombers before breakfast! Isn't that something worth saying "Thank you" for? These hours of freedom sacrificed before the war may yet prove the nation's salvation.

1940 Ellesmere Port Pioneer (newspaper)

Article from Ellesmere Port Pioneer, 29th September 1980

Battle of Britain Airmen Recall the Good and the Bad.

12th August 1940 dawned cold and clear. At Biggin Hill 610 (County of Chester) Squadron was on early morning stand-by. The call to scramble came at 7.31 am. It was 'Hitler's Alder Tag' the Battle of Britain had begun. Eleven waves of bombers escorted by fighters, were crossing the channel. 610 intercepted a group of Dernier 17s and in the following melee Me109's raced towards the Spitfires to keep them from the bombers. The 12 Spitfires were vastly outnumbered but 610 battled on. For almost 20 minutes chaos reigned, then all went quiet as the Messerschmitt's retreated to France to refuel. Eleven Spitfires arrived back at Biggin Hill at 8.30am. The twelfth had been hit and the pilot bailed out. He was picked up in the Channel, safe but with burns on his face and hands.

The score at the beginning of this major battle, which was to set the course of the whole war, was two unconfirmed hits, six unconfirmed, two probable's and one damaged. All pilots had returned safe and only one Spitfire had been lost. The 610 Squadron an Auxiliary Unit, was formed in February 1936 at Hooton Park. It was formed as a light bomber squadron equipped with Hawker Harts, Avro Tutors and later Hawker Hinds.

On 1st January 1939 the Squadron was transferred to Fighter Command but due to the sudden and rapid expansion of the Air Force and the consequent shortage of aircraft, there was some delay in the arrival of their first fighters, and some confusion as to what type they were to be. Initially it was to be a Defiant unit, but by September no Defiants had arrived. For three weeks the Squadron flew Hurricanes but in October it was supplied with Spitfire 1s. The Squadron spent the 1939/1940 winter as a 12 Group Unit based at Wittering, Northamptonshire. There they worked up to operational perfection before spending a short time at Prestwick, Scotland. Early in May they moved to Biggin Hill to replace 79 Squadron in the actions covering the British Army's retreat from France and evacuation from Dunkirk. During this period they notched up eight kills, and four probable's, but lost six aircraft – half the squadron because of this they were withdrawn to Gravesend to rest and re-equip. 610 returned to Biggin Hill in July when it bore the brunt of the ever-increasing Luftwaffe raids. Following the beginning of the Battle of Britain, the squadron was almost continually in the air, sometimes for almost 16 hours a day, against what must have appeared overwhelming odds. The squadrons finest hour was on 18th August when it intercepted a massive formation of German bombers, and prevented what probably would have been the heaviest raid on Biggin Hill ever to be made.

Convoy Duty

The pace of the battle left the mark on the men as well as on the machines and at the end of August 610 was sent North to Acklington to recuperate and rest. Following that they spent a few months on North Sea Convoy duty before going back South to Tangmere Wing at Westhampnett in Sussex. It was here that they received Spitfire 11s and was mainly engaged in offensive sweeps over the Channel. The squadron moved North once more, this time to Leconfield, where it once again joined in shipping patrols. It was at Leconfield that the squadron received the canon firing Spitfire Vb, and with these it concentrated on bomber escort work. It also took part in the Dieppe raids of August 1942, and for this it was based at West Malling in Kent.

During 1943 the Squadron moved around the country on a variety of operations, during which time it made many fighter sweeps and raids over France and spent a short time in Cornwall.

In January 1944 it was based in Exeter, and it was there where it was the first unit to take delivery of the Griffon-engined Mk X1V Spitfire the fastest version of the plane to date. Having mastered the use of these new machines, the Squadron moved to West Malling and Ludham. There for three months the Mk X1V's were put to good use agains the pilotless V1 'Doodle Bugs' which were threatening our towns and cities from their launching sites on the French coast. By late August 1944, when the 'Doodle Bug' threat was over, 10 had 'accounted for 50 of them

Following this success, the squadron put 'drop-tanks on its aircraft and was involved in long range sweeps over Germany, turning out the Luftwaffe wherever it was to be found. In December of that year, 610 joined the Second Tactical Air Force at Evere in Belgium. Here it continued the long-range sweeps and moved with the advance towards Germany, with a break back in England in February 1945.

The allie's progress was so rapid at this stage that 610 was not required to return to the Continent and the squadron was disbanded at Warmwell in March 1945.

July 1946 saw the reformation of 610 as an auxiliary squadron when it had returned home to Hooton Park. The first post war machines it had were Spitfire X1s again but it was not long before it received Mk F22, and then the more modern Meteor F4s and F8s. The squadron remained at Hooton Park until it was disbanded in 1957, when the auxiliary air force lost all its squadrons.

Of the local men who joined the 610 Squadron when it formed, Mr. William Swinnerton of Sutton Way, Ellesmere Port, was the sixth to enrol on the 24th April 1936. Others who joined him were Mr. Joe Banton, of Wolverham Road Ellesmere Port, Mr. Ross Clowes of Thamesdale, Whitby, Mr. William Jones also of Thamesdale, Mr. Roy Blackburne of Hillcrest Drive, Little Sutton, and Mr. Edward Skelding of Malvern Road, Ellesmere Port.

'Reunion of Former Members of the 610 Squadron.'

Former members of 610 Squadron raised their glasses to the times they battled together. Pictured (left to right) when they met at Little Sutton RAFA Club are: Mr. J. Banton, Mr. W. Jones, Mr. R. Blackburne, Mr. A. H. Clowes, Mr. E. Skelding and Mr. W. Swinnerton.

Former members of 610 Squadron raised their glasses to the times they battled together. Pictured (left to right) when they met at Little Sutton RAFA Club are; Mr. J. Banton, Mr. W. Jones, Mr. Blackburne, Mr. A. H. Clowes, Mr. E. Skelding and Mr. W. Swinnerton

'A few of them attended the Battle of Britain 40th Anniversary Reunion at Biggin Hill recently but all were present at the Little Sutton RAFA Club on 29th September where they relived the good old days over champagne and ale. It was almost impossible to interview the gentlemen as they all had so much to reminisce about. Each time we seemed to be getting down to a definite story one would remember an incident connected with it and go off into a tangent. I did however manage to glean some items and incidences which showed me the devil may care spirit which must have pervaded Biggin Hill from 1939-1945. They remembered with a mixture of pride and thanksgiving, sadness and humour, making light of the dark days to which few would care to return. Did you

know for example, that it was 610 Squadron who, while they were based at Westhampnett escorted the plane which flew a new pair of legs out to Douglas Bader when he was a prisoner of war in Germany? Or that later when Douglas Bader was based at Shell in Ellesmere Port he rounded up as many members of the 610 as he could find? At one stage during the war he was the Squadron Wing Commander. Mr. Blackburne remembered a time after a bombing raid when they helped to dig out men whose shelter had been the target of a direct hit, 'All their faces were black,' he said. Our shelter was only a few yards from theirs.'

Mr. Clowes will always remember his 21st birthday, it was while they were at Biggin Hill, they worked an hour before dawn and an hour after sunset. They had to work hard to get time off, but when they did get time they made their presence felt in no uncertain terms.

Their days at Biggin Hill were so full the men only had time to 're run ad re fuel', but that didn't mean that there wasn't time for emotion. Mr. Swinnerton remembers when one of their squadron Harry Peter from Northwich had his leg blown off outside the shelter, there was a time bomb down there, we were supposed to go down and diffuse it but when I got down there I decided it was time to go, we charged two shillings a time for the lads to go and hear it ticking and we gave the money we had to Harry. ' The men I met were the lucky ones, I was told of the two lads who arrived from Blackpool at about 2pm one day. They were thrilled to be at Biggin Hill and to see the planes, but that was the last they ever saw because both were killed soon after they arrived. Many members of the squadron went on an exacting pilot training course, only to return in charge of a plane and never to be seen again. One of the pilots who landed for refuelling was insistent that they hurry up as it was safer in the air than on the ground!

One incident they all recalled was the sight of a single jeep moving on the two airfields after a raid, with two people in it, one of whom was a WAAF. the jeep loaded with steel spikes carrying red flags, and as it passed mounds of earth on the airfield, the WAAF jabbed a spike into each mound. they carried on until the whole area looked like a poppy field and it transpired that they were marking unexploded bombs! Days off were spent in places like Brighton and skating proved to be a popular pastime. During one of these visits to the resort, an air raid sounded and some of the men ran to a shelter which was being displayed in a shop window. At least it proved the efficiency of the design by giving a practical demonstration on unexploded bombs!

Mr. Banton related the hair-raising experience of standing in a shelter watching bombs being dropped and counting them as they fell. 'There were six of them and we suddenly realised the next one should have hit us, but it did not drop, ' he said. Even during the war days, emphasis was always on smartness. Mr. Swinnerton recalled the time they were going out and used to check in the guard house where there was a mirror, to make sure they were dressed correctly. One night they were on their way out as usual when they discovered that not only was the mirror missing but the whole guard house had been completely destroyed.

Roy, along with Mr. Joseph Banton and Mr. A. H. Clowes, trained together at St. Athan in 1940, (pages 42, 43). 810132 Skelding, Edward lived in Ellesmere Port post-war, 810006 Swinnerton, John William was Corporal in the Orderly Room.

Biggin Hill was affectionately known as the 'Bump' because of the airfield's geographical situation on top of a hill between two valleys. Mr. Banton recalls being ever grateful for that because he was taking off in an overloaded plane, 'We took off and if it hadn't been for the valley at the other end of the runway we would never have got up, ' he said.

When the 610 Squadron arrived for the first time at Biggin Hill they were visited by a plump fellow dressed in a dark siren suit who said, 'So this is the Cheshire Squadron,'. In those days Winston Churchill lived not far from Biggin Hill and visited the station regularly, little did he know then that he was with some of the men who were to serve Britain in 'Her Finest Hour' and of whom he was later to say, 'The gratitude of every home on our island in our Empire, and indeed throughout the world...goes out to the British airmen who, undaunted by odds, unwearied in their constant challenge and moral danger turned the tide of the world war, they their prowess and by their devotion. Never in the field of human conflict was so much owed by so many to so few'.

HOW THE BATTLE OF BRITAIN WAS WON

by Group Captain Douglas Bader, CBE, DSO, DFC

MEMORIES of those tremendous Battle of Britain days of August and September 29 years ago . . . kaleidoscopic pictures crowding back.

Two Hurricanes converging on the same Junkers 88. You can't shout a warning because there is no common radio frequency. The Hurricanes touch, a wing breaks off and floats away like a falling leaf.

One pilot bales out. He lives to fight another day.

You are closing on a Dornier [illegible] sixth sense makes you look up . . . to see a Spitfire diving from above.

As you sheer away the Spitfire hits the Dornier fair and square. It wraps itself round it and they both go down on fire, quite slowly, it seems, like a ball of paper that has been set alight.

A stream of bullets crashes into the dashboard of your Hurricane and you nearly die of fright as you wrench it round. You see the Messerschmitt that nearly got you go past in an ever-steepening dive.

On its tail is the Hurricane that has killed it.

Memories that can still stir the blood all these years later . . .

To the young of today it all means very little, but now it's all been [illegible] [illegible] recreated [illegible] a film [illegible] [illegible] [illegible] [illegible]

The film [illegible] [illegible] to make, and [illegible] [illegible] a little licence. It's a [illegible] ful representation of these tremendous days. I have seen it and it is a [illegible] almost unreal experience to relive those times.

Slang

Like other [illegible] in air history, the Battle of Britain became important only in retrospect to those who fought it. In that desperate year of 1940 only the Prime Minister, the War Cabinet, and the Commander-in-Chief of Fighter Command knew without doubt what was at stake. The pilots certainly did not.

They were a good bunch, those pilots—young, light-hearted, prone to understatement to hide their feelings. They coined a new slang some of which has now become part of the English language.

Their pattern of life during the high summer of 1940 was readiness from dawn to dusk, long hours, boring hours, hell on the digestion, but broken up with moments of exhilaration.

You sat around the airfield near your aeroplanes, playing cards, gossiping, reading, playing the gramophone.

Meals were trouble. You were just finishing lunch when the alarm [illegible]

[illegible] as he was known, took over Fighter Command in 1936, his aerodromes were fields. In the first winter his fighters were bogged down.

Typically when some technical expert told him that bullet-proof windscreens were too heavy to be fitted to the Hurricane and Spitfire fighters, the C in C replied: "If a Chicago gangster can have bullet-proof glass in his motor-car, why can't my pilots in their aeroplanes?" He got them.

When France was tottering to surrender in 1940, [illegible] pressure was put on Dowding by the [illegible] to send precious Hurricanes and Spitfires to France.

Dowding replied: "France is finished. We shall need every one of these fighters for the battle to come."

He gained his point, but made political enemies.

In November, 1940, he left Fighter Command and was not again employed by the Air Ministry. Not until 1943 was he made a Baron.

What has rankled with the R.A.F., and still rankles, is that he was never made a Marshal of the Royal Air Force.

Stuffy Dowding was gruff, monosyllabic, sometimes inarticulate, but his fighter pilots of 1940 were not deceived. They recognised the gold beneath the stuffy exterior which had earned him his nickname.

How the Battle of Britain Was Won

By Group Captain Douglas Bader, CBE, DSO, DFC

Memories of those Battle of Britain days of August and September 29 years ago…kaleidoscopic pictures crowding back.

Two Hurricanes converging on the same Junkers 88. You can't shout a warning because there is no common radio frequency. The Hurricanes touch a wing breaks off and floats away like a falling leaf. One pilot bails out, he lives to fight another day. You are closing on a Dornier your sixth sense makes you look up…to see a Spitfire diving from above as you sheer away the Spitfire hits the Dornier fair and square, it wraps itself around it and they both go down on fire, quite slowly it seems like a ball of paper that has been set alight.

A stream of bullets crashes into dashboard of your Hurricane and you nearly die of fright as you wrench it round. You see the Meschersmitt that nearly got you go past in an ever-steepening dive. On its tail is the Hurricane that killed it.

Memories that can still stir the blood all these years later. To the young of today it all means very little but now it's all been excitedly overrated Slang

Like other battles in our history, the Battle of Britain became important only in retrospect to those who fought it in that desperate year of 1940, the Prime Minister, the War Cabinet and Commander-in-Chief of Fighter Command knew without doubt what was at stake, the pilots certainly did not.

They were a good bunch those pilots-young lighthearted, prone to understatement to hide their feelings. They coined a new slang some of which has now become part of the English language.

Their pattern of life during the high summer of 1940 was readiness from dawn to dusk, long…. boring hours, hell on the digestion…with moments of exhilaration

You sat around on the airfield near your aeroplanes, reading…. the gramophone. Meals were brought you were just finishing lunch when the alarm would go.

Lucky

The fighter pilots were overpraised by the great Winston Churchill superlative and now historic phrase about 'The Few' we loved him for it and are everlastingly proud. We knew then and with greater certainty afterwards that every man and woman in the British Islands won the Battle of Britain, we were the lucky ones who could fight back while others on the ground took it – the incendiaries and high explosive bombs and all that went with them. The real memory that endures is of a united British people. On Saturday September 13th, there will be a television programme which records the making of the film. It is fascinating and there is one small incident which caught my attention above all. The name Air Chief Marshall Lord Dowding is probably unknown to most of the younger generation. Yet it was because of him above as much as any other man that they have been brought up in the English way of life and speak the English language.

He was Commander-in-Chief of Fighter Command from July 1936 until November 1940. In 1938 he should have been made Chief of Air Staff. For some unaccountable reason he was passed over and remained at Fighter Command. This was the greatest good fortune for *the country. Without his vision Fighter Command might have been unable to win the Battle of Britain. By the narrowest of margins, the Luftwaffe failed.*

When 'Stuffy' Dowding as he was known took over Fighter Command in 1936 his aerodromes were fields. In the first winter his fighters were bogged down.

Typically, when some technical expert told him that bullet proof windscreens were too heavy to be fitted to the Hurricanes and Spitfire fighters, the CinC replied, 'if a Chicago gangster can have bullet-proof glass in his motor car, why can't my pilots in their aeroplanes?' He got them.

When France was tottering to surrender in 1940 great pressure was put on Dowding….to send precious Hurricanes and Spitfires to France. Dowding replied, 'France is finished, we shall need every one of these fighters for the battle to come.' He made his point but made political enemies.

In November 1940, he left Fighter Command and was not employed again in the Air Ministry, not until 1943 was he made a Baron. What has rankled with the RAF and still rankles is that he was never made a Marshall of the Royal Air Force.

'Stuffy' Dowding was gruff, monosyllabic, sometimes inarticulate, but his fighter pilots of 1940 were not deceived. They recognized the gold beneath the stuffy exterior which had earned him his nickname.

Heroes' return for air aces...

THE Ellesmere Port contingent with the Mayor of Chester. They are (from left) Ian Turner, Joe Hampton, Danny O'Leary, Roy Blackburne, Dan Dunnett, Russ Clowes and Vin Jones.

BATTLE of Britain war aces, many of them local men, received a heroes' welcome when they returned to Chester for a reunion dinner last week.

War veterans from the RAF's 610 County of Chester Squadron were given a Town Hall reception to mark the 50th anniversary of the battle of the skies.

Scores of former members of the Hooton-based squadron who played a major part in the Battle of Britain travelled from all over the country for the occasion where many old friendships were renewed and adventures remembered.

Among the heroes present were flying aces Johnny Johnson, John Storror and John Ellis, who all commanded the squadron at various times.

Organiser Doug Darroch said it was probably the last time all three former COs would be together.

Air Marshall Johnson, who boasts he once flew a Spitfire under the Eiffel Tower, won a place in RAF history after shooting down a record 38 enemy planes.

'We have come to renew old friendships. These friendships are stronger than any in peace time be-

By GILL ISTED

cause we shared some tremendous experiences together,' he said.

Chester vet John Storror, who also won honours for his flying record, shared memories with old friend John Ellis.

Everyone agreed there was more time for socialising last week than there was during the war. But the reception was not just for the pilots.

More than 60 members of the squadron killed during the war were remembered in a roll of honour presented to the Mayor of Chester, Councillor John Bramall.

Among members of the squadron's ground crew, many of whom were killed during a raid on Biggin Hill airfield, were a number of Ellesmere Port men, many of whom have kept in touch through working together at Shell.

One of them, Mr. Dan (Jock) Dunnett of Great Sutton, recalled with amusement 'how his path and that of Mr. Roy Blackburne of Little Sutton repeatedly crossed over the years.

'I was present in the Far East when Roy was flown home after being a prisoner of war,' said Mr. Dunnett. 'But it wasn't until we met again when we were both working for Shell that we realised that.'

Also present was Mr Ian Turner, of Eastham, and his uncles, Alex and Arnie, who, along with Ian's father Sid, also served in 610.

'In fact,' said Ian, 'the occasion when my father and brothers joined was the only time there were three brothers serving together in 610, and when I joined the Turner family became the only one to have two generations serving in the squadron.'

Some of the proudest people there were the members of the present 610 Air Cadet Squadron based at Chester who formed the guard of honour for their distinguished predecessors.

Another local on the scene was local artist Mark Holmes who specialises in painting aviation scenes. Ten of his paintings were on show and the ones depicting the squadron's spitfires bearing the distinctive 'DW' code were especially popular.

Article from Ellesmere Port Pioneer

27th September 1990

Battle of Britain War Aces, many of them local men, received a heroes' welcome when they returned to Chester for a reunion dinner last week. War veterans from the RAF's 610 (County of Chester) Squadron were given a Town Hall reception to mark the 50th anniversary of the battle of the skies. Scores of former members of the Hooton based squadron who played a major part in the Battle of Britain travelled from all over the country for the occasion where many old friendships were renewed and adventures remembered.

Among the heroes' present were flying aces Johnny Johnson, John Storror and John Ellis, who all commanded the squadron at various times. Organiser Doug Darroch said it was probably the last time all three former COs would be together. Air Marshall Johnson, who boasts he once flew a Spitfire under the Eiffel Tower, won a place in RAF history after shooting down a record 38 enemy planes. 'We have come to renew old friendships. These friendships are stronger than any in peace time because we shared some tremendous experiences together' he said.

Chester vet John Storror, who also won honours for his flying record, shared memories with old friend John Ellis.

Everyone agreed there was more time for socialising last week than there was during the war. But the reception was not just for the pilots.

More than 60 members of the squadron killed during the war were remembered in a roll of honour presented to the Mayor of Chester, Councillor John Bramall.

Among members of the squadron's ground crew many of whom were killed during a raid on Biggin Hill airfield, were a number of Ellesmere Port men, many of whom have kept in touch through working together at Shell.

One of them, Mr. Dan (Jock) Dunnett of Great Sutton, recalled with amusement ' how his path and that of Mr. Roy Blackburne of Little Sutton repeatedly crossed over the years.

I was present in the Far East when Roy was flown home after being a prisoner of war, ' said Mr. Dunnett. 'But it wasn't until we met again when we were both working for Shell that we realised that.'

(Roy was never taken prisoner of war, although he had been in Burma, a mistake by Mr. Dunnett).

Also present was Mr. Ian Turner, of Eastham, and his uncles, Alex and Arnie, who, along with Ian's father Sid, also served in 610.

'In fact,' said Ian, 'the occasion when my father and brothers joined was the only time there were three brothers serving together in 610, and when I joined the Turner family became the only one to have two generations serving in the squadron.'

Some of the proudest people there were the members of the present Air Cadet Squadron based at Chester who formed the guard of honour for their distinguished predecessors.

Another local on the scene was local artist Mark Holmes who specialises in painting aviation scenes.

Ten of his paintings were on show and the ones depicting the squadron's spitfires bearing the distinctive 'DW' code were especially popular.

A new exhibition has opened commemorating the bravery of Cheshire's own 'Few' who helped to drive the Luftwaffe from the skies of southern Britain.

Seventy years ago, the pilots of No. 610 (County of Chester Royal Auxiliary) Air Force Squadron, formed at Hooton Park in 1936 as a bomber unit were courageously hurling their Spitfires at the oncoming enemy over the Channel and home counties.

By the time the Prime Minister Winston Churchill had uttered his famous words in Parliament the squadron, operating from well-known Battle of Britain bases including Biggin Hill, had destroyed 40 enemy aircraft in August of 1940 alone during the legendry Battle of Britain. The loss to the squadron was 11 pilots killed during the battle.

The collection of images from the life-or-death struggle during the darkest days of the conflict can be seen at the WW II aviation museum in Fort Perch Rock, New Brighton, which has a long association with the squadron. They tell the story of the unit, whose members were drawn from across Cheshire, Wirral - then part of the county - and Merseyside.

Apart from the officers, those flying the fighters included sergeant pilots, facing the enemy for just 12s 6d (62.5p) a day.

The squadron was re-mustered as a fighter squadron in 1939, moving to Scotland in Spring 1940. A month later the Germans invaded the low countries and the unit was rushed south to cover the evacuation from Dunkirk.

The Battle of Britain saw the squadron's skilful ground crews working miracles to keep the Spitfires airworthy with the aircraft rarely unserviceable for more than a few hours.

The following year saw pilots countering enemy raiders making *heavy night attacks on London and by the end of 1942 their score of victims had risen to 120 aircraft destroyed, 40 probable's and 37 damaged.*

The approach of D-Day saw sweeps over northern France before the pilots turned their attention to destroying Hitler's flying bombs, eventually accounting for 50 of the rocket-propelled weapons.

The squadron flew over German soil for the first time in September 1944.

At the end of that year, it once more came under the control of legendary Group Captain Johnnie Johnston, triple DSO and double DFC holder, and in February 1945 destroyed an early German jet.

It was disbanded shortly afterwards, re-forming at Hooton in 1948 with later model Spitfires which then gave way to Meteor jets.

The Squadron finally disbanded in 1957, when the Royal Auxiliary Air Force ceased to exist.

The exhibition also includes flying logs, which give a first-hand account of aerial combat by the pilots themselves.

Wirral based aviation enthusiast and photographer Robin Bird said 'I don't think many people realise the 610 Squadron took part in the 'The Battle of Britain' to such a degree. Many people think that the Battle of Britain was all about down South, but 610 was a local squadron that moved down from Hooton Park to Biggin Hill to be in the thick of it.

'It's such a great untold story. It was very much a homegrown squadron with pilots and ground crew drawn from across the region.

He added 'The photographs and flying logs on display offer a fascinating insight into 610 during the war, a squadron that we can be proud of.'

Roy's faded 610 Squadron Association membership card found in his wallet following his death, his interest and support for the Squadron and its members still very dear to him sixty-six years from when he first joined in 1939 as a volunteer at Hooton Aerodrome.

Ground crew signatures

Courtesy of 610 (County of Chester Squadron

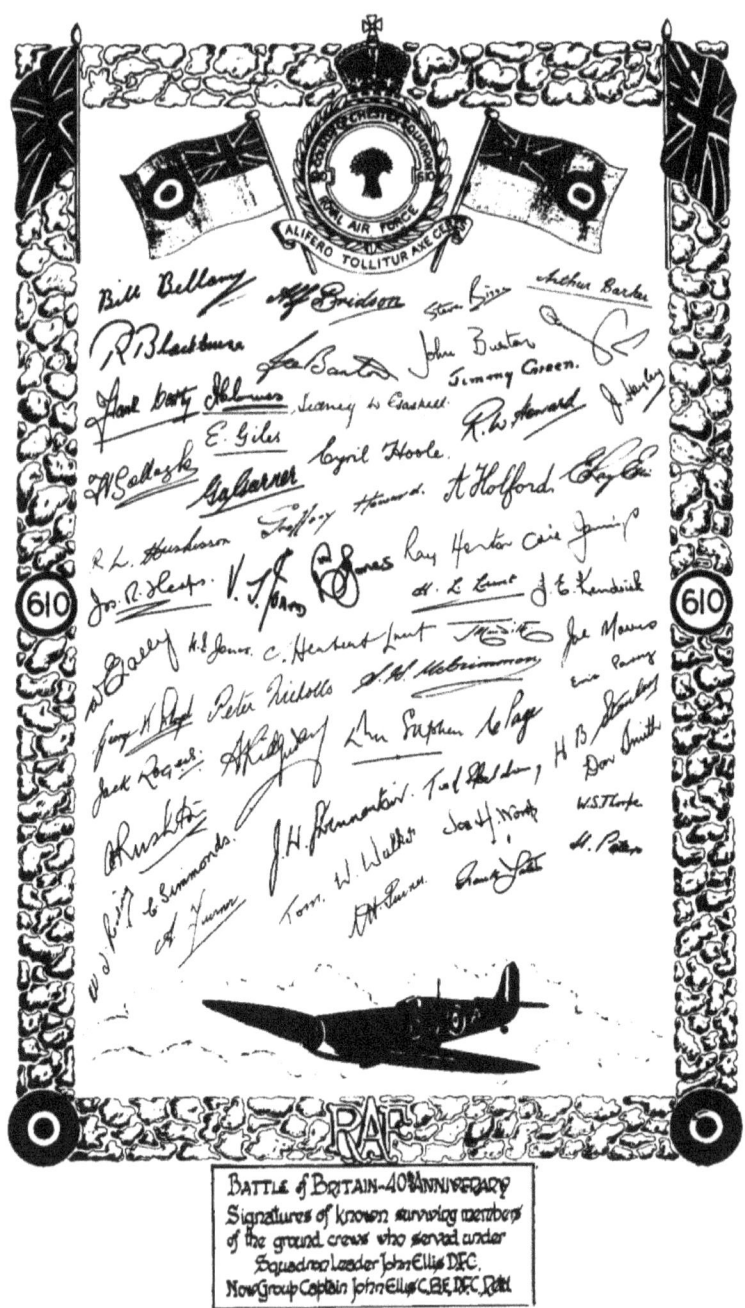

610

(County of Chester Squadron)

Royal Auxiliary Air Force

Formed at Hooton Park, Cheshire

on 10th February 1936

In remembrance of those who gave their tomorrows for our todays

and of all who served with 610

1936-1957

Situated on the hallowed walls of Chester Cathedral is a bronze plaque dedicated to the memory of the 79 pilots and ground crew of 610 (County of Chester) Squadron, Royal Auxiliary Air Force who gave their lives during World War Two.

(Royal Auxiliary Air Force Foundation. 14/08/2021)

Remember Him

He was no Galahad, no knight sans peur et sans reproche Sans peur? Fear was the second enemy to beat. He was a common, unconsidered man, who for a moment of eternity held the whole future of mankind in his two palms and did not let it go.

Remember him, not as he is portrayed but as he was, to him you owe the most of what you have and love today.

Air Chief Marshal Sir Christopher Foxley-Norris, Chairman of the Battle of Britain Fighter Association

THE KINGS   EDWARD. GEORGE V & GEORGE VI

For King and Country

ABOUT THE AUTHOR

**Sandra Hemsworth
née Blackburne**

Born in 1952 in Little Sutton on the Wirral Peninsula, Sandra, a happy and adventurous child had a strict education at Berwick Road, Church of England primary school and later at Ellesmere Port Grammar School for Girls. In 1974 she qualified as a nurse and worked in the Accident and Emergency department at nearby Chester Infirmary and subsequently as an industrial nurse at Bowater's Paper Mill.

She and her husband travelled extensively over the years, initially living in Johannesburg, South Africa where she became Matron of The Frida Hartley Shelter, a home for destitute women. Sandra with her husband and growing family lived in New Zealand for three years, followed by two years in Singapore, and 35 years in Australia where they still live.

Every family should have a family historian. Sandra elected herself to be just that and in 2014 after traumatic life changing events, she turned something negative in to a positive by putting pen to paper. Sandra's enforced convalescence gave her an extended period of time to write undisturbed, resulting in the research and writing of family history books followed by an article, 'Memoirs of a Little Sutton Baby Boomer' for a book being compiled about the village where she grew up, the article later being included in the contents of a Time Capsule.

Sandra's father Roy was involved in two of the wars most defining moments, The Battle of Britain and the Burma Campaign, hence An RAF Time Capsule was written to honour his contribution and those many others like him.

ACKNOWLEDGEMENTS

A special thank you to Dr. Randall Hendricks and Professor Peter Bremner and staff of the ICU at St. John of God Hospital Murdoch without whom I would not be here today. They were a light in my darkest hours. A thank you to my GP, Dr. Stephen McKelvie, my husband Terry, family and friends both home and abroad who supported me throughout this truly traumatic time.

Thank you to my siblings, Enid, Susan and Peter for their ongoing support and encouragement whilst writing this book. In particular, Peter for the kitbag photograph and my brother in law Frank Proctor for the photographs of the medals.

With my knowledge of the R.A.F. and its war years being limited to that of a layperson, I would like to acknowledge the invaluable help of expert Michael Lewis, Chairman of 610 Squadron Association for his time, expertise and encouragement throughout the first part of the book, I could not have done it without him. I would also like to thank Alan Thomas and Liz Deery of the Air Historical Branch (RAF), Ministry of Defence, and Michael Barrass of the RAF Historical Society whose knowledge and input helped guide me in the right direction regarding my father's time in Burma; an almost impossible task with the little information I possessed.

My thanks to Karie Aszkielowicz for her invaluable help with the initial referencing of this book. My dear friend Tom Dowling editor of *'All Together NOW!'* newspaper (UK) for his ongoing support and encouragement. Carl Collier, an archivist, for his research into the bombings in and around Ellesmere Port during 1940-41. I also acknowledge Claudette Pope of Footprints Publishing for her hard work in editing and publishing this book.

REFERENCES

1. Donald P. Leinster-MacKay, 1981, 'The advance of basic education: Some reflections on private commercial schools of Victorian England', The Vocational Aspect of Education, 33:84, p. 23 Accessed 22/07/2020 at https://doi.org/10.1080/10408347308001441.
2. 'Training in Scotland', Cheshire Observer, 20th August 1938. pp unknown. P. 24
3. 'Flying Practice', Cheshire Observer, 20th August 1938. pp unknown. P. 24
4. 'Recreation', Cheshire Observer, 20th August 1938. pp unknown. P. 26
5. Mark Oliver, www.610squadron.com. P. 28
6. 'The Squadron's Badge', 610 (County of Chester) Squadron, 2015, access from http://610squadron.com/the-squadrons-badge/ on 4th August, 2020. P. 28-29
7. Hooton Park, Abandoned and Little-known Airfields in Europe P. 31
8. The motto of 'Alifero Tolitur Axe Ceres' translated means, 'Ceres (The Goddess of Corn' Rises in a Winged Car (chariot) and is a quotation from Ovid P. 29
9. Hamilton, John (Ed)., ABC of the RAF, The Amalgamated Press Ltd., London, 2019, p. 12-13. P. 32-34
10. Hammerton, John, ABC of the RAF, The Amalgamated Press, Ltd., 1943, p. 12. P. 34
11. Airfix, Aerodrome Magazine, Keep 'em Flying/Ground Crew Support Operations During WW II P. 35
12. Overy, Richard James, The Air War 1939-1945, Stein & Day, 181, pp. 138-140. P. 39
13. "Keep em Flying' – Ground Support operations during WW II', Horny Hobbies Limited, Airfix, 11/12/2015 https://www.airfix.com/uk-en/news/aerodrome/keep-em-flying-ground-support-operations-during-WW II/. P. 39
14. Davidson, Martin & Taylor, James, Spitfire Ace, Pan Macmillon, 2015, p. 104. P. 39

15. Blomvall, Laura, 'Digitally mapping the WW II: regional representation, distant reading, and public engagement with the archives', War, State and Society, accessed from http://www.warstateandsociety.com/Bombing-Britain on 5th August 2020. P. 40
16. Rickard, J., 'Westland Lysander', History of War, 21 November 2007, accessed from http://www.historyofwar.org/articles/weapons_westland_lysander.html on 6th August 2020. P. 48
17. 'RAF Reserve Classes', Air of Authority – A History of RAF Organisation, http://rafweb.org/Organsation/Reserve_2.htm, updated 09/06/17.
18. 'Battle of Britain 80th Anniversary', Royal Air Force. Accessed at https://www.raf.mod.uk/our-organisation/our-history/anniversaries/battle-of-britain/ on 27th June, 2020.
19. 610squadron.com
20. Davidson, Martin & Taylor, James, Spitfire Ace, Pan Macmillon, 2015, p. 108.
21. Ibid.
22. Goss, Chris, 'The Many: RAF Ground Crew in the Battle of Britain', A History of Conflict : Britain At War Magazine, 23rd August 2018, accessed from https://www.britainatwar.com/2018/08/23/the-many-raf-ground-crew-in-the-battle-of-britain/ 8th September, 2020. p. 54
23. The Battle of Britain, An Air Ministry Account of the Great Days from 8th August – 31st October 1940, Published by His Majesty's Stationery Office, London, PP. 6 – 7.
24. Davidson, p. 107.
25. Birtles, Philip, Battle of Britain Airfields, Midland Publishing, 2010,P. 49.
26. 'Battle of Britain Airmen Recall the Good and the Bad'. P.58
27. C.N. Trueman, 'RAF Biggin Hill', History Learn Site, Accessed from https://www.historylearningsite.co.uk/world-war-two/world-war-two-in-western-europe/battle-of-britain/raf-biggin-hill/ on 27th June 2020. P. 59
28. Ibid. P. 59
29. Davidson, p. 111. P. 62
30. Bishop, Patrick, Battle of Britain, Quercus Publishing, 2010, p. 362 P. 63

31. Ibid., 230.
32. Caygill, Peter, 'Chapter One – Early Days', The Biggin Hill Wing ,1941 : From Defence to Attack, Pen & Sword Aviation, 2008 – accessed online from Amazon. P. 64
33. Ibid.
34. Birtles, p. 50. P. 68
35. Bader, Douglas, unpublished book, p. 226. P. 70
36. Rickard, J, No. 32 Squadron (RAF) : WW II, 17th September 2008, accessed from http://www.historyofwar.org/air/units/RAF/32_WW II.html on 2nd July 2020. P. 70
37. Crone, Jack, 'Designer of the iconic Spitfire thought the name was 'damned silly' and wanted to call it the SHREW, claims new book,' Daily Mail Australia, 20th June 2015, accessed from https://www.dailymail.co.uk/news/article-3132500/Designer-iconic-Spitfire-thought-damned-silly-wanted-call-SHREW-claims-new-book.html on 2nd July 2020. P. 71
38. 'Spitfire – History of the Spitfire's design and development,' Military History Matters, 4th March 2011, accessed from https://www.military-history.org/articles/world-war-2/history-of-the-spitfire.htm on 2 July 2020. P.71
39. 'The Spitfire and the Hurricane', Royal Air Force Museum London, p. 1. Accessed at https://www.rafmuseum.org.uk/documents/London/Downloads-and-worksheets/Spitfire-and-Hurricane.pdf on 9th September 2020. P. 72
40. Bishop, pp. 336-7. P. 73
41. Fyfe, Maclolm, RAF Acklington, Guardian of the Northern Skies, Fonthill Media, 2017, p. 9. P. 73
42. Ripley, Roy & Pears, Brian, North-East Diary 1939-1945, Brian Pears, 2011, accessed frp, https://ne-diary.genuki.uk/Inc/ISeq_10.html & https://ne-diary.genuki.uk/Inc/ISeq_11.html on 28th May 2020. P. 74
43. Bailey, David, 610 (County of Chester) Auxiliary Air Force Squadron, 1936-1940, Fonthill Media, 2020, p. 425. P. 74
44. Fyfe, Maclolm, RAF Acklington, Guardian of the Northern Skies, Fonthill Media, 2017, p. P. 74
45. 'Ellis, John', Traces of War,2020, accessed from https://www.tracesofwar.com/persons/46085/Ellis-John.htm on 3rd July 2020 P. 81

46. WW II Pilots of No. 610', 610 (County of Chester) Squadron, www.610squadron.com P. 82
47. Ibid.
48. Ibid., p. 225.
49. Fyfe, p. 150. P. 84
50. The National Archives (TNA), Air 27/2106. P. 85
51. "Keep em Flying" – Ground Support operations during WW II', Horny Hobbies Limited, Airfix, 11/12/2015 accessed from https://www.airfix.com/uk-en/news/aerodrome/keep-em-flying-ground-support-operations-during-WW II/ on 9th September 2020. P. 88
52. 'Battle of Britain Airmen Recall the Good and the Bad', Ellesmere Port Pioneer, 29th September 1980, p. 227. P. 89
53. 'Battle of Britain Airmen Recall the Good and the Bad'. C.N. Trueman, 'RAF Biggin Hill', History Learn Site, Accessed from https://www.historylearningsite.co.uk/world-war-two/world-war-two-in-western-europe/battle-of-britain/raf-biggin-hill/ on 27th June 2020. P. 89
54. 'RAF Honiley,' Our Warwickshire, CommunitySites, accessed from https://www.ourwarwickshire.org.uk/content/catalogue_her/raf-honiley on 4th June 2020. P. 94
55. RAF Honiley', Forces War Records, Clever Digit Media Ltd., accessed from https://www.forces-war-records.co.uk/units/4561/raf-honiley/ 4th June 2020. P. 94
56. 'RAF Honiley,' Our Warwickshire. P. 94
57. Bickers, Richard Townshend, The Battle of Britain, Salamander Books, 1999, p. 52 P. 97
58. 'Aircraft of the Royal Air Force', Battle of Britain Historical Society, 2007. Accessed at https://www.battleofbritain1940.net/0012.html on 9th September 2020. P. 98
59. Howard, Allen M., (2011, March 17), Freetown, Sierra Leone and World War 11: Assessing the Impact of the War and the Contributions Made. Accessed from https://www.ascleiden.nl/news/freetown-sierra-leone-and-world-war-ii-assessing-impact-war-and-contributions-made on 10th September, 2020. P. 103

60. Edwards, Martin, 'HM Troopship Somersetshire', Roll of Honour, 2008. Accessed from http://www.roll-of-honour.com/Ships/HMTroopshipSomersetshire.html P. 106
61. Jackson, Allan, 'A Troopship Revolt', Facts About Durban, 2007. Accessed from https://www.fad.co.za/Resources/troop/ship.htm. P. 107
62. Nortje, Ricky, 'Durban in the World Wars and many other things...' Facts About Durban, 2006. Accessed from https://www.fad.co.za/Resources/hillary/nortje.htm P. 105
63. 'MV Christiaan Huygens 1928-1945', Derby Sulzers, accessed from https://derbysulzers.com/shipchuygens.html on 9th September, 2020. P. 135
64. Martin, NA, 'The Madness at Deolali', J R Army Corps, 2006, 152, p. 152. P. 114
65. The National Archives (TNA), Operational Record Books (ORBs) Air-29-1073-3-001. P. 115
66. 'RAF Stations – A', Air of Authority – A History of RAF Organisation, 2020. Accessed from https://www.rafweb.org/Stations/Stations-A.htm#Ambala P. 115
67. 'Hawker Audax', BAE Systems PLC. Access from https://www.baesystems.com/en/heritage/hawker-audax on 9th June 2020. P. 116
68. TNA, ORBS, No. 303 Maintenance Unit, Ambala, Air/29/1073/3 P. 118
69. TNA, ORB Air/29/1073/3/013/2 P. 118.
70. TNA, ORB Air/29/1073/3, 17th October 1942. P. 118
71. TNA, ORB Air/29/1073/3, 27th February 1943. P. 118
72. TNA, ORB, Air/29/1073/3, 31st October 1942. P. 119
73. TNA, ORB Air/29/1073/3/00/2/2. P. 119
74. Franks, Norman, RAF Fighter Pilots Over Burma, Pen and Sword Aviation, 2014. P. 144
75. Lewis, Caroline, 'A Crucial Port – Liverpool in World War Two', Culture 24, 2004. Access from https://www war-2-1108404-2017-12-19 on 15th September, 2020..culture24.org.uk/history-and-heritage/military-history/world-war-two/tra28260. P. 147
76. TNA, ORB Ambala, Air/29/1073/3. P. 147

77. Pearson, Michael, The Burma Air Campaign, 1941-45, Pen and Sword Aviation, 2018, p. 138. P. 150
78. Fail, J.E.H., '322 Maintenance Unit and the Demolition of SEAC Liberators', Robert Quirk's Home Page, acced from http://www.rquirk.com/fail/322mu/322mu.htm P. 149
79. '75 years of World War II Japan bombing of Kolkata: How the city of joy fought back', India Today, 19 December, 2017. Accessed from https://www.indiatoday.in/education-today/gk-current-affairs/story/japan-bombing-calcutta-world-80. Pearson, Michael, The Burma Air Campaign: 1941-1945, Pen and Sword, 2018, p. 139. P. 159
80. Ibid. P. 159
81. This information was obtained through personal email from Malcolm Barrass, author of website www.rafweb.org P. 160
82. Department of Defence, 'Burma Star', Australian. Government, accessed from https://www1.defence.gov.au/adf-members-families/honours-awards/medals/imperial-awards/world-war-two/burma-star on 1st December, 2020. P. 161
83. 'World War II The Burma Campaign', United States Public Health Service Department of Defense Education', 4th January, 2018. Accessed from https://usphsdeparmentofdefenseeducation.wordpress.com/2018/01/04/world-war-ii-the-burma-campaign/ on 15th September, 2020. P. 161
84. Ibid. P. 161
85. Daugherty, Leo J., The Allied Resupply Effort in the China Burma India Theatre during WW II, McFarland and Company Inc., Publishers, 10th February 2017, eBook, p. 164. P. 161
86. Ibid. P. 161
87. Daugherty, p. 165 P. 162
88. Franks, Norma, RAF Fighter Pilots Over Burma, Pen and Sword Aviation, 2014, p. 165. P. 164
89. Slim, Field Marshall Viscount William, Defeat into Victory, Cassell & Co Ltd Field Marshal Sir William Slim (published in 1956) (Kindle location pg.1271, RAF Fighter Pilots over Burma, (Images of War). P. 165

90. 'The Circumstances of the War in Burma', Burma Star Association. Accessed from https://www.burmastar.org.uk/burma-campaign/ on 22nd September, 2020. P. 168
91. Calder, Angus, The People's War: Britain, 1939-1945, Pimlico, Vintage Publishing, 1992. P. 199
92. King, Sue, 'At long last, going home', British forces in Palestine, accessed from http://www.britishforcesinpalestine.org/goinghome.html on 15th October, 2020. P. 199
93. 'General Register Office: National Registration: Correspondence and Papers', The National Archives, access from https://discovery.nationalarchives.gov.uk/details/r/C13353 on 15th October, 2020 P. 244

Every effort has been made to trace copyright holders and obtain their permission for the use of copyright material. The author apologizes for any errors or omissions and would be grateful to be notified of any corrections that could be incorporated in future editions of this book.

Roy's Notebook

Lance Corporal Roy Blackburne.
Aged 23yrs
The propeller badge on his sleeve denotes he is a
leading aircraftman

CAPITAL Note Book

810/83. L.A.C. R. BLACKBURNE.
Junior. N.C.O' Course
UPPER TOPA
MURRE HILLS

Rifle

Cocking action.

When the bolt is to the rear the positioning stud is in the short cam. On pushing the bolt forward the lower face of the bolt pushes the round out of the magazine and into the chamber. This action is quite easy until approx ½" from fully closed. The reason being is that the sear has come into engagement with the full bent of the cocking piece. On exerting further pressure on the bolt, the cocking piece remains to the rear and of the firing pin spring becomes compressed. On turning the bolt lever down the solid rib rides in front of the resistance shoulder and locking lug rides into the locking lug recess

~~TRIGGER MECHANISM~~.

This action has rotated the long and short cams so that the positioning stud is now in line with the long cam: the extractor has ridden over and gripped the rim of the round ready for the extraction

Diagram labels: BOLT, FIRING PIN, LOCKING PIECE, LOCKING LUG, LONG SEAR ARM, HALF BENT, SHORT SEAR ARM, U SPRING, POSITIONING STUD

CORDITE { 35% NITRO GLYCERINE
         { 60% GUN COTTON
         { 5% MINERAL JELLY

TRIGGER MECHANISM

On taking the first pressure the lower rib of the trigger comes into contact with the short arm of the sear. The first pressure continues until the upper rib comes into contact with the arm of the sear also. This action has rotated the sear on its axis pushing the short arm of the sear forward and the long arm of the sear down to the edge of the full bent. On taking your second pressure the upper rib of the trigger pushes the short arm of the sear forward and the long arm of the sear down out of engagement of the full bent. This allows the cocking piece to ride forward

lug recess. This action withdraws the bolt for 1/8 the extractor gripping the rim of the empty case withdraws the empty case for 1/8 loosening it in the chamber and allowing any gases to escape before the bolt becomes fully unlocked.

Half Cock

On pressing the trigger the cocking piece moves forward, the positioning stud on the cocking piece burrs against the divisional stud of long and short cams preventing the cocking piece from going fully forward. On striking the bolt lever down the long and short cams are fully rotated and positioning stud rides in the long cam. The cocking piece is

prevented from going fully forward because
of the sear which is in the raised position
entering the undercut half bent. This
action prevents the bolt from being opened
and the trigger from being pressed.

Before the bolt can be opened the
cocking piece must be pulled back.

Rifle is the basic weapon of
British and Indian soldier.

Rifle is 9lbs in weight. 3.8½" in length
Knox form strongest part of rifle 19's to
S.M.L.E. MARK 3
3 butts - large, small, medium and Bantams
Barrell length 24"
Barrel rifling L.H. Turn one full
turn every 10" 2½ turns in barrel

Sights 200-2000 yds

Characteristics (1) accurate, rate of fire (2) When coupled with bayonet good for fighting at close quarters.

Three rules of aiming
(1) Keep the sights upward. (2) Close disengaged eye (3) Look at the target the line the tip of the foresight in the centre of the u of the backsite and in line with the shoulders and is at the lowest central portion of the aiming mark provided on the target.

A<u>IDS TO GOOD SHOOTING</u>

Physical fitness. Head still. Hold rifle firmly with both hands in shoulder. Have bolt clean and slightly oiled. Tilt rifle to right when reloading. Count number of rounds. Sustain breathing. Take first and second pressure. Make sure you have comfortable position and that your body is oblige to line of fire.

S(OPA3ES)(1) Misfire caused through faulty ammunition

(1) bullet u/s (2) broken spring pin (3) empty magazine (4) Defective magazine lips (5) defective m Spring.

When breach is opened and cartridge fails to fall out. Defective Extractor.

CARE AND CLEANING OF RIFLE.

Pick up rifle and make sure it is not loaded. make sure it is your own rifle.

Take out bolt magazine and sling. Examine rifle from muzzle end to the butt for BREAKAGES. SIGHTS DAMAGED. or screws loose; repairs are done by armoury only.

Cleaning Requisities. Oil bottle - pull through cord - and clean rag 4"x 2" 6 4" x 1½". Loop on first pull through for armourers - 2ND for you and 3RD. fore wire quage comb only be used by permission of officer or armoury. To clean barrel fold rough edge of flannelette inwards: place in centre loop put weight through bridge charger guide

ARMY
you
PERM
ISSN

Holding butt with left-hand rifle upside down. Put rifle butt on floor place thumb so as to guide rope and must be one pull through no stopping.
Clean bolt and slightly oil with G.P. oil, remove oil dust and grit from bolt way and metal parts on rifle. Only armourers oil woodwork with linseed oil.

Cleaning rifle before Firing. oil barrel with flannelette. Clean with clean flannelette. Leave bolt with slight touch of oil. Make sure gas escape holes on bolt head and knox form are clear. — CLEANING AFTER FIRING —

Place small funnel in Chamber - four five to six pints of boiling water through barrel this will remove all dust and firing ferling after the above procedure use pull through 4"x3" till barrel is dry: then use 4"x1" oil flannellete and use 4"x3" again & dry barrel, do not use oil or

Plains. Clean all working parts & slightly oil with G.P oil
If no water available clean with T.P.B oil, this oil must
not be left in barrel after ten minutes as it has a
corrosive effect. Use pull through 4"x3" and dry barrel:
again: 4"x1·3" oil flannelette pull through barrel: use
4"x3" to dry again: use 4"x1·3" to oil then 4"x3" to dry.
carry this treatment out for 4 or 5 days after
firing else rust will set in.

AIMING FOR WIND. (1) Fresh Wind 5-10 miles per hour (10·12)
aim of 6". Strong Wind 10-15 M.P.H (15·20) aim of 9"

We start aiming of at 200 yds.
after 400yds & finish aiming waste of ammunition
With Fresh Wind   200yds 6"   300yds 12"   400yds 18"
"   Strong   200yds 9"   300yds 15"   400yds 27"
Man moving fire at 200yds only. Above 200 yds you
may not hit him. Man running at 200yds. range
fire 2 widths in front of him.
Wind in same direction of man walking fire at man.

at Vehicles fire at 300 yrs only. at 50 miles an hr.
fire one width in front of vehicle. use a tree as guidance.

5 points for a bull. 4 for inner
3 for magpie   2 for outer

4" Group of 25 points
8"   "   " 20   "
12"   "   " 15   "
12 and away 10 - "

{ TO INDICATE BULL SHOW WHITE DISC
{ FOR INNER SHOW MOVES ACROSS
{ FOR MAGPIE TWIST BIG ONE

6FT RED FLAG.
TOP BUTTS

4FT RED FLAG.
When flag is up yours goes up
When yours is down they pull
theirs down and commence firing
After this flag is flying no ammo in magazine
Entrance of range should be guarded

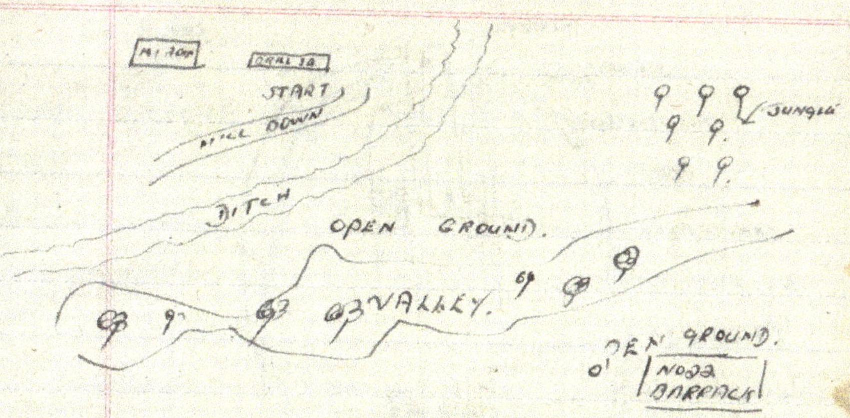
START
HILL DOWN
DITCH
OPEN GROUND.
JUNGLE
VALLEY.
OPEN GROUND.
NO22
BARRACK

VELOCITY OF BULLET ·303
MAX. 2440 FT PER SEC
AVER. 2200 FT " "

BULLET DROP

100 YDS	3.1 INS
200	3 "
300 "	35 "

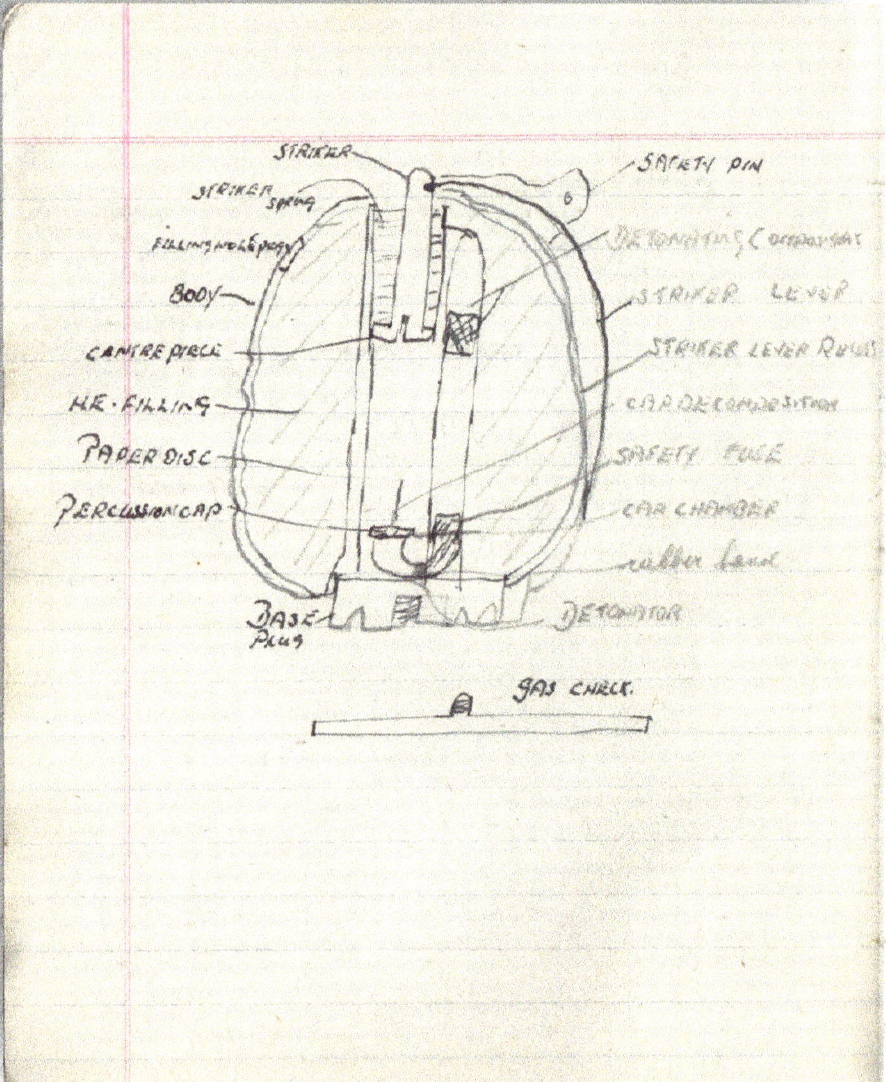

Labels on diagram:
- STRIKER
- STRIKER SPRING
- FILLING HOLE PLUG
- BODY
- CANTRE PIECE
- H.E. FILLING
- PAPER DISC
- PERCUSSION CAP
- BASE PLUG
- SAFETY PIN
- DETONATING COMPOSITION
- STRIKER LEVER
- STRIKER LEVER RIVET
- C.E. DECOMPOSITION
- SAFETY FUSE
- CAP CHAMBER
- rubber band
- DETONATOR

GAS CHECK.

MILLS NO. 36. GRENADE H.E.

Purpose of Grenade to bring enemy out from behind wall - building, fill ban trench or in open where rifle can finish them off.

1st type. Drill purpose grenade (D.P.) painted white has five holes bored in body. weight 1¾lbs shaped like pineapple.

2nd type live grenade. Chocolate or dark brown in colour. a red band painted round the top denotes it is a live Grenade. round the centre is painted a green band which denotes tropical filling round filling cap are three red crosses which denotes that it is already filled with Barritole. length 4" - 2.4" width. weight of live grenade 1½lbs.

Names of parts, base plug - two

outer small holes are for tightening plug up before throwing. Large centre hole gas check. **Striker** small recess at top for lever. In centre small recess for gas escape. At bottom two small lugs. **Striker Spring**. **Lever**, on lever two small lugs or trunnions.
Safety pin and ring.
body made of cast iron & inside the centre piece made of aluminium. Next to centre piece is the **detonater sleeve**. Shoulders of Grenade - on them two recesses for lugs on lever. 2 small holes for safety pin and ring.
Detonater or **igniter** set.

(15f) four second fuse. White in colour with small rubber band.

rubber band to distinguish grenade Detonator in the dark.

7 Second fuse. Yellow in colour. no rubber band. used when grenade is fired from rifle and cup discharger.

Detonator consists of .22 rim fire cap.

Cap Chamber The fuse (7 or 4 second) seperated from detonator by 10" better firing

Explosive in Detonator fulmanite of mercury. or P.E.T.N

3 types of Explosive Charitole (does not detonate) Aminole. Aritole

Characteristics of the Grenade
(1) Weight 1½ lbs (2) A MAN will only carry 5 to 6 grenades

STEN

a high trajectory and steep angle of descent.
4. It is segmentated to split up into small fragments
5. Danger area on soft ground 20 yds to 40 yds
6.   "   "   " hard   "   50 yds to 100 yds AND OVER
7. When thrown by hand 25 - 35 yds
8. Fire from rifle with cup discharger. it will go 80 - 100 yds.
9. very useful weapon at close quarters

Safety Precautions

(1) Remove base plug to make sure the grenade is not primed.
2. Make sure there are no grease grit or cracks in centre of detonator sleeve.
3. Examine body for cracks
4. That the lever is flush in the groove.

that the safety pin is in correctly and
that the shoulders are not damaged
in any way.

Cleaning the Grenade

Strip grenade down with oily rag and 6"
nail or wood, remove all grease from spring
lock sleeves: test striker and sleeve
and its ok for assemble.

Mechanism of the Grenade.

The pin is withdrawn and when grenade
is thrown. the striker goes down
under the influence of the striker
spring during that movement the lever
flies off. The two nipple on the striker
strike the point .22 rim of the cap:
the cap is set off and ignites the
fuze, the fuze burns round and ignites

the detonator. the detonator ignites
main charge.

<u>Command for throwing the grenade</u>
Pick up grenade.
Prepare to throw (withdraw grenade from pin.)

Sten Machine Carbine MARK III
Fixed barrel
Mark I has at front of flash
Eliminator and hand grip
Mark II has detachable barrel
Nane sten from Sheppard and
Turkin.
Description; is operated by recoil
assisted by gasses
Length is 2' 6" weight 6¾ lbs length of
barrel 8". fires all types of 9 mm.
rimless ammunition
Rate of fire approximately 600 rounds
per minute
Has a change lever for automatic
and single shots. one magazine holds
32 rounds but you only load with 28

Names of parts
(1) Butt. on the butt is the Butt stud and hole for recess of plunger and also hand grip

(2) Recoil Spring - recoil spring cup - recoil spring cup retainer with or two lugs. Plunger

Breach Block - or st. fixed firing pin - Extractor with loaded spring - two outer grooves for riding over magazine lips - centre one for fixed ejector. Cutaway on side for trip clearance recess for cocking handle
Extension or projection part for

recoil spring — cocking handle. centre groove for fixed ejector. Two outer grooves for rising up magazine lips

barrel R.H rifling 6 grooves ⅞ of 1 turn. Part over barrel- barrel casing – part sticking out- finger protection— on left hand side. magazine housing with catch and spring inside the chamber.

Body and cocking handle recess. Charge lever on it written A = automatic and R for repetition.

foresight. peepsight. 8"

To fire automatic change lever from right to left.

inside is Trip lever behind this the sear
the trigger guard trigger and trigger
spring

Inside - body tin recesses for retainer
Foresight and backsight
Characteristic R.A.S.C.
R.A.S.C. (1) High rate of fire — great stopping
power with considerable skill (2) accuracy
can be obtained up to 50 yds or more.
3 Short barrel enables targets appearing
in any direction to be engaged immediately
4 C. Combined with element of surprise
it has a great demoralising effect
on the enemy.

Stripping

Press in plunger of spring cup
pull butt down
                    retainer
press spring cup down and turn
anti clockwise it comes out the
              recoil
Spring cup comes out then spring
pull back cocking stud in line with
safety recess, pull out cocking stud
tilt gun press trigger and
Breach comes out.

Assemble

put in Breach block make sure
cocking stud hole is in line
with cocking stud way, press
trigger and Breach block slides
forward, Replace recoil spring
then spring cup - spring cup retainer
turn to turn clockwise, replace butt

bearing down on plunger, slide in —
Gun now ready

- Stoppages -
1. Cocking stud full forward
2. Anywhere else

No 1 misfire - immediate action - recock gun
carry on firing - gun does not fire
broken firing pin - You have to
replace breach block as firing pin is
fixed

No 2 stoppage - Defective round -
remove magazine - remove damaged
round - When remedying a stoppage
always put cocking stud in safety
recess.
broken extractor and broken extractor
spring.

Broken Extractor – remove magazine and empty case and replace Extractor
Broken Ejector – new gun altogether

– Automatic –

On pressing trigger the sear becomes disengaged from the bent of the breach block which allows the Breach block to go forward under the influence of the recoil spring.

The feed rib strikes the base of the round in the magazine pushing it into the chamber, the Extractor gaps the rim of the round – on the Breach block going fully home the fixed firing pin strikes the base of the round which explodes: – direct recoil takes place forcing breach block to the rear. The extractor gripping the empty case withdraws it from the chamber. The ejector riding in ejector groove strikes the base in the empty case - and ejects it through ejector opening. During this movement the recoil spring has been compressed. The circle of operation will continue until pressure is released off the trigger or empty magazine or stoppage.

Single Shots

On squeezing the trigger the sear becomes disengaged from the Bent of the Breach block the breach block is now free to go forward under the influence of the recoil spring. As the breech block goes forward it rides over the depressed sear: strikes the trip lever knocking the trip lever downwards. On the trip lever being knocked downwards the sear again rises in the path of the breech block ready to engage the bent on the breech block when it comes to the rear.

— Load and unloading — Tiring Orders.
(1) Pick up Carbine — 1 pay forward.
(2) Load. (pull back cock handle place in slot.) Place magazine in slot.
3 Check change lever for single shots Target in front 3 single rounds (or more rounds remove cocking handle.

Take up position from hip - three single
shots fire.
Check change lever for automatic
at the target short burst fire.
Command Unload. pull back cocking handle: place in
slot. remove magazine.

HISTORY OF R.A.F

Manual of air force law.
Divided in two parts. Chapt I. Chapt II. Sect 2
Para 18 onwards.
Chapter 3. Chronicle of R.A.F. A.M. Pamphlet 152
Balloon Phase (first passage 1783 by Frenchman.
Chatham balloon School 1897. Later moved South Farn
1909 Frenchman flew Channel in plane.
1911 Italians used balloons against Libya
1912 R.F.C. formed air & naval wing
1914 R.N.A.S. formed
1918 R.A.F. created by General Smuts.
First airship flight 1910.
Cardigan to Montreal R.101 3 days back
5½ days.
Capt Smith Lt Smith flew from Hanstir to
Darwin 9 days.
1929 Parachutes installed in aircraft

1933	Empire air day
1935	Review of R.A.F. by King George V
1935	Spitfire Hurricane Wellingtons Lysander came in.
1936	Shadow factories turning out Pegasus.
1937	Last air display - number of Employees doubled
1920	R.A.F. smashed the mad Mullar Iraq.
1922	R.A.F. took over Iraq
1924	Palestine came under R.A.F. jurisdiction
1926	Tribes invaded Iraq R.A.F. closed them off.
1929	Another Waziristan campaign
1925	R.A.F. took whites out of Kabul
1928	China Command formed.
1932	Disarmament talks
1933	1 APRIL INDIAN AIR FORCE FORMED.

AIR COUNCIL.

Air Council. Split up into Civilian & service part.
(1) Secretary of state for air.
2. { Under Secretary, 1 in House of Lords
                      ,   commons.
4. Permanent under S state for air
5. Advisor in Financial affairs
6.   -   -   Teknical affairs
7. Liason officer between air council and chief of aircraft production.

Service (1) Chief of staff (2) Vice Chief of air staff. (3) Air member for personel (4) Air member for supply and organisation (5) Air member for Training.

```
          AIR COUNCIL
          AIR MINISTRY
 ┌─────────────────────────────┐
 HOME                        ABROAD
  ↓                            ↓
 GROUP                        GROUP
  ↓                            ↓
 STATION WING                STATION WING
  ↓                            ↓
 UNITS                        UNITS
  ↓                            ↓
 SECTS                        SECTS
```

A. O. COMMAND.

```
                    A. O. COMMAND
         ┌──────────────────┴──────────────────┐
      AIR BRANCH                            AOA.
                                           ADMIN.
                                    ┌────────┼────────┐
PLANS. OPERATIONS TRAINING       ADMIN   ORGANIZATION   PERSONNEL
AND INTELLIGENCE.                PLANS
                                          │
                                    ┌─────┼─────┐
                               EQUIPMENT          MOVEMENT
                               SUPPLY   QUARTERS BALLETS
                              DISCIPLINE  OFFICERS   AIRMEN
                                   PROVOST AND LABOUR
                                          │
                                   MAINTENANCE.
                               ┌──────────┴──────────┐
                          WORKS SERVICE         GRAVES
                          CANTEEN               MEDICAL
                          PRINTING              PROVOST.
                          STATIONERY            ACCOUNTANCY.
                          SUPPLIES              EDUCATION
                          TRANSPORT             TRANSPORTATION
                          CHAPLAIN              POST.
                          MAINTENANCE.
```

AIR BRANCH
ADMIN SERVICES.
SIGNALS
SERVICE
ARMAMENT.
PHOTOGRAPHY.
NAVIGATION
METHOLOGY.

A.P. 837 Sect 3

Deals with letter writing and applications to see the C/O.

Para 80 of Manual

R.A.F. B.H.Q. BOMBAY.
DATE

Application for Privilage Leave

Sir, I have the honour to request.

" "
" "

I have the honour to be Sir
Your obedient Servant.
J Jones
810204 A.C. J. JONES.

To officer Commanding B.H.Q. Bombay
letter used in R.A.F.
FORMAL LETTER

ADRESS
DATE.

REF B.H.Q. BOMBAY. 1112/18

Subject What it is

Sir I have the honour to request

" "
" "

To u/s State for Air
London

I have the honour to be Sir
Your obedient Servant.
B Jones G Capt.

2. INFORMAL TYPE

From BHQ Bombay R.A.F.
To HQ 207 Group R.A.F.   Date.
Ref. BHQ B/112/1

Posting F/O Thomas.

With reference to the above
              "
              "
                              A Jones
                          Group Capt. Comm.
                              BHQ. Bombay.

FORMAL TO CIVILIAN.

Reference   address
   BHQ/Bombay/1147/air   Date.

Low Flying Complaint.

Dear Sir,
    Sorry about low flying over your
house — "
         "
                  Yours faithfully
                   K. Jones. F/Lt.
                  for G/Capt Comm.
                      BHQ Bombay.
To Mr Taylor

A.F.I. 195/HH 1939/117 Stars & afsam

War Service Chevrons 170/441
8 wound stripes

One officer to another officer

From —

To

Date Ref. —

Subject

Dear Brown
                                  Yours
                                  Smith 7/Lt.

G C badge   1ST 7½" above cuff
            2ND 8"   "   "
            3RD 8½"   "   "

National Emblems and papers must be worn on head dress on appropriate days. Flags can be worn on lapel on real flag days.

Black bands can be worn for funerals and private mourning on left arm above elbow 3¼" wide   254 - 264 K.Rs. A 472/44 Service Stripes and Chevrons.

Wound Stripes Gold braid (Red for last war). If wounded in different battles this war, 1 for each battle. For service chevrons worn on right arm ¾" long nothing between seams. W/O's wear them above badge on rank.

Badges

Badges an eagle must be worn on all blue uniform. eagle facing the rear 1" below shoulder
$\overline{O/O}$ wear on all uniforms 7" above sleeve cuff
Chevrons between Elbow and Shoulder
Band fitter to be worn on sleeve 7" above cuff. If he is voluntary bandsman he wears crest above tapes and spider
Combined ops badge to be worn on below shoulder
Bomb disposal worn on right sleeve between Elbow and shoulder.
Pathfinder badge worn on left of breast pocket.
Air Sea rescue only by ASR cluster above badge of rank. If not NCO between Elbow & Shoulder.
Air crew must wear badge he is at a present duty - i.e. air gunner - air gunners badge. If a pilot and on A.G. duties wears A.G. badge.

Responsibilities of an N.C.O.
Chapter 15 K.R. Discipline General.
1081 A Redress of Grievance
1095 No Smoking after lights out. no Gambling in Billet

Dress Regulations-
K.R. A.C.1 Chapter 6 A.P. 837 Sect. 63.
A.P. 818A & C.R.O. Command Routine Order
Why the same uniform. For recognition same thing together. same basis together. Uniform must not be worn at fancy dress ball. N.O. cannot permit anyone to alter uniform. No trinklets allowed. e.g. pens sticking out of pocket.
K.R. 190 OBEDIENCE REGULATIONS.
K.R. 189 No beards or sideboards all clothing to be clean

Best blue should be worn for all
Ceremonial Parades - Guards - Court Martial
  Identity Discs K.R.3537.
  Tropical Dress.
    C.R.O. 3/43 Further attendment 13/43
      Standard Combinations of dress.
A. Blue serge service dress uniform
B. K.D. Service dress uniform
C. War Service dress.
D. Khaki Serge battle dress
E. Khaki bush shirts plus slacks or shorts.
F. Khaki Shirts with Slacks or shorts.
G. Great Coats or Capes.
    War Service Dress
Sergeants and above wear collar & tie
Below Sergeant buttoned up. no collar
and tie.

A.C. ADMIN ORDER 59/NH

Khaki Serge battle dress can be worn with skirts and slacks.
R.A.F REGIMENT A.D.O. 328/NH.

A.P. 837 PARA. 1422.

Plain clothes may be worn if you going to participate in any sport.
NO MIXTURE OF UNIFORM ALLOWED.

If on leave after twenty four hours you can wear plain clothes.

Station Duties

K.R Para 820 - 826.

(1) If more than one N.C.O on Station one N.C.O. detailed for Duty N.C.O.

2. Station duty officer F/Lt and above.

K.R 821 he represents C/O after working hours.

3. Orderly officer. performed by officer below rank of F/Lt F/OG below

KRA 820

duty of orderly officer. See airmens messing
complaints - cooks clean cookhouse utensils
clean i/c fire alarms till Senior arrives

4 Duty Pilot
5 Look out K.R. 834 duties connected with
   (Section or Watch)
   flying and aerodrome procedure under D Pilot.
6 Duty Flight K.R. 834
7 Guards Sentries and Police 836 K.R.
8 Orderly Sergeant. reveille - take sick
   report. attends fire piquet parades - goes
   round with orderly officer visits canteen
   (responsible for defaulters not drinking beer)
   attends staff parade which consists of fire
   piquet - defaulters - etc
9 Orderly Corporal similar as Orderly
   Sergeant.
10 N.C.O i/c Fire Piquet

11. Institute N.C.O. to see the institute is opened and closed at definite time. Will attend staff parade.

12. Guard Commander
N.C.O. i/c Detention Room K.R.1216 to see prisoners wash daily - change linen - bath etc.

Leave.   Officers N70
A.C.S.E.A. K.R. 165/44.
Leaven in India starts 1st January
Privelage Leave. FLYING PERS. 56 days.
normally in periods of 14 days also 2 lots of
28 days providing they can be spared.
NON. FLYING PERS 28 days. 2 periods of
14 days if C/O permission can have full 28.
Casual Leave an airman can have
this periods of ten days - up to 4/5.
Sick Leave - up to 21 days sick leave.
Recommendation of M.O.

Compassionate Leave

14 days by an officer not below rank
of Wing Commander. IF MORE REQUIRED HAS TO HAVE GROUP

Railway Warrants.

Airmen in full concession a
two warrants per year. other than cha
one a year

15.11.44

Saluting

K.R.A.C. Chapter 5. Ceremonial 142 - 148. 150
Friendly Greetings   A.P.A. 818A Part I & II
The only time we salute the national anthem is when the Royalty is present. The Viceroy or any Governor General of countries.

Service M.T.   K R XIV

A.P. 837 - Sect. 20
ACSEA 66/NW Responsibilities of MT officers
Establishments 379/43 A.F.O.
A.F.O. 309/43 Control of R.A.F Regimental Vehicles
ACSEA ORDER 67/H Maintenance of R.A.F "
Duties of A.C.H. / M.T. I.AF) minimum of 2 hours driving a day(s) The first three months they must exceed 20 m.P.H.

Marking on Vehicles

A.F.O. 254/43.   camouflage
K.R. 1996 Identification No's

A.F.O 215/43 R.A.F. Roundel

A.F.O. 215/43 Group Identification letters.
painted 3" in Light above Roundel and at back

A.F.O. 215/43 Unit Identification letters
painted white on black background.

A.F.O. 215/43 **Bridge** weight marking 9" Yellow
circle — [sketch] — with of grey on trailer and front axle
figures denote weight of front axle on right

K.R.158 Flags. Air officers will fly
their own flags.

A.L.SEA.ORD 60 Carrying Capacity of
personal - always numbered.

A.L.SEA ORD 64 Maximum Speeds always
painted in cab.

M.T. Gen I. Tyre pressure etc. always in
cab.

1629. M.T Driver Identity card.
Issued on unit basis. to be in [illegible]

or posting and forward with airmans docs. Form 637. Issued to a person who is required to drive vehicles occassionally. This must be signed by unit commander and counter signed by group.

A Military motor vle driving licence signed by Station Comm. for use fore 12 north.

Flight and Section for Admin.

Absentee report form 581.
K.R 336 Church Parades.

ARREST AND CUSTODY.
    M.A.F.L. Chapter IV
    K.R. Chapter XV Sect 283
Regs I.A.F. INST. 240/254.
    A.F.A. Sec: 45.
I.A.F.A Sect 48
A.P. 837 – Sect 93

What is arrest

curtailment of liberties of an airman prior to being on the charge

1. A man is innocent till proved guilty
 - Close arrest in the cooler
2. Open arrest a few more liberties

Close Ar. for drunkeness: insubordination: violence for his own personal safety. If it is considered for the stations discipline

An airman drunk. 1st offence 5/- 2nd 10/- 3rd 15/- 4th £1 can be awarded c/c instead

Form 252.

NO. 1. SCTS				
UPPER TOPA				
12·3·45	L.A.C. A/CPL	BROWN	S.J.	S.P.(V)
MURREE	W/W	WHEN ON ACTIVE SERVICE *	FOR WITNESSES	

HIS. NO. RANK. NAME. TRADE. INIT. TRADE GROUP.

*(Simple absence)

<u>W.O.A.S.</u> absent from 0001 hrs on 1st January 1944 untill 08·00 hrs 0800 hrs on 1st January 1944.

(absent 7 hrs. 59 mins)

+ apprehended by Cpl Smith (when broke brought back by S.P.)

2nd run <u>W.O.A.S.</u> Absent from Guard duty from 18·00hrs on 1st January 1944. untill 18·30 hrs on 1st January 1944.

P. 19

thereby causing his duty to be performed by 1234567 O-r Jones. S

INSUBORDINATION CHARGES

1.O.13.S. Not leaving the canteen by 22.30hrs on 1st May 1944, when ordered to do so by Corporal Brown. at 22.15 hrs on 1st May 1944.

1.O.13.S. When ordered to leave the canteen by Cpl Brown at 2215 hrs on 1st January 1944, say "I'm staying here" or words to that effect.

38' Minor offence report Sub Commander C/Sgt F160

Summary punishment Officer accused
log. the accused can asks c/o 6 Nader
Minor punishment - c/c late parades

A Subordinate commander cannot award Detention or sfot. money.   OR IN DAYS DETENTION IF APE IS ABSENT IN DAYS
A c/o off 7/LT and below award only 7 days
A c/o above S/LDR cannot award 28 days
ACSEA. 728/31 . 29/7/44

GOOD CONDUCT BADGES
K.R. 1175 -1186 A.P. 337. Sect-35.
AF.(S) 206/42
all punkers over 7 days. stop the G.C. badge for 31 days
Entered 5-6-40. due for G.C. 6/6/43.
8 days c.c. 6.8.43. " " held 9 days
If he gets 10 days break v.g. time for two years there he has to do 2 years good c.
due on 20-3-44. 11 onwards
any award above ten days he has to be good for 2 years.

Extend 5-6-40 due for G.C. 6/6/43
14 days C.C. 1-6-41   6-9-43.

Admonition.
Reprimand N.C.O.
C.C. not exceeding 7 days
Deductions from pay to make good loss
or damage
~~If he get admonished~~
Loss of 91 days
Severe reprimand ˟ C.C. 8.9.10 days
Field punishment ˟ detention ˟ imprisonment ˟
Forfeiture pay as a Punishment ˟
Civil convictions (when entered on Charge Sheet) ˟
and forfeiture of pay for absence over 2 days ˟
Fines for drunkness ˟
Reduction of an N.C.O for an offence ˟
11-14 days C.C. ˟

X) DENOTES DOING EXTRA TWO YEARS FOR G C BADGE.

Enlisted 5·6·40
9 DAYS cc 6·8·41 { geti admonished and 2
days pay 1·9·42
                                    + 91 days for cc.
                                    + 2 DAY FOR PAY.

Enlisted 5·6·40
9 days 6·8·41
Admonished   bring back 2 years
3 days pay stopped   g.c.

Enlisted 5·6·40
8 days cc 6·7·41
14 days c.c. 5·8·42
1st Badge 19·5·44

BELOW 7 DAYS NO DELAY IN G.C. BADGE. ABOVE 7(8-10) stop
91 days or AIRMANS G.C. ABOVE 11-14 STOP 2 YEARS.
IF AIRMAN GETS 14 DAYS IN HIS FIRST YEAR HE IS OK

Depriving a man of his badge
Field Punishment
Detention
Imprisonment
Reduction for an offence of an N.C.O.
as order of C.M.
Conviction for desertion

4 Types of M.T. Journey
a routine duty journey K.R. 1954/ ACSEA 63
same stopping place - same time - same visit
to distant M.O.S office same time.   FOR PROLONGATION
1st week in Jan 1st in July. and 1st starter

(1) the routine duty journey 2d.
2 Frequency of the journey
3 Time the journey is to commence
4 Type of Vehicle to be used
5. Duty for which journey is authorised
6. Destination and or/ route to be covered
7 approximate mileage
8 Group reference as c/our authority
    a 658 is necessary but it rarely
    requires a signature for transport.
(2) A.C.S.E.A. O. 68   Individual Duty Journey.
(3) A.F.I. 167/43. Recreational Journeies

Airforce station commander can utilise transport neighbouring towns, organised sport, private residences for organised hospitality to nearest railway station for airmen on (privilages-organised)

They must be over two miles and not over ten miles an airman is allowed 1 recreation night per week.

Over ten miles racines sanction must be got by A.O.C.

A.C.SEA.O. H2 Safety precautions gang's will observe number of passenger

A.C.SEA.O. 21 Officers and W.A.A.F. may travel free in transport, other ranks will not be displaced to make room for officer

Repayment journey K.R.1956 ACSEA.068. these journeys are closed for duration except in furthering the war effort. to descretion of C/O

Q 793 is used for transport or repayment made out in triplicate. 1st to DRIVER. 2nd to accounts officer 3rd to person who wants run.

Q 658 is a request for transportation

A.C.S.E.A.66. says 658 must be in 24 hrs in advance

M.T. accident report form NN6. will always be carried on every service vehicle

— Equipment —   A.P. 837 SECT. 7
                  A.P. 830

A.P. 1036. Price Vocabulary of R.A.F Equipment

— CLASIFICATION —

Stores A. usually of technical nature, always on charge
          CANNOT BE RENDERED ENTIRELY USELESS
       B. treated as a class. stores. BY FAIR WEAR & TEAR
          articles of a consumable nature
       C. ~~exchangeable articles~~ not on charge

— Grading of Equipment — APPLIES TO A 2.3. STORES

Grade A. NEW AND UNUSED EQUIPMENT ONLY
      B. FIT FOR IMMEDIATE RE-ISSUE
      C. SERVICEABLE TO FUNCTIONAL TESTS

GRADE D) REPAIR, REQUIRES WORKSHOP FACILITIES BEYOND YOU.
" E BEYOND ECONOMICAL REPAIR.

674. is an internal demand issue voucher

675 is an internal and return and receipt Voucher

673 is an exchange Voucher

Form 37. Flight or Section Inventory an officer or n/o in charge of all the Eng in workshop kit: when a person is posted he must have a thorough check with his successor

a form 668 record of loan to individuals

108 Temporary Loan card, all Equipment out on a 108 must be returned in on his

Form 29 supplies for way anti barrack Equipment.

A.P.830 Organisation of Stores R.A.F.

674) Voucher

Demand) N°. 100.   28.11.44.

Sect 86 Ratoth. Unit. SL1313.

Ref No.	Sect 23Q. Rnd⸺ 1/10 cons	Denomi. 1000	Demanded. 9/1000	For which Demand). For exginie Spare.
6748				

Flightlar Sect. Com demander
R Blukhere.   Signed B/.
                                                      Receiver.
Stores 3 vouchers Sanctification

(3)   Normal Peace time basis is or statu

Modified Basis, Short notice operations (2)
       Operation, (1)

PUBLICATIONS

R.A.F.   I.AF.

A.P. 958   K.R. A.C.I
A.P. 837.   M. of ADMIN.
A.P. 804   MANUAL OF AIR FORCE LAW.
A.P. 1301.   ROYAL. AIR. FORCE. WAR MANUAL PART. II
              Organisation and admin.
A.P. 1081. — R.A.F. POCKET BOOK.

{ R. IAF INST.   { AND MANUAL OF INDIAN LAW
{ R. 117F RULES { INDIAN AIR FORCE. ACT.

Pay allowance Regs India
Passage regulations
Movement Instructions India

{ K.R. A.C.1   K.R. PARA. 1070
{ Air force act. – K.R. 1101
  airman must have access to always

(IAF)

P1. Sheet Roll
P2. Combatant's enrolment form.
P3. non Combatant's enrolment form.
AFB 122A. Conduct Sheet
Form. 955. Service and Casualty form.
" 1158 Verification Roll.
" 167 Result of trade test.
" 243 Results of Course.

Character As K.R. para 2148.
  V.G.
  Good
  Fair
  Indifferent
  bad
  also V.G*.

Form	1580	Record of service	}
"	280	Cat of "	} Service Docs
"	120	Service Con. Sheet	}
"	131	General Con. Stat.	}
"	445A	Envelope	
"	48	Medical History	
"	64	P.1871 Pay Book	
"	976	Will	
"	1250 or F557 A	Identity Card	
"	1383	Deficiency chit	
"	365	Bed Card	
"	373	Record of service (aircrew)	
"	381	Leave record	
"	667	Flying clothing card	

Trade prof para 2141
  Exceptional
    Superior
    Satisfactory
    Moderate
    Inferior

A R Chapter XXIX
A.R. 837. Sec 57.

```
        INTERVAL      INTERVAL
  4th  o o o o o o o         o o o o
              ↓ DISTANCE
   2   o o o o o o
   3   o o o o o o   THIS REAR RANK
         when turned about to file
```

Above, faintly:
...up 5 (3) broken spring pin (4) Empty ...
magazine lips (6) defective w Spring

Below, faintly:
rough edge of flax alters inward f le...
loop put weight through bridge cha...

— Station Fire Organisation —

A.P. 957. K.R. XXIII Sec 3.
AP 837. – Sec 19.
AP 1334 all fires will be noted to Air Ministry

Tour of duty of fire piquet not to exceed 168 hours.

Discipline in Warfare

AP.1301. Morale of troops   Propoganda
is the general spirit or state   Diplomacy
of mind of a group of men   Economic pressure
as reflected by men under   Military   "
all conditions

How is good Morale produced. Enthusiasm and
Discipline

Judging a good unit
Do all carry out W.R.O"
Bearing is it good
Saluting, did the airmen or officers salute properly.
What is heard about the place.

1. What have you seen personally on various unit on this command.
2. Are you perfectly satisfied with what you have seen.
3. If you are not satisfied with what you have seen in the command : what are you going to do about it.

Statement not on oath cannot be
cross examined
on oath yes the statement can be
examined

— Lessons of the trial —
Accused brought to trial without delay
                                    Read Para 2.
Subordinate Commander attends with
accused's documents
                        K.R 1127. (5)

C.O. has T.160. T252 - K 1127 (3)

Accused must be present throughout
trial   R.P. 3.A.

During trial, accused deprived of his cap.
K.R. 1111 (8)

Accused may demand that all
evidence be taken on oath. R.P. 3.B

Accused may cross-examine any witness
R.P. 3A

Accused may make a statement, either on oath or not. R.P. 3. NOTE 3.

Accused may call witness in his defence R.P. 3A

CO examines F121 only after deciding guilt A.P. 837 Para 729.

In a summary punishment (or a minor which entails a forfeiture of pay) is contemplated. Accused is given option of trial by court martial A.F.A. 146.(8)

A statement made in oath the accused can be cross examined

A statement not made in oath cannot be cross examined

This is used to communicate a charge to the person who is to deal with it → [252]

The subordinate commander will take the charge on this → [7281]
If he remands to the c/o he uses a 252a to send the details. These are entered on 7100 (Guard Report) on which c/o takes the charge.

c/o punishment is entered on the 252 and the guard report. The 252 is returned to the Subordinate Commander for information. He completes the 7281 from it and airmans conduct sheet as well then destroys the 252.

RECLASSIFICATION.

(1 - IV)

TEST - UNIT - CO.

ADJ:(DR.O) T.T.B. { 1 officer
                    1 W/O
                    S.N.C.O'

D.R.3. time and place.

one copy of 7.107   PRACTICAL AND ORAL.
        (EXCEPT FOR CLERKS, EQIP. AND W. OOPS written)

60% A.C.1 79%
80%+ L.AC

When passed out. P.O.R.2

paid from 1st of month following board

Documentation pay books

Group V   (1112 A.P. on TT.B.)

ACH/GD. A.C. S.E.A ADMIN ORDER 3.3/44

AC.2 - AC.1   normal 2 years

Reclassification   1. AF.

NOT REPEAT NOT. A UNIT MATTER.

           3.14/43.

Recommends to Group quarterly   ACSEA 0.223/HH
              23/44
P.19. Triplicate.

For Board S/LDR present.

1 Group

3 BPO.

1 copy to unit

  JLAC unless and untill he takes
Education test. with 18 months of having
his props

     Group V
     C.O. UNIT.
A.C.2. A.C.1. — 6 months   IF MAN
            IS SUITABLE.
A.C.1. L.AC. — 6 month

― Remustering ―

Not a unit matter.
― Discussion Groups ―
(1) Object. Reason for war.
           "   Hasting victory.. getting in Rut
    Show possibilities of post war world
(2) Value. proves your efficiency
           Make people familiar with civil
Government
           Discussion Group will occupy your
spare time
― Remustering ― R.A.F. & I.A.F.
    D.R.O. (for names) (Vacancies)
    Nominal Roll Group
    F.167 (Trip)
Group. Carb Copy
1 flimsey D.P.O. Cov. receipt of letter fam D.R.O.
1 flimsey Unit.   P.O.R
                        Remustering

A.C.S.E.A ADMIN ORDER. 333/44 promotion
officer can promote LAC's Corporal anytime

Groups have the authority of promoting Cpl.
to Sergeants - according to vacancy in
Group.

Records Sgt - 7/Sgt - 7/Sgt - W/O

Groups allowed to make acting paid 7/SGT & W.O.
A.C.H promotion made by B.P.O only.

Inverty Check
 Flight office sends 731 to Store Equip.
they check with there A in a Ledger
any articles outstanding — they send a
copy back to you

Drill.

Word of Command (A)	(B) Slow Time	(C) Quick Time	(D) Double Time
HALT		Right foot passing left.	
TO THE FRONT SALUTE		do	
CHANGE STEP ON THE MARCH		do	
RIGHT TURN		do	
RIGHT INCLINE		do	
RIGHT FORM		do.	
ABOUT TURN		Left foot passing right.	
LEFT TURN.		do	
LEFT INCLINE		do	
LEFT FORM		do.	
MARK TIME		do	
STEP OUT.		do.	
QUICK MARCH (WHEN STEPPING OUT OR SHORT)		do	
SLOW MARCH (WHEN STEPPING OUT OR SHORT)		do.	
STEP SHORT.		do	
EYES RIGHT LEFT OR FRONT.		do.	

WORD OF COMMAND A.	SLOW TIME B.	QUICK TIME C.	DOUBLE TIME D.
TO THE RIGHT OR LEFT SALUTE		LEFT FOOT PASSING RIGHT	
BREAK INTO QUICK TIME. QUICK MARCH	RIGHT FOOT PASSING LEFT.	—	
BREAK INTO SLOW TIME. SLOW MARCH.		LEFT FOOT PASSING RIGHT.	
BREAK INTO DOUBLE TIME		do.	
HALT WHEN MARKING TIME.		LEFT FOOT BEING RAISED.	
FORWARD WHEN MARKING TIME.		— do —	
CHANGE STEP (WHEN MARKING TIME)		RIGHT FOOT BEING RAISED.	

— GAS — LIQUID

1. Get under cover
2. Mop off any gas on you or swabs liquid
3. Rub in anti gas ointment on hands then rub on exposed parts of skin.
4. Remove outer clothing
5. Apply more anti-gas ointment
6. Irrigate the eyes
7. Adjust Respirator
8. Wash with soap and water

<u>Principles and Methods of decontamination</u>

D destruction   BURNING, BLEACHING, BOILING   (H.M.S.4)
R removal   HOSING, MOPPING, SOLVENTS, HEAT.
A avoidance } (S.W.R.)
W weathering } SUN, WIND, RAIN.
S sealing   (W.E.E.P.) WATER-GLASS, EARTH, EARTH AND BLEACH, BLEACH AND PAPER.

<u>Deciding factors</u>   (D.A.F.T.)

(1) Degree of danger to personnel.

2. Amount and type of contamination
3. FACILITIES AVAILABLE
4. TYPE OF SURFACE.

M.T. Vehicles Standard System of Servicing.

The organisation of the above have much in common with aircraft procedure. Each unit through the Engineering officer is responsible for the mechanical efficiency of its vehicles, but secondary responsibilities is delegated to an officer W/O or N.C.O.

— Servicing System.

Inspection periods:—
(1) D.I., (2) 500 miles), (3) major inspection or two thousand miles, (4) Partial overhauls as laid down in M.3.0. part 2 based on Volume 2. Inspectors may be delayed up to 1 hundred miles, but delay over 1 hundred miles must be authorised by M.T. Officer.

Fire tenders, ambulances, cranes, tractors and auxiliary vehicles, may have inspections carried out on the hours run basis where 1 hour = 10 miles.

M.T. 1st, 2nd, 3rd Line Servicing.

Units

1st Line. servicing of M.T. Vehicles is undertaken by units and will cover daily servicing, minor repairs and inspections up to (and may include 2000 thousand miles).

2nd Line Servicing is undertaken by M.T. repair depots, and will cover major repairs and modifications 2000 miles and over and partial overhauls.

3rd Line. Servicing is undertaken by I.B.A.C. and covers complete overhauls and re-builds

Note: no further major repairs will be

undertaken after a vehicles life of three years as expired.

Transfer of R.A.F Vehicles between R.A.F units.

1. Prior to transfer vehicles are to be inspected for serviceability and passed by officer i/c M.T.
2. Complete form 656 and transfer entries into log book no. of log book 7.813.
File old form 656 and raise new 656 and transfer with vehicle
3. Check inventry 748 and form 464
4. Log book signed by officer i/c M.T. brought up to date.
5. Return the vehicle to Stores on form 675
6. Stores raise form 600 transfer

the M.T. vehicle.
7.748 M.T inventory
7813. M.T vehicle logbook
7656 M.T. vehicle Servicing form.
7464. Issues and withdrawals.
7675 Internal return Voucher.
7600. raised by stores is an external
demand issue and receipt Voucher.
7446 Reporting of an accident. Driver will
report to police and get witnesses; he
will sketch scene and describe in his
own handwriting the accident

— Drivers Responsibilities —
1. Starting and running of engines
2. Security of loads and loss of equipment.
3. Liabilities of drivers :- ours, carrying of
   authorised persons, correct no and etc:
   Filling in 658 on return

4. Speed regulations, he is to be aquainted with Speed.
5. Lighting regulations
6. Highway code.
7. War time immobalizing of vehicles as a rule distributor.

N.C.O's Responsibilities
1. Selection of Routes.
2. Painting of R.A.F. Signes on Vehicles
No. of passengers which is authorised and maximum loads that they can carry. Restriction for certain types of vehicles Ambulances. Fire tenders bomb disposal. have blue light on top of cab or wing and leave one full light on.

– Economy in the use of transport –

1. The use of service transport.
2. The hiring of M.T. vehicles of any description
3. The issue of motor mileage allowance.
4. When ever service transport is used the smallest powered vehicle is to be employed.
5. The use of M.T. to carry officers and others to railway stations must be limited to cases of extreme emergency.
6. Use of public conveyances

   Repayment Services and Journeys Form 793
   Under certain circumstances: i.e. when public services cannot be utilised the C/O cannot permit service transport or repayment to sports team

7656 M.T. Servicing form.

Covers the period of one month a seperate form being used for each vehicle it is raised by N.C.O. i/c Sect.

Road Tests, are normally carried out by an N.C.O. but may be carried out by an authorised driver upon the authority of officer i/c Sect after:-

1, 2000 miles or higher mileage inspection and partial overhauls
2, any exchange of major components
3, adjustment of brakes or steering
4, Any other repair work effecting the running of the vehicle

Daily log 7.656
is a record of speed ometer readings daily mileage and mileage to date.

issues of petrol and oil. D.I's.
This is completed by the driver there
is also a column for check instructions
by the officer or N.C.O i/c.
All entries will be transferred into
the log book A.813.

Mileage inspection and periodical
certificate.
A record of tradesman signatures for
the inspectional operations laid down
space is also provided for the
initial of the person carrying out the
road test if applicable

M. T. S. O's
Part I are compiled and issued by the unit unit
c/o. They deal with organisation co-org
anisation of workshop procedure with

regard to Technical matter and define individual responsibilities

Part II — command — These are issued and compiled by unit c/o, they detail inspectional operations at the various mileage and periodical inspections they are based on the schedule of each type of vehicle.

— Disposal of u/s Vehicles — 7523.
The unit will raise form 523 and forward three copies to nearest M.T.R.U. M.T.R.U will check the form 523. or the actual vehicle and recommend disposal. If repair is recommended one copy of 7 523 will be sent to Group. If disposal out of the service is recommended one copy of f 523 and the log book 7813. will be sent to command

7749.) S.T.C.L. — Standard Transfer Checking List
INVENTRY } are being prepared for all M.T. Vehicles.
Part 1 will detail the tools and loose
equipment. part. 2. the easily removable
and attractive items.

Vehicles for repair will be transferred
complete to part of S.T.C.L. (Standing
Transfer Checking List)

Loose tools to part 1 will be vouched
to the nearest M.T. S.U. quoting the
vehicles registration NO.

When a vehicle to part No 2 of S.T.C.L.
is received from M.T. R.D. the necessary
tools will be demanded from the
nearest M.T. S.U.

AIRCRAFT	M.T.
7 1575	7658
7 700	7656
APP. A65.A.T.L	7.748 C.S.T.C.L. PART I & PART II
7701. L cards	7813. LogBook
719	7 814 Monthly return of Journeys. Monthly return of Petrol consumption
7361	7 361 & 7814B. M.S.P.
7171 & 7765 C	7446
Screwing 1st- 2nd and 3rd lines.	U.S.O Part I and Part II
226 Group deposit account	Command Group deposit account.

(C. G. D. A.) Command Group deposit accounts Transfer of a/s vehicles to C.G.D.A. (not overhauls) and report to Command. action taken by group

Carrying capacity is laid down in A.M.O's A 1090/43 958/44.
Airfield M.T vehicles 390/44 486 A.M.O's A

A.D. 113 holds all forms used in R.A.F. always refer to it for

Refueller & Road Tanker
alter 7656 B } Aux Eng.
alter 7813 B }

F 6560 } for P.M.
7 8130 }

Ac Sea letter C.M.a./8451/4/D.M.T.
31/6/44

Stores Procedure

__Organisation of Equipment Branch in India__

A.C.S.E.A. Delhi

Master Provision Office

Embarkation units at Ports.

Air Transit Sections at Aerodromes.

Reinforcement Centre

Equipment Depots

| aircraft Storage unit | air Stores parks. | Equipment Parks. | Repairable Equipment Depts | air armament parks | R.S.U | M.T.S.U | I.S.U. |

Units

Sub Stores.

Master Provision office is at Delhi in touch with A.C.S.E.A. headquarters any formation of new squadrons they organise their equipment.

When the following come in they handle

but as not disperse, aircraft, aero-engines Pyrotechnics & armament. Mechanical transport, Fuel oil.

Embarkation Units and Air Transit Sect. work Seperately but may be attacked.

Air Stores pack. 40 mile Radius generally supply a few Squadrons have 1 months supply of Equipment, likewise Equipment parks

Repairable Equipment dept receives equipment and services it. NOT aircraft

R.B.S.U. deal with salvage and repair of aircraft

F.R.D.	Forward Repair Depots (Mobile)
B.R.D.	Base " " (Static)

Equipment Regulations A.P. 830.

Vol. I lays down procedure for Administration and accounting (Home)

Volume I India
Vol II Storage and packing
Vol III 5 parts Scales of Equipment — A TOOLS
    India Command Equip Regs
    B BARRACKS
    C CLOTHING
    D M.T. MARINE
    E MISCELLANEOUS

A.P. 1086 Vocab of Equipment 15 parts
A.P. 1086C. American Stores
Vol III of Technical pubs
⋂ obsolescent
O obsolete

    Sect. 12 E.
Ref No. 125.   DETAIL NOMENCLATURE   DETAIL.
    Gauge   N.S. Patt No. 1320.

Use nomenclature and denominator of quantity as laid down.

Equipment Account Sect.
Recording of transactions of Equipment
Detection of Weakness.
Fixing of responsibility for custody of Equipment
Estimation of expenditure

Stores A major items which do not wear out in use.
   "   B major items which wear out in use and can be repaired
   "   C Consumable articles

In India a and b class stores come under the same heading

Form 101 Tally cards, a tally card for each type of class equipment

Non-recurrent issues   Red Ink.
    recurrent issues   Black

Authorised by Equipment officer

articles described &full
Held as S or R.
Holdings laid down
All receipts and Issues recorded.
Dues in out out recorded.
A in a Ledger ≠ to the Equal- A/s List
all AEB Stores

Internal Demand and issue Voucher 674 BLUE LINES

DEMAND SERIAL NO. WR1 6/6/11
FURNIDR SEE... AFLT. 10 CTC

ISSUE VOUCHER NO
PERIOD OF ACCOUNT.

REF.NO	DESCRIPTION	Item	Demand	Balance	POSTED	RATE	PER	RS	AS	P	PURPOSE REQUIRED
	SECT 3.A.										
1234	— — —	Doz	1/12								CARBS
	IF PART NO SAY SO. NO.—										

592/44. A.C.S.E.A. ORDER says than when ordering parts an alternative item can be quoted underneath if no room on P.T.O.
When getting spare back items N/AVAN.

If anything you order is not available raise immediately on form 674 a re-demand. & as when it comes into stores you shall get it soon.
mark in remarks column Redemanded on 1/v

If an item is urgently required mark "urgent" dated and sign it can be done in red ink.

673   Internal Exchange Voucher. 7673

Exactly similar items

Serviceability must be certified by Sect. officer (SPECIALIST)
the item labelled.

If you require a new old leg and before you take the old one off a form 108 can be landed in with the 673.

A.P. 830 Vol.1 Chapt.12. Para 42

     Internal Return   7675.
similar to 674.

     Form 91.
     Conversion Voucher.

used for 117. Transferring stores from Main Stores to Sub Stores (2) and transferring stores from

Section to Sect. (3)

(3) It can be used for checking surpluses against Deficiencies (2)

(4) Changing o/o state of items (1) copies

Cont. (1) The transfer of stores from main stores to sub stores are done on a 731 Conversion Voucher the stores receiving signing for the stuff

Cont (4) Change of items e.g. stuff has deteriorated in Stores they can be Struck off on 731 with permission of Technical Officer or if you have surplus tools and down or others

Two N.IV. 20s in this command 1 from command. If one locally N.IV.(L) all N.IV's must have a number. items not in vocab are rendered for Board.

7600 Demand Issue and Receipt Voucher. (External)

Demands from Unit → M.U.

Black, blue and red copies go to M/U, when M/U send Bl. notifying there sending the goods. The red copy is sent with the goods and checked with the blue. The blue is then sent back for M/U's use in Equipment Sect. Black copy goes to Equip Sect.

Returning goods

```
M.U.                              UNIT
                                   BK
                                   BL
        POST NOTIFICATION          RD
BL ←                              ← BL
           GOODS
RD ←
   ↳ Equip
     H.Q.
     Sub...
```

The form 600 is in sixsuplicate and used in the formation of a new unit.   ACSGA

Form 604   Packing Note
raised in Duplicate - original in package duplicate held for record
requires two signatures packers and witness

7674.   Disposal

Section Commander prepares in Triplicate.

T. retained

To Equip Sect. — Flight or Sect.
E. Acct issues goods
O. D. duplicate with goods go → Compares and completes 3 B T. /D&T

EQ. A/c   O D   E. A. S.   T BACK   Checked and stamped
Sect compaithu

If any inventory a/c is to be compared it is to be done when duplicate is sent back with goods to Flight or sect. He prepares period of A/cs a triplicate from Duplicate.

Form 603 used for issues out of R.A.F. Barry: civil
Form 530. issues to R.A.F. from casual
contractors —   Voucher Register
F611 Return   (67? & 600)
F612. Issue.   (674 & 680)
F614 Conversion (673 & 701) 6746. 734
(F 1777.   A.O.S. Register)
It gives the Equipment Officer an idea
of what vouchers are issued and what
number can be issued

War System A	War System B	War System C
Vouchers in triplicate. Inventories held in Sections. SNCO sign Store 674. F673	Vouchers in Duplicate. Inventories held in E.A.S. Sect. Commanders sign 7674 & 675. For a and b Stores 7 & 675	No inventories. Sect Command sign for A & B. Vouchers in single copy NO 7673. 7674 used marked exchange. S.N.C.O's can sign 7675. E 674 E. 6674 but not Titen items
Inv. Holdings only sign for A & B Stores		

Titen items are items which are in short supply, all units are notified from Group which are titen items, only officer can demand titen items

A.O.G.

7674 endorsed in Red A.O.G. signed by ENG OFFICER.

Signal — Signal sent to Equip Depot (repeat H.Q) Starts A.O.G. & gives Sec/Ref and aircraft Type & No.

The words A.O.G gives signal priority. On receipt Equip Depot despatches goods sending signal advising, Goods marked A.O.G. and get priority, Signals used as vouchers.

If the Equip Dept cannot supply — Signal is sent to M.P.O (repeat unit) disclosing inability.

M.P.O can with full authority

(1) Divert to another E.D. or M.U.
(2) ... unit
(3) ... bonnano

(4.) Demand direct from makers
(5) If possible have it done by local manufacture
If another A/c is robbed of spares for another aircraft H.Q. is to be notified.

M.R.R.
Used by A/Cs when progress is held up for repairs. 3rd Priority

I.O.R. Immediate Operation Requirements
For equipment not: repeat not: airborne but without which aircraft will be grounded

Strike off is issue out of R.A.F. after item has served its life. Strike off is charge against the public

Write off Removal from records before useful life is completed — a crash for instance F.T.S. must have authority of C/O aircraft or engine in this war referred to as strike off not write off.

<u>Write down</u> when equipment has deteriated through lying in Stores not due to fair wear and Tear its value can be written down on authority of board of surveyors or Chief Technical Officer.

Raising a f34. Statement of Equipments lost or damaged.

Specialist Officer will raise a report & Engineering officer raises F34. they are forwarded to c/o

c/o raises F34 Quint Quadruplicate

four copies of F34 are sent to H.Q.

1 copy sent back (signed) as authorised

F34 & F31 given C.V. CONVERSION VOUCHER number.

If c/o is not satisfied with it he calls for.
  Board of Survey 7681
He notify's HQ.
they send down officer to unit to be president of B.of S, the c/o details a specialist officer as member.

The Equipment is disposed off after being boarded If they cannot come to conclusion or sent to an m/u for further ~~information~~ opinion
The report of board rendered in Duplicate

— Petrol and oil issues —

— The stores keep a tally of their petrol in bulk issue on f.458

― Petrol & oil issues ―

Petrol issued to R.A.F is usually in bulk from contractors.

7458 Record of issues from Bulk. KEPT IN STORES

1361 Flight petrol book is carried by petrol conveyance on aerodromes.

The flight commander will render a 674 daily for petrol and oil issues he received the previous day.

Labelling and marking of R.A.F Equip
It is the responsibility of the dring officer.

Packing. Specialist packing e.g cases in Vocab Sec: 40, A.P. 1086 Vol III

Marking of the case
all the old markings have to be obliterated
(1) R.A.F. Marking (2) Case no. (3) Consignees
address if s-after case no it means its
sealed (4) Weight (5) Vocabulary section and
reference no

Markings to be precise as:- Instruments with
care

Labels F534. Consignment Label.
    " 532A. Handle with care
    " 532B Glass handle with care
    " 532C. This side up
            Handle like eggs

On receipt of a U.R.R demand a form 600 will
be raised to cover.

— Flight or Section Inventory — 737.
A.P. 830 (1) Chapt. 12. Sect (7.)
Equipment Офрs Sect can check
whereabouts of A & B class stores
1 Copy of sheet 1 held in Equip. Офs Sect.
Sheet 1 under peace time system and
war system A two copies are raised —
one copy to inventry holder of sheet I
and one in E. A. S.
Description of Sheet 1. Front side
Signature Certificate of 737 holder.
Reverse side, top half names of personel
holding F668 & 722'.
bottom half of Sheet 1 is Equip Officers
Signature for no of Sheet II
Sheet 2. Front side, Stores, See:
Ref: nomenclature, denomination, quantity

Columns made up in question pencil, Last vacant column is made up by Equip Officer in ink.

Reverse side of Sheet 2. Distribution log of numbers F-668 & 22².

Sheet 3 continuation of Sheet 2 front side is only half copy

Sheet 4 continuation of Sheet 2 back side

Responsibilities of an inventory holder.

1. Ensure serviceability & maintenance of items on Charge
2. Additions and withdrawals must be recorded in black lead pencil with appropriate voucher no.
3. Must allocate a responsible person to check items held on 7668²
4. 737 & 7668² are kept under lock and key.
5. Responsible for periodical checks.

Taking over Procedure

(1) The 37 Notification, promulgated in D.R.O's of person to take over.

(2) F 37 is taken to E.A.S for checking with a/c in a/c ledger.

(3) E.A.S copy of Sheet I is returned with the form 37 to the flight or Sect plus a list of surpluses and deficiencies.

(4) Check a/c of Sheets II

(5) Check your 668's and 22's against F 37.

(6) Physical check re 7668's & 722's

(7) Transact business regard Surplusses and deficiencies with E.A.S.

(8) Person taking over sigs both copies of Sheet I

(9) Last thing they do is send the E.A.S. copy back plus list of surplusses and deficiencies

Sheet I

Checks.

1. <u>Independant Check.</u> C/O details an Officer or NCO to check 737 annually. He must-be from another flight or Section.

<u>Periodical Check.</u>
Carried out by the inventory holder within six months of the independant check

<u>Taking over check.</u>
When inventory holder becomes absent from duty or posted

Endorsing Vouchers. F614 & 675.

737 action
Serial No.

F668 issues <u>within flight or Section</u>
articles on loan to individuals he can check

his tools about every month

766413 Repayment Voucher for lost or damaged Equipment

raised in duplicate by inventory holder
if a person has lost an article, a 66413 is raised.

raised in three copies by O/C or Section Commander,

Individual signs on original, the 3 copies are passed to C/O for approval and signature
Original and Duplicate sent to Equip Off.
Triplicate sent back to T/Commander to put in
I.V. number and period of A/c

Duplicate goes back to T/Commander
for him to put on the triplicate copy (1)
issue voucher no. (2) period of account,
Duplicate goes back to E.A.S, then original

and duplicate are passed to Iny Offs for action

[Chapter 9]. Sect 2. 830 AP Vol I India deals with 664B action

A.P.830 Chapter 19. _Transferable Equipment._
Items of Equipment which can be move transferred with the airframe from unit to unit.

— Non-Transferable equipment —

— E.g. Towed target and camera guns

Types of Equipment.

(A) Station Plant Stationary Technical fittings - responsibility of D.C.B. in R. N.E.S India

(B) Station Equipment.
    Equipment which does not accompany unit a change of station.

(C) Unit Equipment. goes with unit on change of station. Trollies. Tents.

Seperate Inventories are held for B and C.
Station and Unit Equipment

War Equipment Schedule

issued as authority for equipping a unit with certain type of aircraft

Airframe will come into the service without removable items.

[Airframe Appendix A is checking list of aircraft
Lists removable items

Item | Descrip | Source | HQ | No of Aircraft | No of Aircraft | Wt

Appendix A is only used when aircraft comes from makers into air force. Appendix B is a check of the aeroplane parts.

When the aircraft comes into air force it comes on F530: with discrepancy

List showing things contractor cannot supply.

If anything is short on aircraft that is not on discrepancy list. R.A.F notify contractors on ~~7A 7~~ 800 Discrepancy List ~~report~~ is sent to a.15 at Contractors

S.A.T.L. They have issued you a standard airframe transfer list from

A.P.F.S. Air publication form store

To save time in checking they have brought out a Standard airframe transfer list it is a list of attractive items in other words easily removable items

Form 464 is an issue and withdrawal 2 copies to each airframe held in Equip Sect.

Engine is vouched through

1086 Engine Checking test - found in
Vol. III aero engine Publication
always refer to last amendment of
aero-engine Checking test.

Packing and Marking
A/Fs. & A/Es. [Part II Sect. 40 A.P. 1086. A/F]

Special cases for different types of airframe. When packing case must bear serial no.

Also special packing cases for aero-engines. aero-engines no. must be on the outside of the case.

Sect 40 B. aero-engines - cases for
Sect 40 C. Propellers   "   "
Sect 40.7. Aircraft   "   "

(1) Packing of Engine and fuselage. Vol II AP 830
(2) Drain all fuel and oil tanks,
(3) Remove main planes and if necessary tail unit.
2 Remove propellers.
3 Blank of all pipe lines

(4.) Relieve tyre pressure.
(5) remove or retract undercarriage
(6) Inhibit Engine. and Label as having been inhibited
(7.) Secure the fuselage in its case by special stands Co. provided.
(8) Remove or secure loose control surfaces.
(9) Pack wings on case provided or racks and secure with wedding. 320/213 used. use felt as pack 320/118.
(10) Prop goes with or without as case may be

Inhibiting Engines. refer A.P. 1464/C.32
To offset effects of corrosion caused by leaving spare
(1) Drain sump and cylinders with pyrene
(2) Inline engines remove cam covers and

spray gears with inhibitor. 33c/777
3. Remove sparking plugs and with piston at B.D.C. spray inhibitor in cylinder & fit dummy plugs.
(5) Label engine to effect that it has been inhibited and signed by inhibitor.
(6) Make an entry in log card that it has been inhibited

Collecting of Packing cases from Railway good yards.

Before leaving the unit the N.C.O i/c the party will obtain from the Equipment officer all the necessary information regarding the package. Case no. Dimensions weight, Packing s(c) Checking list. He will obtain he will arrange the off loading procedure a knowledge of the goods siding. also he will map out a rout indicating bridges or rough roads. by-passes, etc. If necessary he will arrange an enscort: also the N.C.O will have a big enough party to handle the consignment. He will also arrange. transport filling the F658. Before he leaves the station he will arrange. for. late meals for the number of men. he has.

Station Workshops.

The o/c of a station is the figure head of workshops. He nominates the Engineering Officer as I/c the Sect. There is usually a W/O or F/St. I/c of the production these N.C.O' in turn are responsible for the Jnr N/C.O. I/c bays. In a workshop Group men are preferable, but there are different groups where necessities permit.

In these workshops we find the precision instruments — machine tools complete overland kits if workshop is working on Merlins they will be in possession of a complete merlin tool kit.

Kits listed in Vol III appropriate publication

Station Workshops.

Lifting Tackle.

Various lifting tackle are obtainable in Station Workshops. the common ones are. Hand cranes, chain tackle, purchase blocks, jacks, (sheer leg:- A.P.) ropes and slings. Engine slings, propeller slings A.P. 1464/373.
Universal Jacking trestles, certain types for different aircraft A.P. 1469/997

Servicing of Lifting Tackle.

All wire and rope slings are to be destroyed on the first sight of fraying. these are subject to periodical checks as laid down. ALL LOAD must never be left hanging on any kind of lift tackle. particularly on places where anyone is working

Ropes are oiled.
wire ropes greased.
A.P. 1404/G1.

$$\frac{15}{5}\times 2246\times 7$$

1200
224
3640
2240
————
1400

No load must be left unattended and the weight of loads must not exceed that of laid down.

The differential type of lifting tackle must only lift 75% as to that is laid down.

The mechanism hub must be lubricated every 3 months — in a foundary every 1. month, a complete dismantle and overhaul is done every twelve months they are to be annealed when stated by makers — the record is kept by the N.C.O i/c Sect. or E.O i/c Sect. on chain tackle we are permitted 10% wear.

Dia is diameter of link material
Safe loads for chains.

D.A.	1/4"	5/16"	3/8"	7/16"	1/2"
LOADS IN SAFETY lbs	650	1,100	1,500	1,900	2,550

The bigger the area angle of the rope the greater the strain

The larger the angle of the legs between of the sling the less the safe load.

Vertical	Load 1000 lbs
30°	950 lbs
90°	700 lbs
120°	500 lbs

Sheer Legs type A.

will lift a load of 2½ tons fifteen feet.

overhanging jib— ·· ·· ·· 1000 lbs twenty feet.

Wooden structures with jib steel fittings, 7 parts in all + small king post. the purchase is 6.
worm type handle gears. two speed gears

Sheer Legs type B.

has ten cwt. block tackle
weights 185 lbs
can lift 1000 lbs up to 17½ feet.
the structure is made of duralumin
has two legs - jib and is steadied by
the wire rope running from rear
end of jib: to pick in ground.

legs can fold.

Workshop proper

Machine tools held as special
inventory on 1512

Precautions

Machine Shop
(1) butter guards, belts, fences to be correct
all these precautions must be strictly
observed.
(2) When change belts over on the move the
machine must be stopped
(3) When a lathe is running and you
want to change tools or measure
the job. the machine must be stopped
(4) Overhauls should be worn and must
be buttoned up. No loose clothing to
be worn on working machines
(5). On using Emery wheels Goggles

must be worn
(6) No small jobs to be done unless using tongs
(7) Rest must be near stone as possible.
(8) Never grind on side of side stone. as it wears down it and breaks causing damage.

— Blacksmith Shop. from 1468
Hammers, swages, sets, flatters, etc. will be examined frequently to insure that heads are secure and there are no loose splinters to fly off when they are used.

Tongs and tools in frequent use should be cooled off in the water trough immediately after use.
Tempered tools must be hardened.

by competent personel. and steel
should not be cold hammered: until
the temper has been fully drawn.
Cared should be taken when
lighting forged fires to prevent an
accumulation of vapours.
Petrol or parrifin must not be
used to start fires.
Coke used should be free from slate.
which may explode or splutter when
heated. Work that has been heated
should be placed on the floor
to cool and marked off in a chalked
rink with the word HOT conspicuously
in evidence

(8) Respirators must be cleaned frequently
(9) Smoking is strictly prohibited.
(10) Exhaust fans should be capable of changing the whole of the area in the shop in two minutes
(11) Metal frames should be earthed to prevent any static charge due to friction

— Salt bath —

Precautions
(1) Notice 72157 should be displayed conspicuously (N/A in I.O.F).
(2) No person is allowed to touch the bath unless authorised
(3) Contact with the molten salts must be avoided and any burns must report must be treated by M/O.

and only first aid given from the first aid box.

(4) Jobs are to be clean and dry before immersing in salt bath, special attention being given to hollow fittings

(5) All exists and entries to the salt bath are to be cleared of obstruction at all times.

(6) In the case of fire the shop must be vacated and fire dealt with from outside

(7) Fuel cocks and blast valves should be operable from outside

Caustic Soda

Precautions.

(1) The harmful effects of Caustic Soda can largely be utilised by use of

a weak vinegar solution or saline solution.

Anodic Bath

(1) The job must not be touched while the current is on.
(2) Operators must wear appropriate clothing and avoid contact with the acid.
(3) Adequate ventilation must be provided and care taken to avoid inhaling the fumes from the Bath.
(4) The acid level must be several inches below the edge of the bath.
(5) Any skin irritation must be reported immediately.

Brazing Lamps

Use only clean filtered paraffin and fill the lamp not more than $\frac{2}{3}$ full.

Ensure the jets are clear, close the
flame regulator, open release valve
and partly fill heater cup with methylated
spirits and light it.

When the vapour riser is heated
close the air release valve, open the
flame regulator and operate the pump.
A clear blue flame should result.
Normal working pressure is between
80 & 90 lbs per □ in

Vapour filler valves A.P 1454/31
May be broken down by authorised
units only. A small hole is to be
drilled in the centre of the valve head
using a dry drill, & the stem
may be nicked across its axis
with a saw. When the salts

are exposed the valve is dropped into a container holding at least twenty gallons of clear water. The water has to be changed frequently.

Nox. — The Alumino Thermic Soldering iron A.P.1464/D61 are to be used in emergency only. They must not be lighted within 15 yds of aircraft or petrol Installations, nor taken into any building whilst tablet is burning.

Electrical Precautions

All main switches must be clearly marked, and in instances of fire involving Electrical Equipment the current must be switched off at the main and the fire dealt with in accordance with A.P. 957.

Heating apparatus should be switched off when not in use. Fuses are to be replaced by competent personnel.

Petrol.

Petrol is used for cleaning magnets, points, sparking plugs, etc. The quantity of petrol in workshops is kept down to a minimum.

Miscellaneous

Accumulations of waste paper, rags and oily waste must be avoided. Unit salvage orders should deal with their disposal.

Workshop Org.

Form 6 is required for all jobs.
Major. Manufacture top. overhauls. complete overhauls, partial overhauls

to aero-engines and airframes
overhauls to n.t. or a repair (involving)
involving the removal of a major
component, e.g. gear box, transmission
certain major modifications to
n.t. airframe aero engine.
Any minor jobs done in w/s form 6
action

Form 6 Requisition for internal return
Manufacture. or manufacture

Sec/Conv. raises 7614 & attaches
sketch or refers to A.P. or our Diagram
(73 if necessary) forwards to Eq.
DURBIN AND OUT ACTION 7.101.
Off. ↑ who raises form 6 in triplicate
he then forwards 76 to the C/O
for authority.
The original and duplicate go to

officer i/c workshops. The triplicate is
filed in Eq Sect.
The work is completion certified by
Off. i/c work shops and forwarded to
Eq officer with original and duplicate
Eq officer signs original and duplicate
giving it A/S Nº and sends original to
Workshops Duplicate to Eq. A.S. for A in
W. Triplicate is filed by Eq Sect.
the Items issued on 767A.

Major job on aircraft

When a major is required (very rarely
minor) the F/S will raise a S/6 in
triplicate these he will forward to
the C/O for authority.

The F/S transfers a/c to Wks
shop on 721. in triplicate. When the

Job is completed and certified it is returned to Flight on Form 6 -V.

Now if the aircraft is going to another flight the F/C will sign a Form 6. Original goes to E.O. He gives C.V. to all copies.

The Original then goes to E.A.S. sect where it is indexed and Dir A action taken. The Duplicate goes to F/Comm. and triplicate goes to wkshops.

Requisition for Minor Job.

The Flight Command will raise a F6 in Duplicate & forwards to o/c work shops who allotts a serial and job No & date. When job completed returns duplicate to F/C

o/c Workshops certifies on original

*Note: original F6 is in Duplicate and returns to Squad offices for c/O; makes triplicate and circulates to o/c.

and sends Job and original 7.6. to 7/c.
7/c. signs both copies & returns them
to o/c workshops.

Internal Procedure.

76 in 8 760 raised (Workshop Record)
In the sections they raise a form 1083
Job Card. A F-1505 is raised (Cheque Form issue) on
Workshops to sub stores and they say
(If requisition) no stock available

Sub stores raise F1136 Equipment Sheet
in duplicate on Main Stores, (Stocks
available - 1 copy of F1136 is forwarded
to Sub Stores. Sub Stores raise a form
674 (Incomplete stock - notify sub stores
on (F1137 available items) of stores available
a Hastener is recorded on F1138.

A.P. 958. K.R. & A.C.I.
are basic rules and regulations in all
branches of the Service

Chapt. 11 clean. Servicing testing & Inspection of A/c.
" 12. regulations - relating to flying
" 35. - Mt naval craft.

A.M.S.I. aircraft maintenance
and supply instructions
are issued in accordance with A.P. 958.
They have the authority of the air officer
commanding i/c. they are issued in leaflet
form. They are listed as & when they are
published in C.R.O' part 2. They are
essential to this command and deal with
servicing aircraft and (M.T.)

Mechanical transport staff instructions

are much like same as A.M.S.1. but are n.J.

A.P.1464. Engineering Manual for R.A.F.
A.P.1464. A. Vol. I Covers all Gen Eng-g workshop practice.
A.P.1464 B. " Aeroplane and ground equipment & Airdrome equip.

{ Part 1 General index part 2 Organisation and administration
Part 3. General Engineering Equipment, part 4. aero-engine equipment. 5. A/c components. part 6. Mechanical transport components. part 7. M/C components part 8. Ground equipment. part 9. Drawing office.

NOT NEC TO KNOW all the 9 parts.

A.P.1464 D. Vol I Bombs and torpedoes trolleys
A.P. 1464 Vol. II Leaflets orders & Modifications headed A to K.
A.P. 1464 Vol III Spare parts Schedule for ground equipment

Airframe Hand book.
The airframe hand book gives full detail description of the airframe, and installation

details of Engine or Engines, Gun arrches
anx etc.

Vol I consists of ~~ten~~ eleven sections, the first three concern the aircrew and other eight mainly the ground crew.

Vol II has four parts:—

part 1: General orders and modifications

part 2: Servicing inspection record. is split up into two sections { 1. Any authour plant supplementary, 2. Major Minor supplementary. these again are divided into sub-sections

part 3: Instructions for repair which can be carried out by units

part 4: Instructions for repair carried out by Maintenance Units.

Vol III split into 2 parts. part I Vocabulary of spare parts. part II appendix A or

airframe, list of spare parts.
Part IV Weight Sheet summary – not used in war time

Aero Engine Handbook (1570/3)

Vol 1, Consists of 4 Sections
Sect (1) Operational instructions
Sect (2) Starting, running and etc.
Sect (3) Installation Instructions
Sect (4) Full description of engine.

Volume 2 consists of three parts:
Part I General orders and modifications
Part II Fits and clearances.
Part III Instructions for overhaul.

Volume 3 Contains engine checking Schedule list of spare parts, list of special tools and tool kits.

NOTE: The leaflets in Volume 2 part 1 are

subject to amendment and alteration in India Command, by leaflets (India) issued in the command under the same A.P No. and Volume.

Amendments

All A.P's are subject to amendment by official amendment lists published from time to time, amendments for Vol II part 5 are in the form of additional amendments to ao' endowment leaflets which are inserted in their appropriate place.

Amendment lists to the other sects of Vol II and Vols I & III may take the form of manuscript alterations, new replacement Sects or fresh reprints of certain pages. amendments to appendix A are made as required and additional

amendment list is filed in the back cover for reference.
Special form to be used for amending A.Ms

A.M.O's A.O.N.

A.M.O's are issued in pamphlet form from time to time by the air council.

A.M.O's <u>A</u> are standing orders of administration which are applicable to R.A.F units all over the world they remain in Force until definitely cancelled.

A.M.O's <u>N</u>.

are temporary orders and notices giving advanced information on all subjects. a list is published monthly of all amendment list to all A.Ms. reference to this monthly list is necessary to keep each A.Ms up to date, promotions and awards to air force personnel are notified in these orders they are to be filed for reference for twelve month after year of issue? also a list of technical pubs about to come out.

A.7-O.² & A.7.S¹ (S)

These orders are now incorporated in A.6.S.E.A. administration orders. With effect from April 1ˢᵗ 1944. Those published previous to that date remain effective untill cancelled by A.6.SE.A admin orders. A.M.O² A applicable to this command will be notified in A.b.S.E.A. admin orders.
A.M.O'N (of like nature) applicable to this command will be notified in command routine orders.

Command Routine Orders

are issued by the A off. i/c in accordance with K.R.S chapter 3 para 39. and are published in parts to suit the various branches of the R.A.F in the command.
Part(1) deals with Admin. Part(2) Engineering Equipment, machinery and Mechanical transport. It gives new issues of special technical instructions. (S.T.I's) and amendments to same, They also authorise and introduce modifications neccessary to the command in part(3) are listed all other orders from Command and higher authority. They also list M.A.S.I's as and when they are published.

Special Technical Instructions (770.716.)

These are special instructions usually

urgent and issued by Air Ministry they are recorded in 4701 (log card) (and 1662 record of S.T.I?)

A/c Servicing Organisation

1ST Line Unit
2ND. M.U. & R.S.U
3RD Contractor E. C. R. D.

Unit Servicing A/c A.P. 1574.

1st Line — Will consist of Daily Inspection.
Between flt inspection.
Certain types of modifications
Minor Repairs & Inspections & may include major
and repairs to certain crashed aircraft
under category A. B. "A.C." and
Certain S. T. I.'s.

2nd Line — Undertaken by M.U/s and R.A.S.U. includes partial overhaul, major inspections major repairs, certain classes of modifications, category B crashed a/c and certain S.T.Ss they will assist the category B and crashed a/c

3rd line. Done by Contractors and civil Repair Units (CRU)s will consist off complete overhauls and rebuilds. Major Repairs certain types of modification and S.T.Ss 6 certain category s of crashed a/c.

U.S.O Unit Servicing Orders
Part i, is to be issued by St/ban. to co-ordinate the technical work on the station, and to define individual responsibility regards servicing of airframes and aero engines

Part ii is to be issued by Squadron commanders and will be based upon

Vol II, part II. Servicing schedule, part 2.
may detail additional inspections necessary
to meet local conditions

Flight and Section organisation

Station Commanding Officer.
         Station Eng. Officer
         Sqdn. Commander.
         Sqdn. Eng. Officer.

A FLT	B FLT	MAINT. FLT	S/HDQM	M/T
F/SGT.	"	F/SGT.	C/OFT/M	40 or F/SGT
2 SGTS.	"	2 SGT.	SGTS	Sgt. (1)
CPLS	"	CPLS	CPLS	Cpl.
7.M A	"	F II A'	F II A'	F.M.T.²
7.M.E.	"	F II E³	F II E2	M.T.M.
ACM/M.AM.	"	Ancillary trades	F.M II	D.M.T.
Ancil/Trades		8 N.C.O's	N/wires inspect y/mxrecel	Dis. RW.
		Equip. Ast.	M.E.S.O' crops radio/ dental nursing ffff	
AM. R&ST or EQUIP. OFFICER.				

A.P.129. Flying Training Manual.

Flt. Desk.

+700 (A.P.1574. AERO-PLANE SERVICING INST.)
A/c Handbooks E/B Handbooks
Flt. order book. All temporary orders
& notices concerning the flt.

Form 1575, Flt. Authorization Book, is
kept nowadays in the f/sgts office. It
gives the details of a aircraft taking
off — number of passengers — if hooker
Capt. of a/c signs for then all
it records time a/c was in air
the aircrafts mission. If aircraft returns
from mission or engine failure it is
recorded in book. When A/c returns
the Capt. of A/c again signs book.

Flight order book

Contains orders regarding
what has to be done to a/c the

crews may be from Group or Command.
or the T/Cmdr the Flt, the tradesman
or the Flight must read these a
good commander will have a monthly
check on these.

779 Flt. Day Book concerns the
squadron using it, time up time down.
type of sortie - captains name
made out in triplicate (1) for O/C (2) for records Sect 2 (1) H.Q.
         to submit
7/71 Pilots report on forced landing) flying was

700 Aircraft Servicing Form.

Date. Signature of tradesman Flying hrs. F.O.C. Rem. Pilots Signature
1.2. and multi engined aircraft A.M.S.1
ORgAP/Tech/24.

Compilation

Instructions for compiling F700 are contained on the cover of the form, they define individual responsibility for making entries and systems to be adopted.

Opening of form F700

A.11). at Contractors works will open F 700 for new aircraft. The following particulars will be entered on the cover page I

(1) Serial No. (2) Date Commencing (3) A/c Type, mark and No. (4) Engine (5) type and mark (5) Aero engine No's. The total time flown

on test or otherwise, before the delivery
of it, will be entered on the form 700
in the columns headed (Total hours flown)
also in the pilots acceptance flying log.
The remarks "Flying time before delivery"
will be written across remaining columns.
The quantities of oil, fuel and coolant put
into the aircraft for the delivery flight
will be entered and signed for on the
F700 will be entered by the person responsible
The form 700 will accompany the aircraft
on its acceptance flight. When this is
found impossible, the F700 must be
despatched by registered mail.
If a/c is going near enemy territory or over
the sea where it may come down, the F700
is sent by registered mail

On issue of an a/c from A.S.U, the total flying times & any repairs done to the a/c while at the unit are to recorded on F 700.

F 700 A Travelling copy A.M.O. A708/43
When an a/c is expected to be away from its unit for a period of 3 days, a F 700 A will be filled in and will accompany a/c. Any inspections or repairs carried out on the a/c during its absent from its parent unit will be recorded on the F 700 A and will be transcribed into the current 700 on its return to unit, by N.C.O i/c Flight.

F 701 Log card.
Opening a log card. Log cards will be opened for the following items of equipment (5). on construction or conversion from

Log cards
are kept
for —
  mark of series to another, and in the
  case of A/C complete overhauls.
  (1) Airframes (2) A/E (3) Propellors (x R.H.c.s)
  (4) I.C. Turbo superchargers, except when used for
  ground instruction purpose (5) Auxiliary
  Power Plant.
      . Transcription .
  Log cards will be completed by transcribing
  of details from F.700 on the following
  occasions. (1) When each 700 is completed.
  (2) On transfer of or A/C from unit to another
  (3) On transfer of one item from 1 A/C to another.
      . Description of log card.
      The log card contains 5 Sections (1) inspection
  list and modification certificate.
  2. Mods embodied at R.A.F or R.N units
  3. S.T.I.s fulfilled at R.A.F or R.N units

(4.) Brief history and transfer reasons for.
(5.) Running times and details of installation
Form 1125 Inspection test and modification book attached to front of F701 it is contractors certificate

Action on transfer

Before transfer of an a/c from a unit, details are to be transcribed from the current 700 into 701. The transfer certificate on the current 700 cover is to be completed in red by the officer responsible for completion

Daily & between flights inspection,

An a/c may be regarded as being serviceable for 24 hours unless 1. a deffect is reported 2. a deffect is discovered during the between flight inspections (3) The a/c becomes due for periodical inspection. (4) night flying takes place, when a further inspection may be made, right of lying equipment must be inspected (5) if an aircraft has not been flown after a D.I., the Flt Commander may wave subsequent D.I. up to a period of 1 week, when the a/c will again be inspected.

Under these circumstances the engine should be run over every day by hand and its own power every third day.

Servicing Inspection Record. S.I.R form contained in Vol II Part II A/c Hand book S.I.R formused to give a proggressive record of minor and major inspections carried out on each a/c, by each a/man for his work. The copy of Vol II part II is issued to each a/c and comprises

the following two inspections. Sect: 1 between
flight inspections. Sect 2. Minor and major
inspections. The inspection to be carried
out is in numerical order by groups, each
inspection having an adjacent grid to
record the action taken

The grid already referred to is headed
thus:

	30hr		60hr		90hr		120hr	
insp.	A	B	A	B	A	B	A	B
1	RB							
2	X	RB						

now hour required have entered in 7700
The airman carrying out the inspection
initials in column A when he has completed,
providing no retification is necessary.
If a repair is necessary the airman

the time at which the next inspection is due. I.E. if a thirty hour inspection is due at 150 hrs. but is done at 152 hrs the next thirty hour inspection is made at 180 hrs not 182 hrs. The latitude on a major inspection is accumulated i.e. If a 320 hr inspection is done at 325 hrs, the next major inspection is made at 645 hrs and not 640 hrs.

Orgad Tech 14. <u>Permissable Latitude</u>.

The maximum permissable delay for inspectors is to be soft % for the minor inspection period for a 60 hour minor inspection Period the anticipation or delay will be 5 hours giving 60 hrs 5 only. The anticipation or delay for major inspection is to conform with that

master copy of all modifications and S.I.s must be maintained and kept by station Eng Officer for all A/c held on the particular station

of a minor inspection (i.e. for no. te next inspection period plus - minus 5 hrs.

Types of Modifications 20th AM104/A35

Class (1) Essential to the safety of the A/c, embodiment is compulsory, sometimes A/c grounded until not finished

(2) These are urgent modifications essential for full operational use of equipment. Priority amongst commands for embodiment to cover distribution of parts & a balance of working parties may be promulgated

Class (3) Are normally embodied by squadron personnel (simple mods) embodiment left to the discretion of the command

A For airframes modifications that will improve the design.

B does not involve the supply of parts

Class (4) To be embodied by the makers, or when instructed by M/us, repair depots or C.R.O.s

7800 Discrepancy Rept. made by contractors

H.A: M/us   4B Contractors
              Special Order Only Modifications
      For A/c or special work.
              Transfer of aircraft between R.A.F units.
      7594 Discrepancy Report raised by B/O.
      on receipt of a/c from another R.A.F unit
      a/c should be checked APP(M) X.A or S.A.T.L

Transfer Procedure of A/c between units
    (1). Check for modifications and S.T.S's
    (2) 721. modification sets held on inventory
        to A/c.
    (3) S.A.T.L. and form 464 bring close to date.
    (4) Make up log cards for all items
    (5) Enter details of transfer on 700 & 701
    (6) all loose gear belonging to A/c is cased
        and put in A/c. to go with it or sent

separately.
(7). 7675 a/c to stores noting any differences
(8). C/O raises form 600 and parts blue copy to consignee
(9) Red copy to travel with a/c.
(10) Part I S.O.R & part 2/3 to go with a/c
(11) Fuel, oil, and loose items 7600 action
(12) Any unit Equipment is to be vouched separately
(13) Consignee raises 739a for any discrepancies
(14) Notify command of transfer (HOME 71623)
(INDIA) TELEPHONE

Handling and starting A/E A.P.129.

Only qualified persons are permitted to start and run up aero engines they are all ranks of 7^{IIa} $7.M.E^t$ $7.E^2$ 7^{IIs} and also pilots. Allied trades of the rank of Sergeant & above are also permitted but must be

certified as being capable and qualified
by the station engineering officer
Pilots only are allowed to taxi a/c except
where they are being used for ground training
(A.P.129. Hand swinging of light a/c to ws test

Standard stracing drill.

Defect Reports 710.22 & 710.23.
Whenever a failure or defect occurs in
any category of R.A.F. Equipment, it is essential
that a report on the matter is dealt
with the least possible delay to H.Q.
so that modification or other action can be
taken to prevent a repetition of similar
defects or failures.
710.22 is to be raised in the following circumstances
(1) weakness in design (2) faulty material (3)
faulty workmanship 4 Faulty servicing resulting

of an inadequate or incorrect servicing instructions
(5) A report F1022 is not to be rendered
in the following circumstances:-
(1). When it is the individuals of unit take
no F1022 action (2) When new items are
drawn from stores

AP4466/107 F1023 is a recurring defect report, submitted
weekly, to or when notified in C.R.O's
part 3.
Sketch-photog aph-or example should accompany
F1022
When returning items which have had F1022 action
675 should be endorsed. defective item F1022.
to action taken giving a/c No & type.

<u>Instruments</u> REF. AP1464/AH
Instrument failures will always be reported
on F1022 unless the number of hours of time

exceeds 150 in which case they are to be returned to the stores as defective clearly and securely labelled stating dist. and serial no. and total hours of run. Stream line wires A/8 defects and failures to stream line wires will always be reported on F1022, form states state of wire or rod. as well as Ref no and kite it came of

Electric Starter Trolley.

on the his is petrol electric charger set, Heavy armoured cable. Two point plug High voltage ours not been cables but is the heavy amperage. These trolleys are used in A/Cs for starting a/c 12 v. 18 v. 20 v. they cut-off the charge off kite and take over.

(1) Three expansion strips used to

prevent cable from catching the wheel
it is a modification
(2) Plug points to be protected when not in use.
(3) Where 12v. starting is used provision must be made for 24 v. starting

General duty Pneumatic compressor. Type 2
Has a petrol engine driven compressor with hose & dunlop connection - 350 lb per sq in

High pressure pneumatic Compressor.
Mounted on wheeled trolly
Two stage petrol engine driven compressor with hoses and fitments
Air at 150, 300, 450 lbs □"

Low pressure Pneumatic Compressor
Mounted on wheeled trolly.

Two stage petrol engine driven
compressor with hoses & fitments.
Air at 30, 60, 100 lbs □".
These tyres used for fitt. sprays.

Hydraulic Servicing Trolley R 2306. B
Petrol engine driven Hyd. pump mounted
on hand trolley (2 wheels). Has armoured hose
valve box etc. and delivers fluid at 350 lbs
□" or 1,500 lbs □". It uses to your aircr. pump
and hose.

Instrument testing trolley
Petrol engine driven compressor, mounted
on caterpillar track, gives air at pressure
2000 □" or create a vacuum of 3" of mercury.

Cold weather precautions A.P. 1441
Shelter tents - steel frames.
Pneumatic span is blown up, they are then

a small a/c for protection on the engine. For the benefit of ground crews aviation inspections it keeps engine fairly warm at night time. Lamps are put in the cockpit and under the engine.

A/c weather proof covers: Cockpit covers, wings, fuselage, tail plane, rubber propellor. <u>Air intake particular in India</u>. Pitot head. Engine.

Aerofoil covers to be doped with flexible dope 33B/352/153 colours are dark and dark green.
Aerofoil and covers must be dry.
We have special type of engine heater cover used in cold climates for keeping the engine warm. On Hurricane exterior fuse over oil tank.

Flameless Heater, Aladin Heater, Condensor.
Gyle Heater. Catalytic Heater burns lead

Pea Petrol has cotton wool mixture inside evapouryation on lip cause the mixture for plane. used for engine.

Aladin heater used in a/c shelter tent burns paraffin same principle as Davy safety lamp.

Condensation Type heater used in cockpit to absorb all the moisture so keeping it dry as to prevent condensation on instruments.

De-icing fluid or De-frosting 33C 771
For use on the ground only for removal of hore frost and like accretions (thin ice) delivered in Black drums.

Paste De-icing
For aerofoils 33C 886, applied on leading edge of aerofoils (soon to stick) to prevent ice sticking to aerofoils, consists of wet impregnated plastic base which on applying

aircraft paste blue comes last no flying hours

cold contracts and squeezes oil out of the paste thus causing of ice formation. applied with smoothing tool and preheated if necessary. must never heat above 120°F.

33C 327 Propellor paste
applied to all surfaces of propellor and spinner in thin, propellor base in grey. drum last. for 1 flight

Permanent Picketing of aircraft
This system consists of seven 3 ton concrete blocks with integral iron loops arranged in hexagonal formation 20 ft apart, the seventh block being placed in the centre. The blocks or chains stretched between adjacent blocks, used as anchorage points allow for any A/C. to be picketed nose into

wind. The securing points on the a/c can be found by reference to Vol I Afpsn publication 1404/ PART 8 Sec I Chapter II.

Pickets

Screw Picket.

Power Spike picket is a cross piece steel single used mainly for sandy regions, has two holes for apply spike extractor.

(1) Cross piece must be near the ground as possible

(2) the reenforcing web on the single crosspiece must be vertical

(3) locally manufactured spike extractor must be used for extracting the spikes (1460/64)

American type picket put in ground by special tool - the arrow heads are expendable and left in

Temporary picketing can be arranged using sandbags, sand filled petrol drums, etc.

— Picketing procedure.—

(1) Place a/c nose into wind. Exceptions Boston & Hud.
(2) Make sure all switches are off.
(3) Chock wheels front and rear.
(3) Lash chock cords
(4) Apply parking brakes
(5) Remove (Pyrotechnics unless guns loaded)
(6) Lock controls and toggle control surfaces.
7. Place under carriage locking device in position (Toggles for non-plane ailerons A.M.S.I. AC/GEN/97)
                      Issue I

(8) Lash all picket points correctly.
(9) Fit weatherproof and heater covers.
(10) Turn propellor to give greatest ground clearance.

C.M.51/MT/GEN/52

(ii) Check
 Fuel and oil tankers
(1) A weekly check for water content is to be carried out at the same time that the daily dip measurement is taken.
 Water seeking paste (334/310) is to be applied to the end of the dip stick. This paste changes colour in water but is unaffected by petrol.
(2) Half yearly check for internal corrosion
(3) A yearly check when internal surfaces will be cleaned thoroughly and painted with anti-corrosive paint

Notes weekly - half yearly - and yearly -
 Hoses are to be protected by split rubber rings.
 Nozzle cap to be secured by chain

6. Hose of filters to be cleaned daily
7. Bonding precautions must be observed during refuelling and arming operations

The ambulance and fire crash tender should be on duty wherever flying is in progress - including flying by visiting a/c.

Servicing of Ground Eqt. AMOA 120/62
AMS.1 SD/EQT/4

Ground equipment is divided in two classes
A. Equipment needing S. Schedules.
B. .... NOT ....

A. (Air compressor, Trolley, Instrument, Heaters
All items of moving parts monthly inspection checked by C/O or i/c Sect.
3 monthly inspection for all static items
All equipment on the unit will be

marked by the rollers or strong enough structurally to carry the load imposed

Before an aeroplane is moved over bad ground some responsible person should go ahead to inspect the aero. On soft ground plank tracks can be laid to receive the undercarriage.

Taxying single Engined A/C
Pilots signals; to go ahead, Pilots arm with hand straightened held above his head. To turn to right or left appropriate arm extended horizontally from cockpit. to stop pilots arm above head palm forward. to stand clear pilots arm waves from side to side above head.

Person i/c taxying party to salute Pilot when he's sure all is clear

(5) Pick good picketing ground
(6) Use nets if necessary
(7) Keep the camouflage points clear of litter paper rag.
(8) Use varying paths to and from dispersal points
(9) Keep aircraft clear of buildings, fuel dumps, bomb dump, and trees
(10) Provide slit trenches etc. for ground crews
(12) Make adequate provisions for fire fighting

Handling of Aircraft

When a/c are moved on the ground one person will supervise from a position where the a/c can be kept fully in view. When taxying the Pilot will be responsible and will direct operators.

A/c will only be handled at points

Taxying Large aircraft.

Person to stand well forward of A/c in clear view of Pilot, and to guide as follows, come forward on both engines, describe circles with both hands as shoulder height, to throttle down port or starboard engines describe circles with one hand holding the other hand stationery palm towards Pilot. To halt A/c, hold up both hands Palms towards Pilot.

To stop Engines hand swing across body below waist level.

At night time the same signals are used with blue tinted torch held in each hand.

AP1921. REPORTING Guarding, Salvage of crashed A/c
AP 1922. CASUALTY PROCEEDURE IN WAR

1. If a crashed A/c is within ten miles of unit concerned they will mount guard.
2. If beyond that unit nearest military unit will mount the guard
3. See the adjutant for orders if i/c party
4. Person wishing to inspect a/c should be in the possession of a Defence Reg 76 describing the holder and signed by W/C and above.
5. Prevent people roaming round the A/c trying to get souveniers Remove A/c immediately if obstructing any highway, railway, road, runway or canal. Explosive and pyrotechnics should be removed by armourers personel.
6. Fuel in India from crashed A/c should

for M.T.
not contain more than 10% lead. fuel graded grade III in India in England 15%

Reporting of Crashed A/C. Flying accident

7765C
Preliminary one sent 7656, within 48 hours for A/c that has crashed, not brought down by enemy action. in other words A/c that has crashed. ops. F.T.S etc.

Final 765c is raised with 48 hours 4 days.

In a k message to A.M.N.

In India A.C.S.E.A. or B.A.F.S.E.A. - B.P.O.

AP 1921-1922 for reference for letters to describe crash - for letters A - N.

FB. is operational flying casualties
FA. is non operational flights
FC. when they are not sure what mission A/c is on.

E.A. when A/c is on ground subject to enemy action

Categories of crashed A/c (INDIA)

Cat. A repairable on site
" A.C. " " " with assistance of R.S.U
Cat B Fly in to forward Repair depot.
    B.C. It can be flown in but its better to be transported goes to. B.R.D
Cat E5. Beyond economical repair but spares can be used or salvaged
Cat E0. Beyond E. R. no good at all.

AT. HOME

Cat. A. Repairable by unit
   A.C. " with assistance from r/u.
Cat B Repairable but not on site
Cat E Beyond. E. Repair no further use.

Removal of Components from crashed A/C

No spares to be removed from Cat. A or AC A/c
You can remove items from Cat. B & C. providing
you put the parts similar back. they must be OK.D
by Eng: Officer

Group Deposit Account

226 Group India   43 Group (UK.)

A/c are transferred to the G.D.A.
(a purely paper transaction) in order that
operational Squadrons are provided with
serviceable A/c. on the following occasions

(1) In forward area's if A/c is u/s more
than 2 days after receipt of spares.
(2) u/s for more than five days at rear
areas
(3) If going on a major overhaul by maintenance
unit wing

(4) Cat AC & Cat B A/C transferred to G.D.A.
Maintenance Wing will issue instructions when to to take Cat BC or Cat BD A/c off the G.D.A.

Special treatment for A/c that has been submerged in ⁺salt water.   1464/A PART 5. SECT I CH 3

AIRFRAME. Drain A/F remove all fabric: metal parts are washed in hot water to remove salt deposits. Tubular members must be flushed out with water and drained, inspect all parts and move corrosion apply anti corrosive treatment. seaplane varnish - durolac.
Fuel tanks, drain fuel completely, aero
Aero. engine dismantle inspect for damage and corrosion, all magnesium alloy alloys. - piston, con rods, and all high carbon steel are scrapped.

SUMATE
KIMATEX HENDERSON.
CANVAS
RUBBER

<u>Light alloy parts</u> are cleaned in hot water
and dry thoroughly.
If any corroded parts wash in hot water
mixed with tartaric acid   100 gal of water
to 2lb of tartaric acid, other steel parts
wash in hot water.

<u>Guns</u> these can be washed in hot
water and pariffin cleaned and inspected
Instruments, to be washed again in hot
water dryed and immersed into oil
anti <u>freezing Type</u> 9. labelled and sent away
<u>Wireless</u> equipment dipped in warm water for
2 seconds and dryed by hot-air.

PETROLEUM.
OIL IS LUBRKAT OF THIS WAR.

Sometime in the early part of 19th century people of the Southern parts of the U.S.A were troubled with a black liquid which was ruining their crops - it was a menace. it was oil.

When a certain Dr Otto of austrin discovered the internal combustion Engine and used petrol for it. The people realized the value of that black liquid.

Since then drilling all over world and now we find oil and petrol in

U.S.A. Venuzuala, Curacao Dutch West Indi Rumani Russia to Scape guarded by PAT f tunnel banora to Scotland.

How much we pay for it   2D
How much we sell it for   1/0
What we do with it -
Agitator. Distillery. breaking plant.

Refinery –
How long it will last
Experts before war said till 1990
since war reduce it to 1960
oil from coal but too dear w/ a gallon

$$\left(\frac{2}{5} \div \frac{7}{3}\right) \times \frac{4}{21}$$

$$= \frac{2}{5} \times \frac{3}{7} \times \frac{4}{21} = \left(\frac{8}{245}\right) = ANS$$

$$\frac{2}{5} + \frac{3}{7} \times \frac{4}{21}$$

$$\left(\frac{2}{5} + \frac{3}{7}\right) \times \frac{4}{21}$$

$$\frac{14+15}{35} = \frac{29}{35} \times \frac{4}{21} = \frac{116}{735} = ANS.$$

$$\begin{array}{r} 29 \\ 4 \\ \hline 116 \end{array}$$

$$\begin{array}{r} 35 \\ 21 \\ \hline 35 \\ 700 \\ \hline 735 \end{array}$$

www.ingramcontent.com/pod-product-compliance
Lightning Source LLC
Chambersburg PA
CBHW042342300426
44109CB00048B/2728